PSYCHOLOGY OF EMOTIONS, MOTIVATIONS AND ACTIONS

BORDERLINE PERSONALITY DISORDER

UNDERSTANDING THE UNCONSCIOUS FUNCTION OF DELIBERATE SELF-HARM AND MANAGING THE TRANSFERENCE RELATIONSHIP

PSYCHOLOGY OF EMOTIONS, MOTIVATIONS AND ACTIONS

Additional books in this series can be found on Nova's website under the Series tab.

Additional e-books in this series can be found on Nova's website under the e-book tab.

PSYCHOLOGY OF EMOTIONS, MOTIVATIONS AND ACTIONS

BORDERLINE PERSONALITY DISORDER

UNDERSTANDING THE UNCONSCIOUS FUNCTION OF DELIBERATE SELF-HARM AND MANAGING THE TRANSFERENCE RELATIONSHIP

AMANDA COMMONS TRELOAR, PH.D.

nova publishers
New York

For permission to use material from this book please contact us:
Telephone 631-231-7269; Fax 631-231-8175
Web Site: http://www.novapublishers.com

Additional color graphics may be available in the e-book version of this book.

Library of Congress Cataloging-in-Publication Data

ISBN: 978-1-63117-076-8

Library of Congress Control Number: 2014931907

Published by Nova Science Publishers, Inc. † New York

CONTENTS

PREFACE

This preamble outlines the typical difficulties observed with psychotherapeutic treatment of borderline personality disorder throughout my clinical and supervision experience – from clinical engagement issues to incomplete or biased diagnostic practices. The importance of developing a working clinical alliance with the patient, and a consideration of past figures of importance (such as parental figures), is discussed as it can ultimately affect the level of engagement by the patient and the response of the patient to the clinician involved. The narrative style of this preface aims to reassure the clinician of the 'normalcy' of the difficulties they may have encountered in this work, and to assist in developing a considered reflection of one's own clinical practice.

To begin, I want to clearly affirm that the preference in my clinical work is for the focus of therapeutic work to be centred on the individual patient, limiting reference to diagnostic categorisation, particularly with regards to borderline personality disorder (BPD). I mostly avoid the use of diagnostic labelling in the therapeutic setting[1]. As will be discussed in detail throughout this text, the presence of BPD as a diagnosis has had much affect on the way in which clinicians approach patients with this disorder, as well as in their conceptualisation of deliberate self-harm (DSH) behaviours as an indicator of this diagnosis. Throughout the many clinical files I have reviewed, it was apparent that if there was a history of DSH behaviours by a patient, a diagnosis or a differential diagnosis of BPD would have been considered. Once the diagnosis has been considered, there is often much influence this label has on the willingness of many clinicians to become involved in the psychotherapeutic treatment of these patients.

There are many concerns that I have with the use of diagnostic labelling, particularly with the term 'borderline personality disorder', although it is acknowledged that it has its place in the clinical setting. Consider these terms separately: 'borderline', 'personality', and 'disorder' separately. 'Borderline' – on the edge, on the brim, on the boundary of two regions; 'personality' – the state of being a person, individual existence or identity, sum of qualities or characteristics that constitute individuality; and 'disorder' – confusion, discomposure of mind, disease or illness (Finch, 1956). The use of 'borderline' in the term BPD is problematic in consideration of today's diagnostic categorisation of personality disorders; 'borderline' in relation to what? It can often conjure images of being on the verge and unstable – albeit many

[1] Diagnosis clarification is however considered necessary for psychoeducational purposes within my clinical practice.

would agree with this notion – however as will be discussed in the next chapter, the origins of the term borderline with this patient group are indicative of being on the boundary between two regions: neurosis and psychosis (Stern, 1938). This initial depiction is not considered in the current classification system of mental disorders, and therefore the significance of the term borderline has become confused. 'Personality' as a term is also confusing given the way in which the diagnosis of BPD is used to 'clump' patients together into a common psychiatric type rather than, in a more abstract sense, acknowledging the qualities that constitute individuality. 'Disorder' as an idiom is technically more correct – there is a general consensus within the clinical community that there is a discomposure or agitation of the mind in many BPD patients. In pairing these terms, it becomes more problematic. A 'borderline personality' could be considered as someone on the edge of being an individual; 'personality disorder' could be interpreted as a confused state of being a person; and 'borderline personality disorder' could be delineated as a person on the edge of being a diseased or an ill individual – this reads as a series of double negatives and clearly shows the problematic syntax and conceptualisation that can exist with the use of these terms.

Upon review of my clinical experience (in both public mental health, community health, and private practice), and in reflection of my work with many different clinicians across the various disciplines, I believe that many in the clinical community may have been injudicious in their ready need to diagnose and label patients with BPD, and perhaps just as hasty in their need to find a treatment program or form of therapy to cure the patient with BPD. This is understandable given the complexity of the clinical work and it is emphasised here that diagnostic clarification can assist in the choice of treatment pathways (and as such assist in the accumulation of empirical evidence for the treatment of BPD). I believe, however, that what I deem as 'diagnostic enthusiasm' may often be to the detriment of the patient as negative therapeutic responses can often be elicited once the diagnosis is made, and the experience of the suffering of the individual patient may become secondary to the 'suffering' of the clinician who becomes involved in the psychotherapeutic management and treatment of BPD.

In the process of recording symptoms, consulting symptom checklists, applying diagnostic labels, and following standard treatment programs of distress tolerance and harm minimisation, I feel that we may have lost something – understanding the patient in turmoil that brings to us their anxieties, regrets, and sadness. We do have an abundance of research into aetiology and theoretical frameworks that can help us in not just treating the patient, but in understanding their psychical distress. Many theoretical frameworks and treatment modalities have been examined within clinical trials to determine efficacy in relation to the psychotherapeutic treatment of BPD: dialectical behavior therapy, cognitive behavioural therapy, cognitive analytic therapy, interpersonal therapy, solution focused therapy, mentalization-based therapy, and psychoanalytically orientated partial hospitalisation (Clarkin, Levy, Lenzenweger, & Kernberg, 2007; Bateman & Fonagy, 2004; Leichsenring & Leibing, 2003; Sharry, Darmody, & Madden, 2002; Ryle, Leighton, & Pollock, 1997; Chatham, 1985). Has diagnostic enthusiasm however led us to being too quick to diagnose and label patients with BPD without stopping to consider how we can use such theoretical information in the conceptualisation, not just the treatment, of the patient's symptoms? Can we use these frameworks in developing more useful clinical insight into the instability and behaviours of our patients to moderate the threat to the therapeutic alliance often observed from such symptomatology? Do we regularly use clinical history taking as an active clinical process in our professional practice beyond the application of diagnoses? The individual patient's story holds the key to appreciating the development of their intolerance and chaos. Further to diagnostic clarification, we have developed many treatment programs to target the BPD patient's behaviours but in our attempt to jump in and solve the problem, have we perhaps forgotten to actively use these conceptual models of BPD in understanding the suffering of patient and their individual experiences, as well as perhaps appreciating the therapeutic significance (both positively and negatively) our presence can have in their lives?

In sum, I have often wondered: how can we use theoretical frameworks about the aetiology of BPD to move toward a more holistic diagnostic consideration of this disorder? Can we also use conceptual models of BPD to move beyond purely the application of diagnoses to a more considered psychotherapeutic stance in considering the impact the developmental history has on the daily functioning of the patient? Can we thus attempt to sit with our anxieties about our patient's suicidality and DSH behaviours, without impulsively moving to attempt to treat the problem and therefore not consider the significance of the patient's behaviours at that point in time? Listening to the patient about their experiences and appreciating this from a position of *investment* in the treatment (rather than to diagnose or to hurriedly discover a remedy) must have significant advantage to the therapeutic alliance, particularly when many patients with this disorder have been ritually abused, abandoned, and disregarded. The ready diagnosis of BPD and the reactive use of diversion and distraction in the face of DSH presentations must contribute to the perception of being disregarded to the already sensitive and traumatised patient.

From working in the clinical field as a psychologist, I have come to the realisation that although patients with BPD are frequently encountered, these patients may be just as frequently misunderstood (and unfortunately some treated very poorly by different professionals throughout their life). The characteristic dysregulation of affect and mood, and the seemingly unpredictable suicidal and DSH behaviours (among other difficult to manage symptoms) are often common sources of mixed or volatile emotions experienced by many clinicians in direct transference response to such patients. Indeed, the use of the term BPD and the presence of DSH behaviour in some patients appear to be the most common barriers that I have observed in my clinical work to the active engagement of many clinicians to the psychotherapeutic work with these patients. Reticence to engage with patients with BPD has been frequently observed in the allocation of cases to clinicians at routine team meetings. In my experience, the treatment and management of patients with psychotic disorders is often chosen over the treatment and management of the patient with BPD. Why is this so? Why do these patients generate such negative countertransference reactions in trained and experienced mental health and emergency medicine professionals?

Although often misused as a diagnostic indicator, the sometimes horrific and repeated self-inflicted injuries with which this patient group may present to the mental health service or emergency medicine department with are often key sources of this anxiety, rejection, and distrust. At this point I wish to also clearly state that I do not assume that self-harm behaviours occur in all cases of BPD, and the focus on the self-harm behaviours throughout this text is in direct response to the greatest difficulty I have observed in working alongside many other clinicians in contact with patients with BPD. They are the symptom however that creates the most anxiety in the clinician, the psychiatric service, the emergency department, the patient's family, and the community in general. The turmoil of emotions and dreaded thoughts of coroner inquests and management root cause analyses[2] in the event of suicide often test our willingness as clinicians or therapists to become involved in the psychological treatment of patients with BPD. General feelings of inadequacy from the mental health clinician in the repeated application of previously unsuccessful behavioural change programs can also often impact on the level of investment we make in the therapeutic relationship.

Working in emergency medicine, frustration must often be experienced by the medical team when they see the same patient presenting with deliberately self-inflicted injury or overdose. I have known some patients who have re-presented with similar injuries to the emergency medicine department within a 24 hour period, often intentionally removing sutures applied to previous but very recent sites of mutilation. In my experience, the emergency medicine clinician's priority is often given to providing medical attention to 'real' accident or emergency patients who are attending the same department while this patient is often left to wait unless presenting in a critical situation. How can intentional self injury or self poisoning be an accident? It must be frustrating to see the same patient presenting with deliberately inflicted injury or overdose; trying to balance providing medical attention to this 'frequent flyer'[3] whilst moving between other patients who are attending the same department following an accident or emergency – words that describe unforeseen injury or mishap (Finch, 1956).

DSH behaviours can commonly be the catalyst for the introduction of the BPD patient to our health services, and these behaviours can also regularly become the status quo throughout clinical care. The DSH behaviours and strategies of deterrence often become the key focus of our interventions and as such we can miss the fundamental therapeutic needs of the patient who acts in such a way. When self-harm ideation is voiced or self-inflicted injury occurs, this becomes the priority focus of care. Providing crisis response and developing risk management plans is highly time consuming and often it would seem of little benefit in the actual reduction of DSH episodes. The recurrent crisis situation can also prevent us from pausing to conceptualise the development and underlying purpose of the behavioural disturbance, and in taking adequate therapeutic time to invest in the psychological investigation of the behaviours with the patient.

> Because patients engage in so many self destructive and self defeating behaviours, clinicians may find themselves spending a great deal of the therapy setting limits on the patient's behaviours. The risk in these situations is that therapists may become entrenched in a countertransference posture of policing the patient's behaviour to the point that treatment goals are lost and the therapeutic alliance is compromised. (Oldham et al., 2001, p.20).

Understanding why this patient would feel the need to harm themselves, and how such a coping strategy developed, often becomes the missed yet most important therapeutic aim of the therapy and intervention. As humans, we are supposed to avoid pain, not to inflict it; so how and why has this intentional injury come to be the status quo for our patient?

When the patient is diagnosed with BPD, there is often an expectation on the part of the clinician involved in the psychological treatment of the patient that the self-harm behaviours

[2] This is a process followed by the management of psychiatric services in the event of patient suicide where the clinical file is examined for evidence of appropriate care. This is often completed prior to a coronial inquiry, but also as part of good psychiatric practice.

[3] A term that I have heard used by some emergency medicine clinicians to describe BPD patients who have regular patterns of emergency department attendance.

will repetitively occur during the period of care. As such, assigning patients to clinicians or therapists can become problematic. There are few mental health clinicians with whom I have worked with that are willing to become involved in the psychotherapeutic treatment of the patient with BPD. Unfortunately many of these clinicians become involved completely unaware of what the psychotherapeutic intervention will require from them in terms of investment to the therapeutic alliance. Once within the treatment setting, the effect of the patient's distress and behaviours can create turmoil of its own within the countertransference response of the therapist – I have observed this time and time again, even amongst highly experienced therapists and clinicians.

In the process of supervision and peer consultation, I have heard a myriad of anxieties from many clinicians and therapists about their BPD patients: What can I do? What if they kill themselves? What stops them from self-harming? Have I done everything that I can? Upon consideration of this, all of these fears and uncertainties have common themes – what is the possible impact of the patient's behaviours on me, and how can I be involved in such a way to stop the patient from harming themselves? The responsibility for the presence or occurrence of ongoing self mutilation or overdose often becomes transposed onto the clinician involved. The clinician's psychotherapeutic attempts to prevent such behaviours often appear to fail, or the patient often seems to show an exacerbation of symptomatology upon entering treatment. This is often a key factor in the development of clinician anxiety and rejection, and in the limited efforts to attempt and maintain the engagement of the patient in sustained psychotherapeutic treatment. Amongst the instability, the therapeutic question remains: how can we develop a considered approach of therapeutic inquiry in helping to understand the behaviours of the BPD patient without accumulating the feelings of frustration, anger, and hostility that can contribute to disengagement in the therapeutic alliance?

It is also important to clearly indicate at this stage that I do not propose immunity to the discomfort or anxiety associated with the treatment of the BPD patient, particularly when self injury or self poisoning occurs. The difficulty with this fantasy – discovering a remedy for professional anxiety and negative countertransference reactions – is that a therapist or clinician without any anxiety about their tumultuous patient would be of no therapeutic value. Some form of anxiety is needed to genuinely work with, and empathetically understand, patients who live with such inner turmoil. The anxiety of the clinician however needs to be transformed into some sense of curiosity, or a desire to inquire; hence showing our commitment to the therapeutic alliance. As clinicians, we need to learn from and make use of our anxiety (Lacan, 2004). The level of anxiety experienced by the health professional needs to be considered and constrained, negotiating a balance between the two types of clinicians that I have often observed: hardened against the emotional experience of the patient and thus sceptical of prognosis; or panicked and reactive to the behavioural displays of the patient and thus becoming caught up in the instability of the patient – in sum, the 'cynical abandoner' and the 'flustered rescuer'.

A revision of thought around the aetiology and consequent diagnosis of BPD, and the meaning or purpose of self-harm, is required to enable a more measured assessment of risk and committed investment to the therapy that can be offered to such patients. It will be argued here that this can stem from an active process of a consideration of theoretical models applicable to this particular disorder, and a regular review of the growing evidence-based practice literature. The different conceptualisations of BPD do vary significantly, in their consideration of the development of behavioural disturbance such as self-harm, and in their use of the transference relationship. Although it could be argued that all forms of therapy use the transference relationship in some way – and I believe that it is impossible to create meaningful dialogue with a patient without it – many theoretical schools do not acknowledge its existence. The interpretation of the transference response and reaction between therapist and patient however is a feature that I have found to be most beneficial in the psychotherapeutic work with patients suffering from BPD, particularly as negative clinician/therapist responses tend to escalate the occurrence of DSH episodes.

To accept the treatment of the patient, the one that suffers, there needs to be a consideration of the level of investment that is required from the clinician. In order to satisfy the needs of the patient, we need to understand how we personally, acting in our role of clinician, mediate the experience of the patient. I believe that to acknowledge the suffering, and to understand the development of such torment, a great personal and professional commitment on behalf of the clinician is actively required. In undertaking the clinical work, there is an expectation that the patient will offer an account of the conscious concerns in their life; however beyond this, there are also the unconscious workings that require acceptance and consideration.

In the transference relationship, the patient will have the unconscious compulsion to repeat and redirect the feelings from the past relationships of their life (Racker, 2001). This is a concept of the clinical work that many clinicians may fail to recognise with adequate significance. To allow oneself, as a clinician, to be a vehicle by which repressed experiences are permitted, analysed, and worked through requires a great level of investment. A relationship needs to be built in which to enable and interpret the experience, conscious and unconscious, of the patient.

> The patient is not satisfied with regarding the analyst in the light of reality as a helper and adviser who, moreover, is remunerated for the trouble he takes and who would himself be content with some such role as that of a guide on a difficult mountain climb. On the contrary, the patient sees in him the return, the reincarnation, of some important figure out of his childhood or past, and consequently transfers on to him feelings and reactions which undoubtedly applied to this prototype. (Freud, 1940/1964, p.174).

The presence of DSH behaviours, and how we as clinicians can influence the occurrence of these through our presence in the transference relationship, not in the role of advisor with distraction and harm minimisation techniques but as a projected figure from the past, is of great significance in the treatment of BPD. I believe that it is imperative in the treatment of patients with BPD that clinicians recognise and facilitate greater insight into the unconscious processes. This includes greater recognition of the origins and mechanism of behavioural disturbance and of the transference relationship when ongoing mutilation occurs.

It is hoped that understanding the role of the unconscious via appreciating a psychoanalytic theoretical model applicable to BPD, and its conceptualisation of why self-harm behaviours and recurrent suicidal threats or gestures occur, may assist in the ability of the clinician to maintain empathy with the patient in such turmoil. Indeed, in the literature there has already been some preliminary research conducted into the impact of the use of training and conceptual modelling of BPD on clinician attitudes and understanding of BPD as a psychiatric disorder. For example, in a study by Krawitz (2000), completion of clinical training by mental health staff in BPD was shown to lead to an increase in confidence, optimism, enthusiasm, and positive feeling toward working with BPD patients, and shown to be maintained at 3-5 month follow up. Unfortunately many mental health and emergency medicine clinicians may not have received specific training in this complex disorder. It is not highlighted in standard medical and allied health training regimens, despite many clinicians possibly having regular clinical contact with patients diagnosed with BPD. A consideration of psychoanalytic theoretical frameworks assisted me in my clinical work with BPD, and so I am interested in attempting to impart this knowledge onto other health professionals – many professionals whom I have seen struggle at times to provide the necessary therapeutic contact required to adequately engage and treat BPD patients who present with significant suffering.

Recognising and interpreting one's anxiety when dealing with the BPD patient is paramount to the transference relationship and the therapeutic work, and also for containing and interpreting the level of clinician distress. This book aims to assist clinicians in considering the possible reasons why such patients are often unconsciously motivated to attack themselves, and therefore attempt to promote greater understanding and tolerance for these patients. A consideration of how our response to the patient can be linked (either positively or negatively) to the occurrence of repeated DSH behaviours is important to the clinical work. The self-harm episodes and suicide attempts are often assumed to be self explanatory due to the presence of the BPD diagnosis – by the utilisation of circular logic it is by definition what they do. However the reasoning behind the behaviours is often not self explanatory at all. It is common that the patients themselves are unable to identify why they

have deliberately hurt themselves, and are unable (initially) to create a meaningful dialogue around their reasons for self-harm. It is hoped that through this discourse, the clinician involved in the treatment of BPD may begin to better appreciate the damaged psyche of such patients. Acknowledging the years of suffering of the patient, and starting to allow ourselves as clinicians to sit with the anxiety beyond the behavioural displays, may help move toward a more considered diagnostic conceptualisation and approach of therapeutic inquiry. There is much more complexity to the patient with BPD than the observable body of wounded flesh and skin that sits opposite us in the therapy room.

Amanda Commons Treloar, Ph.D.
Alumni of Monash University,
School of Psychology,
Psychiatry & Psychological Medicine
Victoria, Australia
mcandpt@bigpond.net.au

ACKNOWLEDGMENTS

I wish to acknowledge Dr. Leonardo Rodríguez and Dr. Andrew Lewis, for their many hours of consultation, their genuine encouragement, and clinical advice during the compilation of the material used in this text. Their intellectual guidance has been invaluable. I also wish to express my gratitude to the School of Psychiatry, Psychology, and Psychological Medicine at Monash University for the theoretical and financial support of my research work in this area.

I also want to thank my family, friends, and colleagues for their ongoing support during the many years of researching and writing about borderline personality disorder. The time spent editing by Trudy Clutterbok in the early stages of manuscript preparation, by Peter Treloar throughout the writing period, and by Dr. Krystal Bowers in the final manuscript compilation, has also been highly valued.

Special thanks must go to 'Lisa', 'Helen', and 'Eve' who entrusted me with their very personal stories and experiences. Without their participation and willingness to disclose their most intimate experiences, thoughts, and feelings, the enriched illustration of the theoretical concepts to be discussed here would not have been possible. They gave the theoretical framework a 'personality'.

Part 1: A Consideration of Borderline Personality Disorder

These chapters discuss the difficulties in the early conceptualisation of borderline personality disorder, in terms of clinical classification and problems with psychotherapeutic responsiveness. It outlines the current diagnostic procedures for this disorder, and provides working definitions and discussion on subtypes of patient behaviours that could be considered as deliberate self-harm. The third chapter introduces the issue of clinical avoidance by professionals due to the presence of the diagnosis and the occurrence of deliberate self-harm, and suggests ways to remedy this avoidance through obtaining necessary clinical education and supervision. The practice of considering theoretical frameworks is introduced in the conceptualisation of diagnosis and in appreciating their benefits in the execution of psychotherapeutic treatment.

Chapter 1

ISSUES OF DIAGNOSTIC PRACTICE

THE HISTORY OF THE 'BORDERLINE' DIAGNOSIS

Borderline personality disorder (BPD) as a clinical diagnosis has only been used since its inclusion in the *Diagnostic and Statistical Manual of Mental Disorders*, third edition (*DSM-III*) by the American Psychiatric Association in 1980. The growth in the recognition and use of BPD as a diagnosis in psychiatry has been remarkable since this time (Gunderson, 2001). The origin of the borderline diagnosis however has been identified from the early part of the twentieth century, with its clinical observations traced by Adolph Stern in the 1930's. Stern (1938) was a psychoanalyst who recognised a subgroup of patients that did not fit into the existing psychopathological system which consisted primarily of the diagnoses of neurosis and psychosis, introducing the term borderline to the psychoanalytic community. These patients were neither considered neurotic nor psychotic, and in fact conceptualised as being on the borderline to both these subgroups of patient diagnoses. Even from these early times, the clinical thinking surrounding this group of patients was typically problematic – their clinical presentation, symptom profile, and responsiveness to therapeutic interventions was different to the patients being diagnosed (and consequently treated) utilising the established categorisation of psychopathology as neurosis or psychosis. The lack of diagnostic clarity with some patients, who could not be precisely diagnosed with neurosis or psychosis, led to a vast wasteland of patients referred to as borderline. Stern's attempt to describe the possible causes and symptom profile of the borderline patient was the first identifiable attempt in the clinical differentiation and classification of what we now consider BPD.

Nearly two decades later Robert Knight (1953) attempted to further expand on Stern's (1938) observations of the borderline phenomena, introducing the concept of the ego to his descriptions of the diagnosis. The consideration of the ego's function assisted in an appreciation of the borderline patient's specific psychological impairment (in terms of their 'unique' failure to realistically perceive the world around them, and then successfully integrate their thoughts and feelings into effective responses to that world[1]). The difficulty was that from its inception the term borderline was often used to denote difficult and troublesome patients with significant functional problems, who did not appear to progress

[1] And this conceptualisation continues to be the foundation of considering BPD via many of the current theoretical models, such as dialectical behavior therapy (Linehan, 1993).

with psychotherapeutic intervention. Unfortunately this clinical practice did (and does) continue. Despite the identification of an alternate and differential diagnostic conceptualisation of the borderline state, borderline patients continued to defy psychotherapeutic understanding. Although they were beginning to be more clinically appreciated and recognised, the borderline patients remained considered as non-responsive to traditional psychotherapeutic treatment – a hopeless case with poor prognosis. "Use of the term borderline for atypical, clinically troubling cases staggered long in the periphery of psychiatric thinking without notable progress until developments in the late 1960's" (Gunderson, 2001, p.3).

Most notably, Otto Kernberg added to the understanding of what was already considered the troublesome borderline patient through his conceptualisation of borderline personality organisation (BPO) in 1967. BPO was characterised by Kernberg (1967) as one of three personality organisations – psychotic personality organisation, neurotic personality organisation, and borderline personality organisation. The BPO was considered a unique phenomenon – a separate entity on its own, where particular symptomatology or personality structures (rather than treatment response) could differentiate it from other psychiatric diagnoses. Specifically, BPO was differentiated from the psychotic and neurotic personality organisations by the presence of failed or weak identity formation, the use of primitive defenses such as splitting and projective identification, and reality testing that transiently lapsed when the patient was under stress (Kernberg, 1967). This differentiation of trait and state, informing future psychoanalytic thought of the symptom and structure of the patient, helped shape the clinical thinking around such patients by moving toward a theoretical framework for conceptualising the clinical foundation and hence appropriate diagnosis of this disorder. The consideration of BPO provided a platform for understanding the personality structure of this patient group rather than (as was done traditionally) disregarding them as a diagnostic quandary and therefore problematic to clinically work with (in terms of their unresponsiveness to psychotherapeutic treatment)[2].

The identification of BPD or borderline pathology traditionally came from a process of exhausting all other diagnostic options. In response to diagnostic difficulties and the timely and clumsy process of exclusion of other disorders, a new approach to categorising the borderline phenomena was adopted by Patricia Chatham (1985), labelled the eclectic-descriptive approach (cited in Linehan, 1993). This approach considered the recognition of symptoms in criteria sets for the diagnosis to be made, and is embodied in the classification system currently adopted by the American Psychiatric Association in the development of the *Diagnostic and Statistical Manual of Mental Disorders* (*DSM*). The first inclusion of BPD as a psychiatric diagnosis in the *DSM-III* led to a diagnostic process that was to enable a systematic identification of which patients should attract this diagnosis. The clear use of symptom descriptions for the diagnosis of BPD, and indeed other clinical disorders, assisted in a growing consensus with regard to the conceptualisation of BPD, and can be seen by some as a step toward preventing the misdiagnosis of complex patients and the misuse of the term BPD (in an attempt to prevent the clinician in applying the diagnosis to patients who perplexed us in terms of how they behaved and how they accounted for their difficulties)[3].

[2] Much the same as completing a picture puzzle, it is so much harder to places the pieces in the correct place if one is unaware of what the puzzle picture actually is or represents.

[3] Although I would argue that the ready application of the diagnosis of BPD continues in today's clinical environment, despite the use of criteria sets by which to guide assessment practices. The continued placing of

DIAGNOSTIC CRITERIA FOR TODAY'S DIAGNOSIS

The diagnostic criteria for BPD is outlined in the *Diagnostic and Statistical Manual of Mental Disorders*, fifth edition (*DSM-V*) (American Psychiatric Association, 2013). The distinguishing feature of the diagnosis is "a pervasive pattern of instability of interpersonal relationships, self image, and affects, and marked impulsivity that presents itself by early adulthood" (American Psychiatric Association, 2000, p.710)[4]. For the accurate diagnosis of BPD, this pattern of instability and impulsivity needs to be present in a variety of contexts, as indicated by five (or more) of the following: frantic efforts to avoid real or imagined abandonment; a pattern of unstable and intense interpersonal relationships; identity disturbance; impulsivity; recurrent suicidal or self mutilating behaviours; affective instability due to marked reactivity of mood; chronic feelings of emptiness; inappropriate, intense anger, or difficulty controlling anger; transient, stress related paranoid ideation; and severe dissociative symptoms (American Psychiatric Association, 2013).

Consideration of the symptomatologic pattern of the BPD patient does require careful thought around the various presentations of the different patients whom may meet these criteria. Manifestations of issues of abandonment, identity disturbance, impulsivity, affective instability, feelings of emptiness, anger, paranoia, and dissociative symptoms are all paramount to the accurate diagnosis of BPD. At times throughout my clinical experience I have unfortunately seen the label of BPD applied due to recurrent deliberate self-harm (DSH) episodes, with the consideration of the further four symptoms or criteria to be present for diagnosing this disorder being grossly ignored. A total of at least *five* clinical symptoms are required for accurate diagnosis of BPD (American Psychiatric Association, 2013). Reduction of the diagnosis of BPD to a category to be used for patients who present with DSH behaviours and recurrent suicide attempts (often without further examination of the presence of additional symptoms required to make this diagnosis) is not only inaccurate but fosters what I consider as a poor clinical response to patients presenting with these behaviours[5]. Only five of the possible nine criteria listed for diagnosis of BPD via the *DSM-V* are required to be present and this *might not* include recurrent suicidal and self mutilation behaviours. Although DSH behaviour is common in BPD (Zisook, Goff, Sledge, & Shuchter, 1994), Skodol et al.

---

troublesome or perplexing patients into the borderline wasteland has been seen in my clinical practice, even as I write this text.

[4] Within the newly published *DSM-V*, all of the 10 *DSM-IV-TR* recognised personality disorders remain. The criteria sets for the diagnosis of BPD (and all other personality disorders) remain unchanged. There has also been a change made with regards to 'personality disorder, not otherwise specified'. It is now considered as 'personality disorder – trait specified'. The distinct axial presentation of personality disorders (on axis two) has been removed however, allowing for a consideration of BPD as a mental disorder within a single axis with other mental disorders and general medical conditions. The arbitrary boundaries of personality disorder from other mental disorders have been removed. It is hoped that the addition of the diagnosis of 'personality disorder – trait specified', where a personality disorder is considered present but not diagnosed (as all criteria are not met) does not contribute to the current issue of inaccurate or incomplete diagnostic practices, and prejudicial or inaccurate risk management procedures. As BPD (with all personality disorders) should be considered on a spectrum, wouldn't most of the patients we treat then be able to be considered as borderline (trait specified) if meeting some of the criterions for the diagnosis (and therefore show a sub-clinical presentation)?

[5] As earlier stated, I do not assume that self-harm behaviours occur in all cases of BPD, and the focus on the DSH behaviours throughout this text is in direct response to the greatest difficulty I have observed in working alongside many other clinicians in contact with patients with BPD. I believe that DSH is the symptom that creates the most anxiety for the clinical community in working with BPD.

(2002) have calculated that with nine possible criteria, and five criteria needed for diagnosis of BPD, 151 different symptom combinations are possible for the one diagnosis of BPD.

Diagnostic procedures need to consider not only the nine symptom descriptors or criterions for BPD, but also appreciate that the diagnosis relies on a consideration of the patient (and the presence of these symptoms) across a variety of contexts, and therefore consistent with a *pervasive* pattern[6]. Furthermore, the emergence and development of BPD symptoms in the context of the patient's childhood and adolescence (as a precursor to its clinical presentation and diagnosis in early adulthood) is fundamental to the accurate assessment and consequential diagnosis of this disorder. In order to improve diagnostic consideration of BPD (and therefore possibly develop more accurate diagnostic procedures), clinical education has been found to positively influence diagnostic practices. In a recent study, a decrease in the reliance on the behavioural symptoms in the consideration of BPD as a diagnosis, with an increase in the consideration of the interpersonal and aetiological symptoms of the disorder was found following attendance at a targeted education program on BPD (Commons Treloar, 2009c). In presenting clinical information on BPD, including criteria and diagnostic procedures, and case illustrations of BPD, it appears that clinicians may become more aware of the developmental factors and pervasive patterns of the diagnosis, and thus many varied presentations or symptomologic patterns of BPD (Commons Treloar, 2009c).

Reducing the reliance on using the behavioural symptoms of BPD (that tend to dominate screening procedures for the diagnosis), in preference for a consideration of the interpersonal difficulties of the patient and the aetiological factors in the development of BPD, may result in a more measured assessment process by the clinician. This process may then be more engaging for the patient when assessing for BPD (Commons Treloar, 2009c). The interpersonal difficulties and aetiological factors are not readily observable, as are the recurrent suicidal or recurrent mutilation behaviours of the patient. As such, clinicians would need to spend necessary clinical time in providing adequate clinical interview and assessment of the patients in order to consider these factors. The clinician would need to engage and talk with the patient to consider these developmentally significant and relevant dynamics. The change in the consideration of BPD symptomatology could reduce the minimalist screening techniques and eager application of the label of BPD in patients, as the observation of behavioural displays and the recording of symptoms via a symptom checklist would be insufficient for the thorough investigation and accurate application of the diagnosis. Clinicians would need to take the time to use qualitative assessment procedures, such as structured clinical interview with their patients, and obtain a detailed clinical history *prior* to the application of the psychiatric label of BPD[7].

[6] Indeed I have seen adult patients diagnosed with BPD due to a six month history of affective instability, impulsivity, recurrent suicidal gestures, difficulty controlling anger, and issues with abandonment, without an extensive, persistent, or premorbid history of this symptomatologic pattern. Similarly I have seen BPD diagnosed in patients who are experiencing relationship breakdown (and presenting with fear of abandonment, feelings of emptiness, anger outbursts, suicidal threats, and paranoia) but remain functional in all other areas of their life, with steady and rewarding employment, and positive interactions with a good social network that are considered supportive. The clinical pattern needs to be *persistent* and *all-encompassing* for the disorder to be diagnosed.

[7] Further discussion of the importance, clinical use, and technique of this process is provided in further chapters of this text.

From a review of the literature, indeed some researchers have recommended the assessment of DSH behaviours as a diagnostic indicator to distinguish BPD patients from other patient presentations as DSH behaviour was felt to be sufficiently consistent amongst BPD to diagnose this disorder (e.g., Gunderson, Kolb, & Austin, 1981; Perry & Klerman, 1980; Spitzer & Endicott, 1979). Sansone, Weiderman, and Sansone (1998) developed a scale for identifying DSH behaviours and BPD, where the diagnosis of BPD could be considered via an assessment of the patient's behavioural disturbance. The Self-Harm Inventory (SHI) (Sansone et al., 1998) is a self report measure that comprises of 22 items to explore the types of DSH behaviours in which respondents have engaged. Using a cut off score of 5, the SHI was found to diagnose 83.7% of BPD cases correctly (compared to clinical interview). Although the authors report that the SHI shows acceptable clinical accuracy as a screening measure for the diagnosis of BPD, the practice of reducing BPD diagnostic practice to the completion of a 22 item self report questionnaire remains questionable. As noted by its creators, the screening tool does rely entirely on the patient's candour and comprehension of items and "is not based upon a theoretical construct for the disorder, but rather the association between self-harm behaviours and BPD" (Sansone et al., 1998, p.981).

Although considered as a "practical adjunct to the diagnosis of BPD" (Sansone et al., 1998, p.981), it is feared that the use of such a simplistic measure may further reduce the detailed investigation required for accurate diagnosis. It may also lead to further reduction of DSH behaviour as purely an indicator of BPD, and a greater neglect of the other criteria required for the accurate diagnosis of BPD in the clinical setting. It is important to consider that it is estimated that 4% of the general population has engaged in at least one episode of DSH, with approximately 0.3% doing so regularly (Briere & Gill, 1998). Moreover, it has been found that 35% of female patients with a diagnosable eating disorder engage in DSH behaviour (Paul, Schroefer, Dahme, & Nutzinger, 2002) – does this mean that one third of patients with this diagnosis can also be considered as having BPD? [8] Furthermore, it has been found that DSH behaviour is also present in the other personality disorders, despite DSH only being listed as a criterion for BPD (Klonsky, Oltmanns, & Turkheimer, 2003).

In response to simplified diagnostic practices and concerns with the reduction of BPD as a category for DSH, many other researchers have cautioned about the early diagnosis of BPD in clinical samples without adequate assessment being made; they in fact recommend the use of both quantitative and qualitative assessment procedures to determine the appropriateness of the diagnostic categorisation in each circumstance (e.g., Zanarini et al., 2003; Tredget, 2001). Warne and McAndrew (2006) also caution about some symptoms of BPD, including DSH behaviours, being taken at their face value and without an understanding of the possible causation being sought. The use of clear descriptions of the key symptoms of BPD can be seen as a step toward preventing the misdiagnosis and the misuse of the term 'borderline patient'. Despite the development of more rigorous classification systems and assessment procedures, it has however been noted that in today's clinical setting, the observation of symptoms of recurrent self mutilation and recurrent suicidality continue to dominate in diagnostic procedures (Hill, Swales, & Byatt, 2005; Sansone et al., 1998). This preference can

---

[8] Although co-morbidity of BPD with other psychiatric diagnoses is high, the estimation of one third of patients with an eating disorder being able to be considered as having BPD – via the possible use of the 22 item self report tool to assess the patient's behaviour disturbance (Sansone et al., 1998) – is highly questionable. The SHI requires further investigation in terms of its power to be able to successfully identify or differentiate between patients that *do not* attract the diagnosis of BPD.

often result in a problematic neglect of many of the *DSM-V* criterions, let alone broader diagnostic considerations derived from emerging research. "Clinicians have long associated repetitive and chronic self-harm behaviour with borderline personality disorder" (Sansone et al., 1998, p.974). Although some researchers believe that recurrent DSH behaviours appear to comprise a distinct component of personality disturbance (e.g., Livesley, Jackson, & Schroeder, 1989), the reduction of the diagnosis of BPD to a category to be used for patients who present with self-harming behaviours and suicide attempts, without further examination or assessment of the presence of additional symptoms required to make this diagnosis, is inaccurate and promotes a poorer clinical response to patients presenting with these behaviours. Accurate application of the BPD diagnosis requires the presence of further symptomatology, and considering the categorisation of BPD with only the observations of DSH or suicidal gestures is contrary to the procedural approaches outlined by the *DSM-V*.

Prevalence and Aetiology of the Disorder

Regardless of the cause, over the last decade the incidence of the BPD diagnosis appears to be increasing (Hodges, 2003). The statistics on the prevalence of BPD rely on the accurate diagnosis of this disorder using *DSM-V* criteria, and may raise the question of whether the population of BPD sufferers is indeed increasing as a 'symptom' of the lack of quantitative and qualitative assessment procedures being completed in preference for briefer screening procedures, or the need to apply diagnostic categorisation to the utilisers of the current health care system. Within the current Australian psychiatric system, all patient registrations completed upon the patient's entry to the service require a diagnosis to be recorded, using the *International Statistical Classification of Diseases and Health Related Problems*, tenth edition (*ICD-10*)(World Health Organization, 2004). The need to list a diagnosis on the person's registration occurs after only an initial screening assessment process is completed to determine whether the person will become a patient of the Australian health system. Perhaps the increase in BPD rates is not an indication of greater mental health problems in the community, but rather may be a symptom of limited time available for adequate differential assessment or a symptom of the requirements of the registration and information technology processes of today's health system. The accurate clinical assessment of personality disorders is a time consuming process and due to increasing demand on the health system, the lengthy assessment of BPD may possibly be avoided.

In review of the literature, there does appear to be some discrepancy with regards to the calculation of the prevalence of BPD in the community. In North American studies, the prevalence of BPD is generously estimated at 0.2-1.8% of the general population (Swartz, Blazer, George, & Winfield, 1990). What is considered as one of the most empirically-stringent and reliable studies into the prevalence of BPD was completed by Torgersen, Kringlen, and Cramer (2001) in Oslo, Norway. Torgersen and colleagues (2001) found that 0.7% of the community sample was diagnosed with BPD. When one reviews the prevalence of BPD in mental health samples however the rate dramatically increases: 8-11% in outpatient clinics, 14-20% in inpatient clinics, and 60-80% in forensic facilities (Bateman & Fonagy, 2004). "Individuals meeting criteria for BPD are flooding mental health centres and practitioners' offices…Borderline patients are so numerous that most practitioners must treat at least one" (Linehan, 1993, p.3). As a treating clinician this does result in a high likelihood, regardless of the mental health setting one is employed in, that there is already a number of BPD patients every clinician is (maybe unsuspectingly) already treating.

Regardless of the clinical debate on prevalence, much research has been conducted into the aetiology of BPD. Being a disorder of personality, BPD is considered to be developmental in origin and therefore many studies have been conducted into determining childhood experiences that are significant to the later development of this disorder. High rates of parental loss, whether through divorce, illness, or death, have been found common to patients later diagnosed with BPD (Walsh, 1977). Walsh (1977) also concluded that atypical parenting attitudes, such as over involved or over protective parenting, may also be a significant factor. Many patients with BPD have also reported a family history of mood disorders and substance use disorders (Widiger & Trull, 1992) or have experienced childhood trauma and neglect (Zanarini & Frankenburg, 1997).

A study of 358 patients with BPD and a comparison group of 109 patients with other personality disorders[9] was completed to examine the reported pathological childhood experiences associated specifically with development of the borderline personality pattern (Zanarini, Williams, et al., 1997). BPD patients were significantly more likely than comparison patients with other forms of personality disorder to have been emotionally and physically abused by a caretaker and sexually abused by a non-caretaker: 91% reported having been abused and 92% reported having been neglected before the age of 18 (Zanarini, Williams, et al., 1997). Zanarini, Williams, and colleagues (1997) also found that the patients with BPD were significantly more likely to report having a caretaker withdraw from them emotionally, treat them inconsistently, deny their thoughts and feelings, place them in the role of parent, and fail to provide them with needed protection.

In general terms, the significant predictors of BPD in adulthood include female gender and the following experiences in childhood: sexual abuse by a male non-caretaker, emotional denial by a male caretaker, and inconsistent treatment by a female caretaker (Zanarini, Williams, et al., 1997)[10]. With such early developmental experiences, the engagement of the patient to a suitable therapeutic alliance is often troublesome. Fears of abuse, denial, and abandonment (as may have been present throughout the patient's life) impact on this alliance. It is imperative therefore that when determining the development of the borderline pathology in the therapeutic setting, each patient's experience needs to be carefully listened to and acknowledged. A list of childhood experiences needs not to be written down in a file and conceptually disregarded but considered carefully within the psychotherapeutic setting. This inquiry or examination includes investigation of difficulties with relating to caretakers, not just a history of incest as commonly believed. Sexual abuse is neither necessary nor sufficient for the development of BPD in adulthood and other childhood experiences, particularly neglect by caretakers of both genders, represent significant risk factors (Zanarini, Williams, et al., 1997; Van der Kolk, McFarlane, & Weisaeth, 1996).

---

[9] These patients met the *DSM* criteria for at least one axis II disorder other than BPD, including paranoid, schizoid, schizotypal, anti-social, narcissistic, histrionic, avoidant, dependant, and/or obsessive-compulsive.

[10] In fact, in consideration of all the BPD patients I am currently treating, all of them would identify with the experience of emotional denial by a father figure and inconsistent treatment by a mother figure (as well as a few with the experience of sexual abuse). Indeed all three of the patients to be illustrated here account experiences consistent with this too (as presented in part three of this text).

It has been found that typically children who later come to develop BPD:

> have begun their lives in an environment that was extremely intrusive and impinging…there was a serious lack of respect for the integrity and individuality of the child… (and)…as the children got older, such normal acts as self assertion, the keeping of secrets, and the wish for privacy gravely threatened the parents because these capabilities all represent ego-autonomy and apartness…the child comes to feel that not even slight divergences of opinion can be expressed unless the parent can be convinced that it is acceptable. (Saretsky, 1976, p.437).

Thorough consideration of these early attachment relationships is important not only in terms of the development of masochistic tendencies and the behavioural presentation of self-harm but also in the presentation of fear of abandonment, emptiness, and poor self concept observed in the BPD patient. In an attachment study by Fonagy et al. (1996) many BPD inpatients were found to be fearfully preoccupied with attachment[11], with 47% of BPD patients in this study so classified, as compared to 28% of the psychiatric group without the BPD diagnosis and 1% of the control subjects. In consideration of this, it helps give meaning to how or why any small gesture of rejection or disapproval by the clinician can become significant sources of anxiety and preoccupation by the BPD patient (often resulting in an exacerbation of the behavioural disturbance). The residual attachment patterns from childhood remain active in the adult patient and therefore need clinical consideration. They do become of significance to the clinical interaction and the therapeutic relationship[12].

THE CLINICAL PRESENTATION OF BORDERLINE PATIENTS

The presentation of the borderline symptoms occurs by early adulthood, and thus can be considered to have aetiological connections to the child's development. Therefore upon entry into treatment, the adult BPD patient has *already developed* the pervasive pattern that affects the way they relate to the world around them. The psychotherapeutic treatment of BPD is intricate and requires a thorough understanding of the complexity and severity of the disorder to effect symptom reduction and greater behavioural, affective, interpersonal, and cognitive stability. The impulsivity, issues with abandonment, poor self image, and feelings of emptiness (among others) all contribute to the occurrence of DSH behaviour. They are already well developed and entrenched in the patient's interactions (across all facets of their life), and are constantly activated in their response to the environment. For this reason, psychotherapeutic treatment will need to be long term in order to sustain any form of desirable therapeutic response, and an enduring commitment from the clinician will therefore be needed. To understand the patient's symptoms and responses, careful examination of the development of the disorder (from the unique individual experience of the patient) is warranted. Given the damage already caused by other trusted adults in the patient's past, and the extent in which the attachment to these abusers remains activated, an appropriate level of therapeutic inquiry and steadfast engagement to the therapeutic relationship is required (if the clinician is to be successful in tolerating the patient's symptoms and psychotherapeutically treating the patient with BPD).

---

[11] In this study, Fonagy et al. (1996) used the three attachment categories of free-autonomous, dismissive, and preoccupied, as outlined by the attachment classification system of Main & Goldwyn (1991).

[12] Further discussion of this is provided for in later chapters of this text.

As suggested within the delineation of *DSM-V* criteria, the BPD pattern is one characterised by not only behavioural but affective, interpersonal, and cognitive instability. Due to this pervasive pattern, it should be expected that the therapeutic encounter with the BPD patient can be often influenced by this instability. As such, the nature of the BPD patient's pattern of instability requires careful consideration in both treatment planning and in the execution of psychotherapeutic treatment. The issues of abandonment, often a by-product of the patient's developmental history, will commonly be replayed through the transference relationship. Behavioural displays to test the commitment of the clinician to the psychotherapeutic relationship are common. The instability of the interpersonal relationships outside the therapeutic setting can also impact on not only the patient's attendance at therapy but can also dominate the matters raised by the patient in the therapy session itself. The BPD patient's identity disturbance and mood reactivity also contribute to their difficulties in managing day to day functioning, with co-morbid illness such as anxiety and depression being commonplace (Skodol et al., 2002).

With growing numbers of patients with this diagnosis (Hodges, 2003), the avoidance of the psychotherapeutic treatment of patients with BPD is difficult. These patients are major utilisers of services, particularly of mental health and emergency medicine services. The effectiveness of clinical and medical interventions however remains questionable, with this patient group having a mortality rate by suicide of close to 10% (Work Group on Borderline Personality Disorder, 2001). Treatment remains complex and difficult as the clinical presentation of BPD is of severe functional impairment in a broad spectrum of areas, such as employment, substance use, and interpersonal relationships (Work Group on Borderline Personality Disorder, 2001). Impairment in these areas also impacts on the ability to the BPD patient to commit to ongoing treatment or therapy. With no productive or rewarding activity during the day, frequent high use of alcohol and other drugs, and often limited social networks involved to also provide support, keeping the BPD patient in therapy – and effective therapy – is often primarily dependent upon a strong therapeutic alliance with an appropriate clinician.

The Impact of the Application of the Diagnostic Label

As mentioned previously, I caution against the ready use of the diagnostic label of BPD as it can often prevent health professionals from considering the experience of the individual patient and understanding the development and intent behind their DSH behaviours. Unfortunately many clinicians often remain uncomfortable with discussing the patient's experience or the intent behind their behaviour. "A typical dilemma is not knowing whether to interpret or to inquire" (Watson, 1996, p.82). Johnstone (1997) found that once diagnosis of BPD is made, inquiry tends to cease and clinicians often see the disorder rather than the person with the disorder. Again the reasons behind the patient's DSH behaviours are often ignored – it becomes dismissed as something they just do regularly by nature of their diagnosis. It is important to remember that self-harm behaviour does occur with other mental health disorders, such as those with schizophrenia, anxiety, and depression. The presence of DSH behaviour does not necessarily indicate that the diagnosis of BPD should be considered. Indeed, Silburn and Zubrick (1995) reviewed 182 consecutive DSH presentations of young patients aged 14-19 years who attended hospitals in Perth, Australia, and found that 43% of the sample did not met the criteria for any psychiatric diagnosis. Unfortunately the diagnosis of BPD in today's public health service has become not only problematic in terms of its use to categorise patients who present with DSH behaviours and suicide attempts, often without further examination of the presence of additional symptoms required to make this diagnosis, but also in mediating the clinical and/or medical response to patients presenting with these behaviours.

Given that the diagnostic label of BPD can often shape staff responses (Johnstone, 1997), it remains important to consider how this diagnostic label is conceptualised and thus applied in today's psychiatric setting. It is evident that the use of BPD as a psychiatric diagnosis in today's health setting is increasing (Hodges 2003; Linehan, 1993), despite attempts by the clinical community to regulate its use as a diagnosis through the application of rigorous classificatory systems. Although the *DSM-V* application of the diagnosis does not require the active consideration of the interpersonal histories or experiences of the patient, rather criteria sets of symptoms (as such research on childhood and familial experienced does not have statistical or predictive power in determining the presence of the borderline personality pattern in adulthood), the consideration of the patient's history is important in understanding the pervasive pattern of how they interact with the world around them. I believe that the patient's early life experiences do become pertinent to reflect on not only in terms of diagnosis but also in the provision of psychotherapeutic treatment and understanding our clinical interaction with the BPD patient. As to be illustrated here in later chapters, the BPD patient's history does impact on the patient's individual symptomalogic presentation, on their unique pattern of instability and relating to the world, and on their personal ability to appropriately engage in a therapeutic alliance with a suitable health professional.

Chapter 2

DELIBERATE SELF-HARM AND BORDERLINE PERSONALITY DISORDER

CLASSIFYING BEHAVIOUR AS 'DELIBERATE' SELF-HARM

The World Health Organization (WHO) defines -as an act with non fatal outcome, in which an individual deliberately initiates a non-habitual behaviour[1] that without intervention from others will cause self-harm, or deliberately ingests a substance in excess of the prescribed or generally recognised therapeutic dosage, and which is aimed at realising changes which the subject desired via the actual or expected physical consequences (Platt, Bille-Brahe, & Kerkhof, 1992). More simplistically, and the preferred definition for the purpose of this text, the National Collaborating Centre for Mental Health (2004) describes self-harm as self poisoning or self injury, irrespective of the apparent purpose of the act. This definition coincides with the finding of the Australian Psychological Society (1999) who report in their publication of *Suicide: An Australian Psychological Society Discussion Paper* that the term DSH is preferred by many clinicians, without any reference usually made to the intent behind such harm. Indeed the Australian Psychological Society (1999) argues in this discussion paper on suicide that there is often a range of motivations or intentions behind the act of DSH behaviours; the nature of the intent may be shifting and ambivalent. Horrocks, Price, and House (2003) also state that repeated self-harm might not always be for the same reason, or by the same methods, each time. This variation[2] suggests that intent behind the self-harm behaviours needs to be assessed with each episode and not inferred from previous instances of similar behaviours; indeed an assessment of DSH risk therefore needs to be undertaken at each clinical contact[3]. The National Collaborating Centre for Mental Health (2004) supports the regular assessment of each episode of DSH behaviour, reporting that

---

[1] Although the WHO refers to a non-habitual behaviour in defining self-harm, this position is open to question as I have had much contact with BPD patients who have described their DSH behaviours as being habitual or even addictive in nature, and much literature also supports such a counterargument (e.g., McAllister, 2003; Strong, 1998).

[2] I feel that this argument of the nature of the intent behind DSH being shifting and ambivalent, and therefore maybe not for the same reason each time it occurs, is also open to question. The trigger to the DSH episode may be variable in each instance but I believe that the basic function, or drive, of the self-inflicted injury is the same in each instance – this is further discussed later in the text.

[3] An examination of the trigger to each occurrence of DSH is paramount to assist in understanding the underlying function and drive of the behaviour (let alone to also keep the patient engaged in the therapeutic alliance).

assumptions about intent should not be based on previous patterns of self-harm. Each act must be assessed separately to determine the motivation behind the current behaviour, particularly in an attempt to distinguish between DSH and suicidal gesture. Failure to do so can result in the behaviour of self-harm being misunderstood, resulting in an inaccurate interpretation of the act of self-harm that the patient can find judgemental or dismissive.

FORMS OF DELIBERATE SELF-HARM

In general terms, self-harm is classified into two broad categories of self poisoning and self injuring. Self poisoners are more likely to seek assistance following overdose on medication, with 80% of DSH presentations to emergency medicine departments consisting of self poisoning, usually an overdose of prescribed or over the counter medication (Horrocks et al., 2003). In contrast to those that attend emergency medicine departments, self injury is considered to be more common than self poisoning in the general population, with a British study concluding that self injury is more common in teenagers than self poisoning at an estimated ratio of 2:1 (Hawton, Rodham, & Evans, 2002). Cutting is considered the most common means of self injury; however self injury can also include deliberately inflicted harm by burning, stabbing, swallowing objects, insertion of objects, shooting, jumping from heights, and jumping in front of vehicles (Middleton & Butler, 1998). Middleton and Butler (1998) also argue that more abstractly, self-harm can also include excessive risk taking, excessive drinking, starvation, unprotected sex with multiple partners, reckless driving, self-imposed neglect of hygiene or health, and the provoking of violence from others.

Unfortunately repeated DSH patients are often seen as only attention seeking and the risk of further injury and suicide can be grossly underestimated. Following an episode of DSH behaviour, Hawton, Zahl, and Weatherall (2003) estimated that the risk of attempted suicide in that patient increases to 50-100 times the risk of attempted suicide in the general population; in fact, they found that men who have self-harmed are two times more likely to complete suicide as women that have self-harmed. Disturbingly, an estimated 25% of all people who die by suicide have attended an emergency department following an episode of DSH in the previous year (Owens & House, 1994). Based on these findings, I believe that it could perhaps be argued that 'attention seeking' may in fact be a somewhat appropriate term to consider with regard to repeated self injury – 'attention seeking' in that the presence of recurrent DSH behaviours should be recognised as a significant indication that clinical attention *needs to be paid* to the level of distress and turmoil that the patient is experiencing (not only to adequately assess and manage ongoing risk but to enable validation of the patient's distress). In support of this, approximately 18% of people who attend emergency departments following self-harm will self-harm again in the following year (Owens & House, 1994). With entry of such patients into appropriate treatment, this number could be reduced.

As cautioned by the National Collaborating Centre for Mental Health (2004), there is insufficient evidence to support the widely held view that the small minority of people who harm themselves repeatedly, such as the BPD patient group, are less likely to die by suicide. Recurrent DSH behaviours in the BPD patient group may often be also considered differently due to the presence of the diagnostic categorisation. As opposed to an acute reaction to an overwhelming stressor (such as terminal illness or relationship breakdown), chronic DSH behaviour or suicidal ideation is typically in response to "the day's chaotic events", and this is considered as most common in personality disorders (Barbe, Rubovszky, Venturini-Andreoli, & Andreoli, 2005, p.284).

COMPARING RATES OF SUICIDE AND DELIBERATE SELF-HARM

In Australia, death by suicide accounted for approximately three percent of all deaths in 1995 (Australian Psychological Society, 1999). In 2010, the rate declined to 1.6% of all deaths, and there were 2361 registered deaths from suicide, compared to 2286 of such deaths in the previous year (Australian Bureau of Statistics, 2013). Despite the trend of the age pattern changing with an increase of youth suicide (especially in male youth), this figure has remained generally constant over the past century with suicide accounting for 21 deaths per 100,000 for males and 5.5 deaths per 100,000 for females (Australian Psychological Society, 1999). In 2010, the rate of male suicide was 16.3 per 100,000 and 4.9 per 100,000 for female suicide (Australian Bureau of Statistics, 2013)[4]. Statistics for suicides, although dependent on many factors including lengthy coroners' inquests, are more easily determined than that of self-harm. Many incidents of self-harm do not reach the attention of services or professionals (Mental Health Foundation, 1997).

In comparison to the general population, suicidal behaviours are more common with BPD, with mortality rates by suicide as high as 10% in the BPD patient group (Work Group on Borderline Personality Disorder, 2001). Despite many treatment programs being developed to target these self destructive behaviours, as a rule attempted suicide and completed suicide in BPD is still poorly understood (Weinberg & Maltsberger, 2007). There is also often a lack of clear distinction between DSH behaviours and suicide attempts, with reference to intent – the key component of deciphering between these two behaviours – often being overlooked or disregarded. Due to this regular confusion, Weinberg & Maltsberger (2007) argue that self-harm and suicide are significantly different and should be studied separately, regardless of diagnostic categorisation.

In Australia, the Victorian Suicide Prevention Task Force (1997) attempted to calculate the rates of self-harm in the general population in Victoria through the number of people presenting to the state's hospitals with intentional self-inflicted injury or self poisoning between 1987 and 1996. They estimated that the rates of self-harm were approximately 64 per 100,000 for males, and 93 per 100,000 for females; these figures however do underestimate the occurrence of DSH behaviours as the study excluded those presentations that were discharged from the emergency departments within four hours of presentation (Victorian Suicide Prevention Task Force, 1997). Alarmingly, the rate of self injury presentations in the community appears to be increasing with recorded 55 per 100,000 people exhibiting this behaviour in 1987 to a rate of self injury in 1995 recorded at 112 per 100,000 people (Victorian Suicide Prevention Task Force, 1997).

[4] And these rates are generally consistent across many developed countries. For example in 2009 the rates of suicide in the United States of America were 19.5 males per 100,000 and 5.5 females per 100,000 (Kochanek, Xu, Murphy, Miniño, & Kung, 2011); and in 2010 the United Kingdom recorded suicide rates of 17.0 males per 100,000 and 5.3 females per 100,000 (Office for National Statistics, 2012).

With regard to DSH behaviours in the BPD patient group, as compared to the general population, the incidence is much more common. Zisook et al. (1994) found that DSH behaviour was found in 75% of patients with BPD (or as a comparison to the above figures, a colossal rate of 75,000 per 100,000 people with this diagnosis)[5].

REPEATED SELF-HARM AND THE MISUSE OF THE DIAGNOSIS

Recurrent suicide attempts and DSH behaviours are not in themselves indicative of a personality disorder, contrary to the common belief that self-harm is an indicator particularly of BPD and despite one of the criterions for its diagnosis being recurrent suicidal or self mutilating behaviours (American Psychiatric Association, 2013). Although there are such patients within this diagnostic category who do not self-harm, in my experience it is often due to this 'criterion' that they come to our clinical attention. Indeed DSH actions in this patient group often tend to be managed with behavioural techniques such as diversion or distraction, which can be ineffective when the patient's reasoning behind their DSH behaviours are not investigated and their pattern of continued self-harm is misunderstood (Haswell & Graham, 1996). It is important to consider that the reasons described for accomplishing self-harm are often related to punishment, relief of some dysphoric state, or emotional regulation, which is of significance to the provision of psychotherapeutic treatment (Barbe et al., 2005).

With 75% of BPD patients engaging in some regular forms of DSH, and in my experience many of them engaging in extreme forms of DSH (as will be illustrated in the first two case illustrations to be presented here), the tentativeness of the clinical community to become involved in the care of the patient labelled as BPD is common. Johnstone (1997) found that staff often judge patients with the diagnosis of BPD harshly, feared contact with them, constructed their condition as chronic, and therefore felt that these patients were unlikely to change. With this viewpoint, resistance by clinicians to attempt to engage and thus provide effective treatment to patients with BPD remains stagnant.

> ...in many ways, the borderline calls forth strong emotional reactions in a therapist in an attempt to establish and maintain some form of emotional relatedness to the other, literally to 'bind' with the other through the force of emotions. The therapist experiences these binds quite differently, often feeling strongly, but with little or no desire to maintain the interaction. (Watson, 1996, p.82).

Given that the diagnostic label of BPD may often shape staff attitudes and therapeutic responses, it is argued that considering the individual patient experience (as a unique presentation rather than a diagnostic group) may assist in promoting a greater empathy and understanding of the patient's instability[6]. Taking the time to invest in the care of the patient, not in the diagnosis, is essential in the psychotherapeutic relationship. The engagement of the clinician to the process of inquiry, to understanding the experiences of the individual who could be termed as borderline, may then assist in the establishment and maintenance of an

[5] By process of deduction, it is also important to consider that DSH is not found in 25% of cases of BPD. This is important to consider in terms of earlier discussion on diagnostic conceptualisation and procedures.

[6] Although placed into an arbitrary diagnostic classification of BPD, it is the individual patients with whom we have to work.

appropriate therapeutic relationship – a relationship which is needed for the provision of any effective therapy or treatment. Crucial to the prognosis of the patient is the quality of object relations; especially the quality of the therapeutic relationship between patient and therapist – and countertransference problems also make prognostic judgements difficult (Woollcott, 1985). Therefore to understand and manage DSH behaviours and acknowledge the distress of the BPD patient, we need to ensure that as clinicians we can be open to, *and committed to*, the therapeutic relationship with these patients.

Chapter 3

The Professional Response to Borderline Personality Disorder

Professional Attitudes Toward Deliberate Self-harm Behaviours

Given that patients diagnosed with BPD are major users of health services, it is assumed that most clinicians will have some contact (of various forms including routine care or crisis intervention) across the term of their employment. With a 10% mortality rates by suicide, there is clearly room for improvement in the clinical management of this patient group. The challenge in providing effective or even adequate management often stems from the confronting and pervasive patterns of behaviour that affect the way these patients relate interpersonally during their clinical contacts. Impulsivity, issues with abandonment, poor self image, and feelings of emptiness contribute to the presentation of recurrent DSH behaviours and some of the difficulties observed in the ongoing engagement of the BPD patient in treatment planning and service provision. As such, working with patients with BPD has well acknowledged challenges, not least of all is that attempts to prevent further self injury or overdose can appear ineffectual in the context of recurrent DSH behaviour presentations throughout the period of clinical care.

As a result there has been an increasing focus in examining the way that health professionals relate to this patient group. According to the research, attitudes of professionals toward patients diagnosed with BPD tend to be negative and derogatory (Commons Treloar, 2009b; Bowers & Allan, 2006; McAllister, Creedy, Moyle, & Farrugia, 2002; Haswell & Graham, 1996). In my experience, their self-harm behaviours tend to be managed with behavioural techniques such as seclusion and restraint within the inpatient setting, or diversion and distraction in the community setting. This can often be ineffective when the patient's intent behind their DSH behaviour is not adequately discussed or investigated by the clinician involved in their care. As discussed earlier, due to the presence of the diagnostic label and the often frequent presentations to the health services with thoughts or actions of DSH or suicide, the continued patterns of self-harm are often frequently misunderstood and not appropriately assessed (Haswell & Graham, 1996). These pessimistic attitudes and reactive behavioural management strategies then act as a major barrier to effective service provision for this group of patients[1]. Whether these attitudes may be directly demonstrated or covertly disguised, patients may sense negative attitudes through the clinician's demeanour and manner (McAllister et al., 2002), which may prompt further self-harm behaviour (Hemmings, 1999)[2].

Within the literature, few studies have investigated attitudes of different professions or specialists across different settings (McAllister et al., 2002). Platt and Salter (1987) found that when compared with psychiatrists, nurses in emergency medicine were more likely to view overdose as attention seeking behaviour. Although it would be reasonable to expect that clinicians within the mental health setting would have more positive attitudes toward working with patients who engage in self-harm (due to the more regular contact they would have with these patients), the research has demonstrated conflicting confirmation of this assumption. A study by Lewis and Appleby (1988) revealed that patients who were given a previous diagnosis of a personality disorder were seen as more difficult and less deserving of care by a sample of psychiatrists than patients who did not attract such a diagnosis. Anderson (1997) found no differences in attitudes when comparing a sample of nursing staff in a community mental health setting (n=33) to those in an emergency medicine setting (n=33). Both groups reported similar attitudes towards patients presenting with self-harm and suicidal behaviours, using the Suicide Opinion Questionnaire designed by Domino, Westlake, and Gibson (1982).

Regular clinical exposure to BPD patients does not necessarily enable a nuanced consideration of this disorder, or of why these patients may behave in such destructive ways. It is evident in some studies that mental health clinicians can experience ambivalent attitudes towards patients presenting with DSH behaviour. In a study conducted with mental health staff in the United Kingdom in 2000 with 213 participants, 75% (n=60) of such staff reported that DSH behaviour in their patients was difficult to manage and 65% (n=128) of the sample also reported that they found it difficult to build a relationship with patients who present following DSH episodes (Huband & Tantam, 2000). A more recent study by Cleary, Siegfried, and Walter (2002) examined the attitudes of 229 mental health staff in a public mental health centre in New South Wales, Australia. It was found that 80% (n=183) of the participants felt that dealing with BPD patients was moderate to very difficult, and in fact 84% (n=192) felt that the BPD patient group was more difficult to deal with than other patient groups.

Some other studies support that the service setting, or place and reason in which we come into contact with the BPD patient, may be an influencing factor in the nature of clinician attitudes toward DSH behaviours in BPD patients. A comparative study by Suokas and Lonnqvist (1989) examined nursing attitudes towards DSH behaviours across emergency medicine and intensive care health settings. The emergency medicine staff (n=64) reported more negative attitudes toward such patients than their intensive care counterparts (n=73). The nature of care provided – in direct medical care of non-fatal injury and harm, or in the provision of almost fatal injury or harm – appears to be of some influence in how clinicians consider the patient and their behaviours, and therefore be able to empathise with the patient.

---

[1] As to be later demonstrated in this text, inadequate investigation or inquiry about why the patient has hurt themselves can contribute to an activation within the transference and therefore significantly impact on the therapeutic alliance required to achieve behavioural and structural change within the patient. A cumulative effect of distain and mistrust towards the clinician, even as a result of interactions with callous professional involved in the patient's history of care, impacts on the patient's current engagement in treatment.

[2] As to be discussed, the power of the transference in the activation (and/or resolve of DSH behaviour) needs careful consideration regularly and throughout the patient's psychotherapeutic care.

Similarly, Boyes (1994) reported that emergency medicine staff in particular reported frustration at their inability to cure the patient, as they often re-presented with similar non-fatal injuries despite recent medical treatment for their DSH behaviours.

In a more recent study, a number of factors were found to influence a clinician's attitude toward working with BPD patients that engage in DSH behaviours; this included the clinicians' service setting and whether they have undertaken training specific to developing a theoretical understanding of BPD (Commons Treloar & Lewis, 2008a). The attitude ratings of clinicians employed in the mental health service setting were more positive compared with clinicians working in the area of emergency medicine. Again, the significantly more negative attitudes of the clinicians from emergency medicine may be a function of the form of contact this professional group typically has with BPD patients. Emergency medicine clinicians are required to provide urgent medical attention to the patient with BPD following episodes of self injury or poisoning, and this may result in such professionals having a greater difficulty in maintaining an empathetic attitude toward such patients when also in contact with other patients requiring care from non-deliberate forms of harm[3]. The capacity for empathy may also be influenced by the high level of distress that the BPD patient presents with in the emergency department immediately following self mutilation or a suicide attempt. They can be difficult to engage and communicate poorly when highly agitated, particularly those patients with transient paranoia or severe dissociation. Mental health clinicians that provide ongoing management and treatment for BPD may have more positive attitudes toward working with this patient group as a consequence of their more sustained and involved level of care. They are involved in a capacity where the patient would not be actively engaging in DSH and therefore be more able to appreciate the development of the disorder and the specific difficulties experienced in the patient's personal life (in comparison to the emergency department nurse who interacts with the same patient in the context of applying sutures to a self-imposed cut on the patient's body) (Commons Treloar & Lewis, 2008a).

Further to the investigation of the effect of service setting on attitudes, gender of the clinician has also been shown to have some impact on the nature of clinician attitudes. Female clinicians across both mental health and emergency medicine service settings have been found to have more positive attitudes toward patients with BPD that engage in DSH (Commons Treloar & Lewis, 2008a). The ability of female clinicians to empathize with the patient may be related to the traditional sex role of the female being more able to nurture patients with significant emotional difficulties (Henley, 1977). Furthermore, the difference observed in the attitude ratings between male and female clinicians may be related to the higher presentation of female patients being diagnosed with BPD. Men are in the minority of patients receiving the diagnosis of BPD (Wirth-Cauchon, 2001), with 70-75% of patients with the disorder being female (Becker, 1997). Other factors such as the frequency of contact with patients with BPD, and level of university training completed prior to clinical exposure (across mental health and emergency medicine service settings) do not seem to be associated with attitude ratings toward such patients (Commons Treloar & Lewis, 2008a). Although some research has found that years of clinical experience may contribute to a better understanding and empathetic response to BPD patients, as nurses' attitudes toward DSH behaviours (specifically by overdose) were found to be more positive if the nursing clinicians

[3] I have often wondered how hard it must be to feel empathy for a patient who has just used a knife to sever a nerve in their arm when also providing care to another patient who has just amputated their leg in a tragic motor vehicle accident.

held greater years of clinical experience (McLaughlin, 1995), there were no differences found in other studies (Commons Treloar & Lewis, 2008a). In terms of maintaining an empathetic approach and positive attitude toward working with DSH behaviours in BPD patients, this suggests an alternative to the conventional wisdom that it is always necessary to allocate BPD patients to highly trained and experienced health professionals for all aspects of their clinical management; other factors are more predictive of positive attitudes to BPD patients. The individual variance in the therapeutic relationship across different patients with BPD (and indeed at different times of care with that same patient) is influenced by the individual history of the patient and is therefore also significantly influenced by the transference.

Consideration of the Transference and Countertransference

The way the patient interacts with us, and the way the patient perceives we relate to them, is inevitably a by-product of the patient's history – this is not something we can clinically influence in the early stages of psychotherapeutic care[4]. What can and does influence the transference response of the BPD patient at this time is the countertransference; our personal response created from our own history[5]. The form of support required by us as professionals when in clinical contact with BPD patients, whether as a provider of medical care, agent of intensive care, or as a source of psychological treatment, will ultimately have an influence on our countertransference reaction to the patient. As we would not have a thorough understanding of the patient's history, nor the development of a working hypothesis regarding the unconscious conflicts of the BPD patient (as this requires extensive clinical time), the early responses of the patient (and their continued DSH presentations) become a confusing interplay of their transference response with the clinician's response to their behaviour. The countertransference becomes everything to the establishment of, and commitment of the patient to, the therapeutic alliance.

In terms of managing our countertransference response in the circumstances of the patient's entry into psychological care, prior training in the theoretical constructs of BPD has been found to enable to base by which to mediate the clinician's interaction with the patient. Nursing and medical clinicians showed significant improvement in their attitude ratings if they had attended such training (Commons Treloar & Lewis, 2008a). Interestingly, allied health clinicians – such as social workers and psychologists – did report significantly more positive attitude ratings to working with BPD than nursing and medical clinicians (Commons Treloar & Lewis, 2008a). The differences in professional groups may suggest that basic professional trainings in psychosocial factors in mental illness may predispose allied health clinicians to more positive attitudes to patients with severe personality disorders than traditional biomedical trainings. The differences found between the attitude ratings amongst allied health professionals and their nursing and medical counterparts may be related to the limited efficacy in the use of the medical model in the treatment of BPD. Nursing and

---

[4] Nor be able to influence in the period of clinical care where medical attention is provided to the site of self mutilation.

[5] In this regard, countertransference is considered as everything in the clinician's personality, and prior history and experience that can affect the treatment.

medical training may place greater emphasis on the biology of health conditions, including mental disorders, than that of standardized allied health training. Unfortunately the use of psychopharmacology in the treatment of BPD has yielded inconsistent results, with only limited efficacy found for some antipsychotic and antidepressant medications, and mood stabilisers in symptom reduction with BPD (Bateman & Fonagy, 2004).

Although all disciplines consistently strive for evidence-based practice, it could be argued that the training of allied health clinicians in the realm of mental disorders appreciates more the aetiological constellations of personality disorder – and therefore begin to appreciate more the history of the patient (Commons Treloar & Lewis, 2008a). The treatment focus also remains fixed on psychotherapeutic strategies to achieve change in the disturbed behaviours typically observed in BPD, as opposed to pharmacological intervention (Commons Treloar & Lewis, 2008a). The basic training of allied health clinicians appears to promote more empathetic attitudes toward working with BPD, possibly as the training of these professionals is also more likely to consider the unconscious processes of the patients and reflect on the usefulness of considering the concept of the transference and countertransference (more so than their medical and nursing counterparts). Indeed of recent note, there has been a call to reintroduce the psychoanalytic perspective to basic medical school education, fearing that the exodus of psychoanalysis from psychiatric training has led to a reduction of psychiatry to the interactions between a drug and neurotransmitter receptor – the result of which is a less humanistic field (Mintz, 2013). In the end, the practice of psychoanalysis does result in a more empathogenic consideration of the patient's difficulties than that of bio-medical conceptualisations (even of diagnoses other than BPD).

RECOGNISING THE IMPORTANCE OF THE PATIENT'S HISTORY

Further to attitudes towards DSH behaviours and BPD patients, clinicians across different settings do appear to operationalise the disorder in different ways. In terms of screening for the diagnosis, the behavioural symptoms of BPD (such as impulsive behaviours that are self damaging, recurrent self mutilation, and recurrent suicidal threats and gestures) are heavily relied upon across both mental health and emergency department health settings (Commons Treloar & Lewis, 2009). A greater consideration of aetiological constellations in the conceptualisation of BPD as a possible diagnosis has been observed however amongst the emergency department clinicians, with mental health clinicians showing a greater consideration of the interpersonal difficulties of thc patient in the consideration of the diagnosis of BPD (Commons Treloar & Lewis, 2009)[6]. While empirical research suggests that the significant predictors of BPD in adulthood include female gender and interpersonally traumatic experiences in childhood (Zanarini, Williams, et al., 1997), in a clinical setting the symptoms which are more readily observed (such as recurrent overdose or cutting behaviours) are primarily used to screen for this complex disorder (Commons Treloar & Lewis, 2009). Although the DSM diagnostic criteria is used in the clinical setting, it is notable that the classification system which allows the diagnosis based on five symptoms of a

[6] Interestingly, the patient's history was considered as more important in the diagnosis of BPD by emergency department clinicians than those employed in the mental health setting. The mental health clinicians placed more significance on the patient's ability to interpersonally interact with the world around them in considering BPD as a diagnosis.

possible nine listed can be operationalised in substantially diverse ways across the different service settings (Commons Treloar & Lewis, 2009). The use of the diagnosis of BPD is rapidly increasing, and many clinicians and researchers have found the application of BPD to be problematic due to the impact such a label has on professional attitudes and consequent provision of therapeutic treatment. It can be argued that when considering BPD as a possible diagnosis, determining and understanding the *development* of the borderline pathology would have significant advantages. In terms of therapeutic work, a consideration or understanding of the development of the pathology should be the central part of not only the psychological treatment of this disorder but also in the initial and ongoing assessment, and continued engagement of the patient.

Contact with patients diagnosed with BPD who display serious and sometimes chronic patterns of DSH is a common experience for most clinicians, in both mental health and emergency medicine settings. Pessimistic attitudes regarding prognosis and the failure to maintain a positive approach, and therefore respond non-therapeutically, can result in the patient feeling critically judged and dismissed (Commons Treloar & Lewis, 2008a). This in turn limits the efficacy of interventions and may well add to the chronicity of such severe presentations (National Collaborating Centre for Mental Health, 2004). Although traditionally clinicians equate BPD patients with manipulativity and therefore are reluctant to engage with them (Potter, 2006), there is emerging evidence that training and education can assist in the improvement of empathetic attitudes toward working with this patient group. The provision of a theoretical grounding in BPD can assist in understanding the patient's history, and in mediating the transference relationship; ultimately enabling a greater commitment by the patient to the therapeutic alliance. Greater empathy and understanding would result in a more considered and tolerant approach to the patients' behavioural difficulties when DSH occurs – to see the patient who has hurt themselves as a by-product of their miserable history is clinically useful and important to the management of the patient's transference and to our countertransference response.

Clinician Rejection as a Typical Countertransference Response

The impediment to effective clinical interventions derived from negative professional attitudes has been well documented in studies. Alston and Robinson (1992) found that clinicians held negative attitudes toward patients that exhibit DSH behaviours and when faced with such patients the clinicians experienced a multitude of mixed emotions causing them distress and inner conflict, which then disposed them toward an absence of empathy regardless of the patients' need for therapeutic understanding. This was further supported by Vivekananda (2000) and even extended to general public opinion, including family and carers of patients who self-harm, who often experienced shame when their loved one self-harmed. People who self-harm create in us, as clinicians, medical staff, or families and friends, an uncomfortable mix of fear, guilt, anger, and frustration (Levenkron, 1998). As argued by McAllister (2003), to intentionally hurt oneself is seen to go against the core of the basic human values, and people who self-harm are therefore seen to contravene the most basic of human drives – self preservation. The disdain and disapproval experienced by the professional community when exposed to someone who has self-harmed is therefore able to be rationalised; it is morally uncomfortable to have to look upon grievous bodily harm inflicted by choice. This fear and discomfort however, if not managed appropriately, can affect the ongoing engagement of such patients to the therapeutic relationship.

DSH behaviours and suicide attempts are common precipitators for referral to public mental health services, and in fact accounted for approximately 37% of problems presented by patients to mental health services in Victoria, Australia, in 2001 (Auditor General Victoria, 2002). The high rate of utilisation of services of people who self-harm is also seen across other agencies and departments, such as hospital emergency departments, and private practitioners such as counsellors, psychologists, private psychiatrists, and general practitioners (Auditor General Victoria, 2002). Some studies have suggested that within the emergency medicine department, clinicians may make the person wait, express obvious expressions of frustration, anger, fear, and helplessness, fail to empathise, and fail to maintain safety and respect when presenting for medical care following DSH behaviour (regardless of diagnosis) (Johnstone, 1997). Patients who present to casualty are assessed and prioritized according to life threat, yet people who come to the emergency medicine department for medical assistance because of self-harm may not be perceived as good and deserving patients (Sbaih, 1993).

This rejection by the emergency staff is a behaviourally communicated clue of the repeated lived experience of a patient with BPD that many clinicians fail to see. In my experience, patients with psychosis may also experience inner turmoil; however the patients with personality disorder have their inner turmoil more readily experienced externally by others. "There are powerful emotional reactions that come about when treating borderline patients" (Watson, 1996, p.81). With increasing presentations of DSH behaviour to the health services, and given the need to differentially diagnose BPD patients from other patients presenting with DSH behaviours, education and training in the conceptualisation and diagnostic application of BPD is considered highly needed. As indicated in much of the literature on clinician attitudes to BPD, the presence of the diagnostic label can influence the willingness of clinicians to be involved in such patients' care, even predisposing clinicians to an absence of empathy (Alston & Robinson, 1992). "Clinicians tend to equate BPD patients with manipulativity and to forewarn others about them" (Potter, 2006, p.140).

Improving Clinician Attitudes Using Clinical Education

Given the difficulties observed with professional attitudes towards some mental health disorders, such as BPD and even other complex problems such as drug addiction, understanding the theoretical conceptualisation of such disorders may assist in the improvement of such attitudes. According to Fishbein and Ajzen (1975), the knowledge of society's expectations (and desire to comply with these expectations) can improve the likelihood of a behavioural response. In reflection of this, it is hypothesised that clinicians may be more likely to consider the experiences of the patient relevant to the development of their behavioural disturbance (as well as the diagnostic criteria of BPD in the application of the diagnostic label) if they are more readily aware of the explicit theoretical considerations, diagnostic criteria, and clinical practice guidelines (and the interactions of these in the clinical care). The societal expectations to comply with definite and unambiguous guidelines can result in more consistent behaviours (Hormbrey, Todd, Mansfield, & Skinner, 1996). It becomes important to consider that perhaps education may assist in the consolidation of accurate diagnostic practice and effective psychotherapeutic technique and response towards patients diagnosed with BPD. "Improvements in raising the quality of psychiatric nursing services for people with BPD therefore is likely to require training, educational programmes and staff support..."(Deans & Meocevic, 2006, p.48). Although there has been many recent recommendations made for the use of educational interventions to improve clinician attitudes toward BPD patients in the present clinical environment, in comparison little empirical study has been completed to demonstrate the practical effectiveness this can have.

Within the literature, more generic clinical education has shown some effect on the attitudes of health clinicians towards different patient diagnoses, with improvements found in clinician attitude ratings and clinician confidence following completion of training in other complex clinical areas such drug addiction (e.g., Karam-Hage, Nerenberg, & Brower, 2001), and domestic violence (e.g., Harris, Kutob, Surprenant, Maiuro, & Delate, 2002). Following attendance at a one-day educational conference on addiction psychiatry, 52 general psychiatry residents' demonstrated significantly improved attitudes toward working with drug addiction (Karam-Hage, Nerenberg, & Brower, 2001). The use of internet-based education in the area of domestic violence (typically an area that many clinicians are reluctant to work in) was shown to significantly improve confidence in 65 physicians in working with patients who present with such difficulties (Harris et al., 2002).

In terms of promoting more positive attitudes to the complex BPD group, access to training has been a request frequently made by clinicians (across a variety of health settings), and in my experience many clinicians have reported a perceived need for further education and training in this disorder. In fact, Cleary et al. (2002) found that 95% (n=218) of clinicians indicated a willingness to gain further education and knowledge in the management of patients diagnosed with BPD. Recent research has shown promising results, with attendance at specific and specialised training in BPD resulting in statistically significant improvement in clinician attitude ratings towards working with DSH behaviours in BPD (Commons Treloar & Lewis, 2008b; Krawitz, 2004; Krawitz, 2000). More positive attitudes expressed toward working with DSH in patients diagnosed with BPD were reported by clinicians once they obtained knowledge relating to research findings on attitudes to BPD, prevalence rates, *DSM-IV-TR* diagnostic criteria, aetiological factors, definitions and rates of self-harm and suicide, therapeutic responses to BPD, clinical guidelines to working with BPD, and some form of theoretical framework to understanding the purpose of DSH in patients with BPD [7] (Commons Treloar & Lewis, 2008b). It was shown that clinicians from both the emergency medicine and mental health settings were able to demonstrate improved attitudes toward this patient group with access to targeted clinical education (Commons Treloar & Lewis, 2008b). In another study which provided training on BPD (conducted over a two day period), clinicians found an increased optimism, enthusiasm, and positive feeling toward working the BPD patients, which was maintained at 3-5 month follow up (Krawitz, 2000). Further assessment of attitudes using a larger representative sample of clinicians from public mental health and substance abuse services (n=418) also supported a statistically significant improvement in such attitudes (as deemed by an increase in optimism, enthusiasm,

---

[7] It is hoped that this is what this text provides for.

confidence, and willingness to work with these patients) following specific training in the area (Krawitz, 2004). Miller and Davenport (1996) also examined the effect of education on attitudes toward BPD patients. Their sample consisted of 32 nurses, with 59% (n=19) randomly assigned to an experimental group and 41% (n=13) to a control group. They found that following completion of a self-instructional program, significant improvements were found in nurses' knowledge of and attitudes toward BPD patients (as compared to the control group)(Miller & Davenport, 1996).

Although improvements can be made, previous literature demonstrates the chronicity of clinician perceptions of the borderline diagnosis. Many studies demonstrate that emergency medicine clinicians are typically negative in their responses to patients diagnosed with BPD, or those that present to the emergency department for treatment of DSH injuries (e.g., McAllister et al., 2002; Johnstone, 1997; Boyes, 1994; Sbaih, 1993; Platt & Salter, 1987). Similarly, mental health clinicians can also demonstrate derogatory attitudes toward working with DSH behaviours and the BPD patient group collectively (e.g., Bowers & Allan, 2006; Huband & Tantam, 2000; Haswell & Graham, 1996). With archaic views and established biases towards this patient group, improving clinical care to be more empathetic in its approach and include a thorough consideration of the BPD patient's difficulties remains problematic. As evidenced by the growing research, improved attitudes toward this patient group (or working with their difficult behavioural responses of DSH) can be achieved through providing access to targeted clinical education on this complex disorder; however the extent of which this is accessible or even provided to clinicians is questionable. In today's clinical practice, with its preoccupation on evidence-based practice models, the exposure to basic theoretical trainings[8] in BPD appears to be lacking – although having regular clinical contact with BPD, 54% of clinicians sampled had not received any formal education or training in this diagnosis (Commons Treloar & Lewis, 2008b). "To continually develop as a discipline, a profession needs to generate a knowledge base that can evolve from education and practice" (Lyons, 1999, p.29).

USING THEORETICAL FRAMEWORKS TO INTERPRET BEHAVIOURAL DISTURBANCE

Negative countertransference reactions, particularly in response to the occurrence of disturbed behavioural displays, unfortunately impact on the BPD patient's engagement in therapy, and thus the provision and efficacy of treatment interventions. The importance of tolerance and understanding of the patients' difficulties is paramount as unsympathetic responses tend to escalate behavioural disturbance (Sbaih, 1993). Understanding the different theoretical models of BPD and their conceptualisation of why DSH behaviours and recurrent suicidal threats or gestures occur, may assist in the ability of the clinician to maintain empathy with the patient in such turmoil.

In providing clinical education, Bateman and Fonagy (2004) recommend that training in BPD should encompass a robust theoretical framework, but with so many competing schools of thought in the clinical world, determining what frameworks are more useful is clinically important. Many theoretical frameworks and treatment modalities have been examined within

[8] As opposed to a consideration of treatment strategies for the diagnosis.

clinical trials to determine efficacy in relation to the psychotherapeutic treatment of BPD. The use of theoretical frameworks in the improvement of clinician attitudes toward patients with BPD via education programs however has not been a strong focus of the current literature. Recently, Hazelton, Rossiter, and Milner (2006) assessed the use of training in the principles and practice of dialectical behavior therapy (DBT) on clinician knowledge of BPD and attitudes toward this patient group with 94 staff from a regionally based New South Wales mental health service, Australia. Following completion of training over a two day period, the majority of participants showed an improvement in their knowledge regarding detection and treatment, and in their attitudes toward BPD patients. "Overall, the study findings indicate that the systematic development of a training program utilising evidence-based research, in conjunction with adult learning techniques, whilst labour intensive has had a positive impact" (Hazelton et al., 2006, p.128).

Further to the use of the cognitive behavioural model of DBT, a standardised assessment of two different theoretical models (to determine which may be of greater benefit in the education and training of clinicians who come into contact with BPD) was also recently completed. Comparing a DBT and a Freudian conceptualisation[9] of behavioural disturbance in BPD, it was found that the psychoanalytic model enabled a greater empathetic response in clinicians (Commons Treloar, 2009a). Both the DBT and psychoanalytic theoretical framework in understanding DSH behaviour in BPD patients produced an improvement in the attitudes of mental health and emergency medicine clinicians towards this patient group, with a superiority found for the Freudian conceptualisation of behavioural disturbance in BPD as only the psychoanalytic framework maintained a statistically significant improvement in attitudes ratings at six month follow up (Commons Treloar, 2009a). Although the DBT and psychoanalytic education programs both included information relating to aetiology, diagnostic procedures, clinical definitions, and an overview of clinical practice guidelines (which one could consider as responsible for the improved attitude ratings), the assessment of the clinician attitudes at six month follow up provided some evidence as to the isolation of the impact of these theoretical frameworks; only the psychoanalytic experimental group maintained statistically significant improvement in attitude ratings. From this, it appears that the theoretical context of moral masochism provides some basis by which clinicians can consider the presence of behavioural disturbance in BPD, thus possibly reducing frustration and rejection. The suggestion of a reduced awareness of the motivating force behind their behaviours, due to the consideration of an unconscious process, appears to be of greater assistance in the maintenance of an improved clinician attitude (Commons Treloar, 2009a).

[9] A consideration of psychoanalytic theoretical frameworks assisted me in my clinical work with BPD, due to the consideration of the cause of DSH behaviours and how patient-clinician interactions can impact on the presence and occurrence of such behaviours. The framework was used to compile a targeted education program on understanding the function of DSH in BPD and then empirically tested to determine its ability to also influence a more empathetic response in other mental health and emergency medicine clinicians.

The Value of Moral Masochism in Understanding the Patient

It appears that by providing education on the unconscious processes underlying the behavioural presentation of DSH in BPD, both emergency medicine and mental health clinicians can develop a greater ability to empathize with the difficulties of the patient (Commons Treloar, 2009a). The moral masochism framework[10], that posits the origin of DSH behaviour to an unconscious sense of guilt related to past trauma, appears to be of some use in the generating of a more considered understanding of the patient's history and its connection to the current day trauma. It also provides a consideration for the clinician of the transference and the importance of the countertransference in the work with BPD patients. An empathic understanding of DSH harm within the context of personality disorder, with a theoretical basis, is clinically important in today's health system. In order to facilitate enhanced therapeutic engagement with these challenging patients, increasing the health clinicians' understanding of why BPD patients may engage in DSH behaviours can be achieved using the theoretical paradigm of moral masochism, as it does provide clinicians with a theoretical context with which to interpret DSH behaviour (Commons Treloar, 2009c).

Freud's (1924/1961) concept of moral masochism does suggest a reduced awareness for the observed behaviours of patients with BPD, who unconsciously 'choose' to engage in masochistic behaviours such as DSH. In undertaking the clinical work, there is an expectation that the patient will offer dialogue on the conscious concerns in their life. Beyond this however there are also the unconscious workings that need acceptance and consideration, allowing clinicians to develop greater insight into the complexity of the unconscious processes that underlie the patient's behavioural disturbance (Commons Treloar, 2009c). As to be discussed, neutrality or a degree of difference in the transference (enabled only by a recognition and active management of this process) will have significant advantage in the clinical treatment work with these patients. Managing the countertransference and understanding the patient's transference response (enabled via an appreciation of the unconscious workings of the patient and ourselves in the clinical work) is fundamental to the efficacy of our clinical interventions.

---

[10] Greater exploration of the theoretical tenets of the moral masochism framework is provided for in the next part of this text.

Part 2: Interpretation of the Function of Deliberate Self-Harm

These chapters aim to introduce a detailed consideration of the chosen Freudian theoretical framework highlighted in this book. The basic theoretical postulates of the moral masochism framework are examined. Its applicability to interpreting the function of deliberate self-harm behaviour in discharging an unconscious sense of guilt is discussed. It also includes dialogue of how the clinician can become an active agent in the engagement and psychotherapeutic process through thorough developmental investigation and examination practices (via clinical interview). The need to develop an understanding of the connection between the aetiology of the behavioural disturbance (and thus development of the disorder in adulthood) and reflect on the transference and countertransference response of patient and clinician is highlighted here.

Chapter 4

UNDERSTANDING SELF-HARM WITH THE USE OF CONCEPTUAL FRAMEWORKS

APPRECIATING THE PURPOSE OF DELIBERATE SELF-HARM

If the patient is already suffering and experiencing what many term as emotional pain, why does the patient have the need to physically inflict pain upon themselves as well? Looking toward the purpose of self-harm is important if one wishes to treat this behaviour. Strong (1998) uses the term 'self soothing' to denote the intention behind DSH behaviours, and indeed many BPD patients in my clinical experience have described such an experience. Many BPD patients (and also other patients without this disorder that utilise DSH behaviours) have often described the ability of the self-harm to relieve their distress and therefore they are compelled in some way to injury themselves – it can be seen as a coping strategy, or even a suicide prevention strategy (Strong, 1998). It is well recognised by many in the clinical community that BPD patients will continue to self-harm until they receive appropriate and sufficient psychotherapeutic interventions and support (e.g., Strong, 1998). As such, persuading such patients against using this form of 'coping' will be futile until the meaning or purpose of such behaviours can be recognised. "Knowing the idiosyncratic significance of the self mutilating act to the patient will aid future management and treatment" (Green, Knysz, & Tsuang, 2000, p.1396).

Recognising that the self-harm may have come to mean survival for many patients is important. Common affective responses in those that have engaged in DSH behaviours provide some indication of the underlying reason for the presence of such behaviours. Many patients have articulated the feeling of guilt prior, during, and following the act of self-harm (Levenkron, 1998). Expressed ideas of the need for punishment are common, as are the use of terms such as 'release' and 'relief'. Why is the experience of guilt so common and how is this related to DSH behaviour? The significance of guilt in the action of self injury or self poisoning is an interesting concept that is used in varying degrees across different theoretical frameworks of BPD, with many theorists making connections between the behaviours and affective experiences of the patient and their past developmental encounters. "Understanding of self injury needs to be located within the long term effects of trauma, abuse, loss or neglect" (Vivekananda, 2000, p.18).

As previously discussed, it is unfortunate that much of the clinical contact centres around keeping the patient safe when self-harm ideation is voiced or in attending to self-inflicted injury when it occurs. This process can be highly time consuming and often prevents the pausing to consider the behavioural causes. Adequate therapeutic time is required to invest in a more thorough psychological investigation of the behaviours in order to develop sufficient insight (for the clinician and the patient themselves). Understanding why these patients may feel the need to inflict self injury or engage in self poisoning, and why such a behavioural response has developed, often becomes the missed therapeutic aim of the therapy and intervention. It is considered imperative to understand why the patient would engage in such behaviours.

To work with patients that engage in DSH, Goin (2001) argues that the parameters of psychotherapeutic treatment must be clearly present for effective treatment – a specific treatment framework must be established, and psychotherapy must be provided. The use of frameworks can assist in not only the management of the patient's behaviour where a predetermined and designated plan is established to reduce the reactivity of the clinician to the patient's behaviours, but also in attempting to understand the motivations and intent behind the patient's DSH behaviour. A theoretical framework can also be used in moderating the emotional and behavioural response of the clinicians to such patients.

Various frameworks have been used in past and contemporary clinical practice to conceptualise the aetiology, treatment, and prognosis of the BPD patient. Regardless of the school of thought – psychoanalytic, biological, behavioural, cognitive behavioural, neurological – conceptual frameworks have the potential to guide treatment responses by the clinician and reduce the experience of clinician stress (Goin, 2001). If one can identify and mediate the transferred emotions evidenced by the treatment of the often unpredictable and unstable patient with BPD, the therapeutic setting can become a place of inquiry and thus more likely to affect change. The instability of the BPD patient is often emotionally provoking and such patients can often step outside the boundaries of 'rational'[1] behaviour in attempts to externally communicate their internal distress. As effective clinicians, what we need to do is to not only recognise the patient's distress but also conceptualise the source of this distress.

Using Frameworks in Considering the Transference

If one wishes to work with BPD patients that do exhibit DSH behaviours, I argue that the purpose of the self-harm must be carefully and deliberately considered. To enable this, the developmental experience of the patient must be examined and consequently used in the development of insight and in the consideration of the transference relationship. The transference is where the repetition of feelings and desires, especially those unconsciously stemming from childhood, are directed toward a new object (Racker, 2001) – often the clinician now involved in the patient's care. Through investing in the therapeutic relationship with the patient, where the transference can be accepted and interpreted, I believe that the

[1] This term is used to highlight the common judgements I have heard made about a patient's behaviour by treating clinicians in considering the reaction of the patient (within the context of peer consultation and clinical supervision).

clinician may be more able to use their anxiety to facilitate a more considered approach of therapeutic inquiry – an inquiry that will ultimately begin to move toward an appropriate understanding or interpretation of the function of behavioural disturbance in BPD. Recognition of the countertransference reaction, those thoughts, feelings, and attitudes that interactions with the patient bring forth in the therapist (Watson, 1996) is also necessary in order to facilitate an appropriate level of sustained engagement with the BPD patient. Different frameworks of BPD do however vary in their use and recognition of the transference relationship (and indeed countertransference response). This concept will be discussed in more detail later in this work.

As previously discussed, the attitudes of health professionals in working with DSH behaviours in BPD is an area of great interest that has received research attention in the collation of data to examine such responses. As an outcome of these examinations, many studies have suggested the provision of targeted clinical education in an attempt to improve clinician attitudes and produce more consistent and empathetic behavioural response to patients with this particular disorder (e.g., Deans & Meocevic, 2006; Cleary et al., 2002). Having a working knowledge of such frameworks is considered as a means by which to interpret the BPD patient's responses in their interactions with the community and in the therapeutic setting.

As was highlighted here, many clinicians may not have received specialised training in the area of BPD and their knowledge of this personality disorder may have been gained only by a process of exposure to these patients in the clinical setting. Although some consumer literature has identified that many BPD patients find their contacts with health services to be difficult and inconsistent (National Collaborating Centre for Mental Health, 2004), it is believed that a knowledge of theoretical frameworks can assist in a sustained improvement of clinician attitude to this patient group. If an improvement in clinician attitudes can be effected, this may generate a more empathetic response and consistent professional approach when in therapeutic contact with BPD patients.

Guiding Clinical Practice via Theoretical Considerations

Many theoretical frameworks of BPD, from across the various paradigms of thought, provide information on the development of the BPD symptomatologic pattern and instruct on ways in which clinicians should respond to particular patient concerns and behaviours. This modus operandi is of significance in the promotion of more positive clinician attitudes to this patient group, as structured information on the expected professional response to difficult behaviours displayed by the BPD patient can assist in the management of feelings of perplexity and uncertainty (which can be common responses of health professionals in their clinical contact with BPD). The several conceptual frameworks of BPD can vary in their view of the aetiology of the disorder and therefore in their recommendations as to treatment response by the clinician in the alleviation of the patient's symptoms. The implication of these differences should allow clinicians to appreciate the complexity of this disorder from a variety of perspectives, as opposed to increased confusion of how to respond.

The transference relationship with the BPD patient, regarded by some as the most clinically useful tool in the psychotherapeutic treatment of the disorder (e.g., Watson, 1996), is considered and utilised differently across the various theoretical frameworks. Some use the transference as a central therapeutic apparatus in the relief and healing of BPD symptomatology. The importance of the transference in the contact with BPD patients is associated traditionally with the practice of psychoanalysis, however many other paradigms do make reference to the transference, in terms of what is required from the clinician in their personal response to the patient. The cognitive behavioural paradigm of DBT emphasises the need for warmth, responsiveness, and genuine regard from the therapist to facilitate the ongoing engagement of the patient. This collaborative approach is considered central to the therapeutic treatment of BPD (Linehan, 1993). As to be discussed next in detail, the transference response however is not actively utilised as a means by which to *interpret* the patient-therapist interactions, as with the psychodynamic or psychoanalytic paradigms. Much of the useful clinical material that can be discovered in the analysis of the transference response of the patient (and in the countertransference of the clinician) is commonly disregarded[2] as being a direct consequence of the contact with a difficult patient diagnosed with this complex disorder, often without conscious permission or awareness.

Consideration of the Patient's Trauma History

As discussed in an earlier chapter, according to the literature on the aetiological constellations of BPD, the significant predictors of developing BPD include trauma, loss, and neglect as a child (Zanarini & Frankenburg, 1997; Zanarini, Williams, et al., 1997; Walsh, 1977). In contemplation of this, other theorists have attempted to further incorporate a consideration of a traumatic childhood into the development of DSH behaviours and the later development of BPD in adulthood, beyond the consideration of the DBT's primary focus on childhood invalidation.

A child who has to cope with incomprehensible and complicated feelings on their own when confronted with traumatic circumstances often turns inwards (Levenkron, 1998). The invalidation of their emotional experience, as discussed by Marsha Linehan (1993), results in a child who develops into an adult who cannot redress the grievances she has with others, who is afraid to argue and assert themselves, and therefore is unable to articulate what they may be so angry about. With no language with which to describe this to others, Levenkron (1998) believes that the DSH behaviours then become a symbol of this unresolved grievance. The BPD patient's apparent need for punishment and their expression of guilt may be related to this unresolved sense of subjective (yet unconscious) sense of injustice. As argued by McAllister (2003), people who have survived childhood abuse or neglect may have learned to feel somehow responsible for the abuse. Being a participant in the abuse, and even at times self-considered to be an active participant, may then lead to the experience of guilt – and therefore the common proclamation of being deserving of their own self punishment.

[2] It could be argued here however that transference cannot be genuinely disregarded; the patient has an unconscious, as does the clinician.

Hayes, Wilson, and Difford (1996) believe that patients engage in dysfunctional behaviours, such as self mutilation, to avoid painful internal experiences. DSH behaviours can therefore be utilised to stop painful emotions and flashbacks. Often behavioural techniques such as diversion and distraction are utilised to attempt to reduce the occurrence of DSH behaviours. It could be argued however that if the painful feelings are not adequately addressed, the self-harm behaviours will inevitably continue in a chronic and inflexible pattern that results in significant psychopathology (Simpson et al., 1998). Following this reasoning, it could be argued that for successful treatment of BPD and the extinction of DSH behaviours, the painful internal experiences of the patient must be addressed and not continually suppressed through a process of diversion or distraction.

It could also be argued that to understand why this self-harm coping strategy exists, and how to alter these tendencies, one needs to understand the psychical structure of the BPD patient. Rather than focusing on the behavioural level of 'attention seeking'[3] or upon the anxiety provoking acts of the self-harm (which tends to exacerbate clinician rejection and negative emotions), the conceptualisation of the BPD patient from a structural[4] perspective involves a greater consideration of how the coping skill of DSH has developed and the reason as to why these patients may choose self injury or self poisoning as a way to cope with overwhelming affect. This is where the concept of moral masochism becomes an interesting prospect of therapeutic inquiry in the examination of BPD cases.

[3] Again, this term is used to highlight the common judgements I have heard made about a patient's behaviour by treating clinicians in considering the reaction of the patient (within the context of peer consultation and clinical supervision).

[4] I refer to the structural view here with regard to the topographical differentiation of the psychical apparatus.

Chapter 5

A PSYCHOANALYTIC FRAMEWORK FOR CONSIDERING SELF-HARM

THE MORAL MASOCHISM FRAMEWORK

If one reviews psychoanalytic literature and theory, which focuses more on the structural process rather than the behavioural, the pioneer in the recognition and examination of masochistic tendencies in some patients was Sigmund Freud. Freud (1924/1961), based on his view of masochism, argued that the masochistic will always remain in a constant state of pain, actively seeking opportunities of suffering and misfortune[1]. The equilibrium was unusual; contrary to expectation, a neurosis that defies therapeutic effort may vanish if the patient becomes involved in the misery of another misfortunate event such as a poor marital relationship or ill health: "in such instances one form of suffering has been replaced by another; and we see that all that mattered was that it should be possible to maintain a certain amount of suffering" (Freud, 1924/1961, p.166). This is clinically significant when one considers the clinical contact with BPD patients. The resolve of an issue or receipt of reward can often, confusingly, generate a return of DSH behaviour, and this inexplicable logic again leads to an increase of frustration for the therapist[2].

Traditionally, the term masochism was used in the description of a sexual perversion where the sexual gratification or satisfaction of the masochist was achieved through their own experiences of suffering or humiliation. Freud (1924/1961) extended the notion of masochism beyond the perversion as described by sexologists and beyond the origin of the concept, inspired by the work of Sacher-Masoch (1870), *Venus Im Pelz* (Venus In Furs). "[Freud] describes derivative forms, notably 'moral masochism', where the subject, as a result of an unconscious sense of guilt, seeks out the position of victim without any sexual pleasure being directly involved" (Laplanche & Pontalis, 1988, p.244).

---

[1] It is cautioned here that there is a relative position in masochism; it is not an enjoyment of pain, rather a libidinal enjoyment of humiliation or punishment – the experience of pain is not the aim per se. There is a threshold for pain in the unconscious. The patient's aim is to seek punishment, not to seek pain.

[2] And again, the clinician becomes faced with seemingly unpredictable DSH episodes.

This form of masochism – a *moral* masochism – is the particular focus of this text as it is a concept that can offer some insight into the motivation or structural mechanism from which the BPD patient may seek to engage in DSH behaviours.

> Masochism comes under our observation in three forms: as a condition imposed on sexual excitation, as an expression of the feminine nature, and as a norm of behaviour. We may, accordingly, distinguish an erotogenic, a feminine and a moral masochism.... The third, and in some respects the most important, form assumed by masochism has only recently been recognised by psychoanalysis as a sense of guilt which is mostly unconscious. (Freud, 1924/1961, p.161).

The objection raised by Carveth (2001) regarding the problematic notion of unconscious feelings of guilt, as distinct from its associated ideation, is acknowledged: "only ideational correlates can be unconscious" (Carveth, 2001, p.12). Freud (1924/1961) himself acknowledged that it is psychologically incorrect to speak of unconscious feelings (p.166), despite earlier identification of how the affect becomes detached from its ideational representative as in case of obsession, resulting in compulsion repetition, and unconscious feelings in melancholia, provoking the seeking of poverty and punishment (Freud, 1915c/1957). This was further confirmed in his work on the ego and the id, where he wrote that feelings are either conscious or unconscious (Freud, 1923/1961). It could be argued however that there is an unconscious ideation from which the guilt stems, that is associated with the need for punishment; a need that is commonly satisfied through the use of DSH behaviours in the patient with BPD.

> We may, I think, to some extent meet their objection if we give up the term 'unconscious sense of guilt', which is in any case psychologically incorrect, and speak instead of a 'need for punishment', which covers the observed state of affairs just as aptly. We cannot, however, restrain ourselves from judging and localizing this unconscious sense of guilt in the same way as we do the conscious kind. (Freud, 1924/1961, p.166).

Clinical examination of the ideational correlate and the function of guilt inherent in DSH behaviours may be valuable in the course of therapy. This can be achieved through qualitative assessment and clinical interview, where time is provided for adequate exploration of the patient's thoughts and feelings in consideration of their interpersonal experiences in a developmental context. Within this exploration, the unconscious ideational correlate to the affective experience of guilt and a need for punishment may be discovered. Clinical observations suggest that in treating patients with BPD who self-harm, patients often describe a sense of guilt and need for punishment prior to, during, and often following their engagement in self-harm. Such behaviour functions to confirm or verify a core belief that they are bad and deserve to be punished (Rosenthal, Cukrowicz, Cheavens, & Lynch, 2006).

As earlier discussed, the experience of guilt has been spoken about to me by many BPD patients in connection with their need to impose self injury and suffering. Indeed, across different BPD patients the experience or feeling of guilt has been described with different affective tones – with anger, with sadness, with despair, with persecution. The concept of guilt is however considered as much more complex than a feeling or affective state of the patient. The concept of guilt requires a consideration of the transgression of the law[3], where a splitting of the ego between accuser and accused has occurred within the psyche of the patient (Laplanche & Pontalis, 1998):

> It may designate emotional states (varying from the remorse of the criminal to apparently ridiculous self-reproaches) which follow acts that the subject deems reprehensible, though the reasons he gives for doing so may or may not be adequate ones. Or again, it may refer to a vague sense of personal unworthiness unconnected with any particular act for which the subject blames himself. At the same time the sense of guilt is postulated by psycho-analysis as a system of unconscious motivations that accounts for...self-inflicted suffering... (Laplanche & Pontalis, 1998, p.414).

The presence of moral masochism in the patient can account for many of the difficulties observed in the psychotherapeutic treatment of BPD, with regard to engagement, continued DSH behaviour, and non-response to some treatment programs. They can often be seen by clinicians as sabotaging and manipulative, and their acts of self-harm are often extreme to the presenting environmental stressor.

> The satisfaction of this unconscious sense of guilt is perhaps the most powerful bastion in the subject's (usually composite) gain from illness – in the sum of forces which struggle against his recovery and refuse to surrender his state of illness. (Freud, 1924/1961, p.166).

As expected, the patient is often unable to adequately explain their behaviours, with much of the rationale being hidden within an unconscious process. I have observed in treating BPD patients who self-harm that often these patients describe a sense of guilt and need for punishment prior to engaging in this behaviour. It is argued that the true source of this guilt however is not an annoyance in their immediate environment, as is often seen or reported by the patient following the self-harm to justify the presence of their behaviours; rather it is attached to some past trauma.

> The transposing of material from a forgotten past on to the present or on to an expectation of the future is indeed a habitual occurrence in neurotics no less than in psychotics. Often enough, when a neurotic is led by an anxiety-state to expect the occurrence of some terrible event, he is in fact merely under the influence of a repressed memory (which is seeking to enter consciousness but cannot become conscious) that something which was at that time terrifying did really happen. (Freud, 1937/1964, p.268).

The confusing affect and behavioural reactivity of the patient to the current environmental stressor becomes more understandable when we consider that there is an underlying process by which the response to current stressor can be interpreted. The repetition of the trauma becomes a compulsion; the active seeking of misery, misfortune, and pain. The sense of guilt that remains connected to this past trauma triggers the disturbed behavioural

---

[3] The expression of the law here relates to the internal prohibitive law, and consideration of psychological functioning in view of the way internal conflicts are managed. The authorizations and prohibitions of the super-ego, and the way in which conflict against this authority, generates a sense of guilt is needed for consideration. The fear of the super-ego, with its role in ideal formation and conscience, plays the ultimate part in the development of turmoil for the patient.

presentation of DSH behaviours in these patients; however this process is unconscious to the patient. Its connection to the subjective experience of childhood trauma, and the active need to discharge the guilt through the act of punishment and experience of pain, is beyond conscious access to the BPD patient. Instead, the sense of guilt is often displaced to an immediate stressor in the environment so as to explain the experience of the patient[4].

Freud's (1924/1961) concept of moral masochism suggests a reduced awareness of the motivation behind the observed behaviours of the DSH patient who unconsciously 'chooses'[5] to engage in masochistic behaviours such as self-harm, following the affective experience of guilt. The conscious awareness of a sense of guilt, if recognised as a somatic state at all, then requires some form of punishment to discharge itself from the patient's conscious. This is an idea in itself that, if considered by the clinician, should be able to assist with the maintenance of compassion, and help us hold steadfast in our obligation to sit with our own emotions in the interest of our patient. The clinician can feel undermined in their attempt to re-educate the patient on ways to respond to stress. Unfortunately it is not adequately recognised that this is in fact the wrong aim of the psychotherapeutic treatment! Although an early concept in psychoanalytic literature, Freud's (1924/1961) moral masochism does have some significant value in the understanding of the function of DSH and consequently can be used in the psychotherapeutic treatment of BPD.

The masochistic drive[6] in the BPD patient results in:

> feelings of inadequacy, worthlessness, and pessimism…chronic feelings of dysphoria, dejection, and gloom…self blaming, self critical, and brooding; they tend to choose people and situations that lead to disappointment, they respond to positive events with feelings of guilt and depression, they reject opportunities for pleasure (feeling undeserving), and they engage in excessive self sacrifice. (Costa & Widiger, 1994, p.53).

This is often another source of frustration to the treating clinician. Again, looking past this behavioural level to the structural level of the patient may assist in the maintenance of a more neutral[7] countertransference in the therapy. Transference is considered as imperative for any therapeutic relationship to effect change within the patient, and using the transference as a vehicle of resolve for the patient in their conflicts with previous figures of importance, without adopting the countertransference response of rejection and disdain that was once that of these figures, is necessary. "There is theoretical and treatment value of viewing the problem of masochism from the standpoint of the self preservative functions of the ego" (Saretsky, 1976, p.434).

A consideration of this structural conceptualisation may also assist the clinician in viewing the patient as an individual who has developed this disorder through their unique

[4] Which unfortunately contributes to a negative countertransference response of the clinician as on the surface, the stressor does not justify the emotional and behavioural response of the patient.

[5] The term chooses is highlighted here as, in a literal sense, all actions (including unconscious ones) are of choice.

[6] The term drive is used here and throughout the thesis very loosely as masochism does not correspond to the psychoanalytic sense of the term employed by Freud – i.e. having four components of source, aim, pressure, and object being present (Freud, 1915a/1957).

[7] The term neutral is used here to highlight the need to retreat from the urge to negatively respond to the patient's behaviour and become the persecutor (the exact role the masochistic drive within the patient desires from the clinician). The seeking of punishment will continue until the need for punishment can be examined and adequately extinguished.

childhood experience, rather than just another chaotic BPD patient to manage who requires frequent psychiatric intervention and medical attention as a result of their self mutilation.

> We isolate self destructive behaviour from a discussion of structural change for several reasons....change in self destructive behaviour is not synonymous with structural change. Decrease or even elimination of self destructive behaviour could occur without structural change, whereas structural change by definition would involve elimination of self destructive behaviour. (Clarkin, Yeomans, & Kernberg, 1999, p.105).

The need to consider the structural view of the BPD patient is important for the treating clinician to keep in mind as the temporary resolve of DSH behaviours, achieved through the use of coping skills training, does not necessarily indicate or mean a cure. Often unbeknown to the clinician, the patient can often engage in alternate masochistic behaviours to achieve the aim of punishment. The occurrence of self injury or self poisoning can appear to be extinguished when, without structural change, it becomes replaced by another means of suffering. The structural change in the BPD patient, which can be achieved through long term psychoanalytic psychotherapy, is the closest guarantee to permanent behavioural change and resolve of symptomatology. Identification of the ideational correlate motivating the cyclic pattern of the seeking of punishment and persecution is required. The removal of the clinician from the reactive position of persecutor to the adoption of the position of examiner is needed in order to make conscious what can be addressed therapeutically. What is unconscious to the patient and therapist is what automatically pilots the masochistic pattern of recurrent DSH behaviour.

RECOGNISING THE UNCONSCIOUS FUNCTION OF DELIBERATE SELF-HARM

Deliberate acts of self-harm and the invoking of misfortune by the BPD patient are a way that earlier trauma is repeated, communicated, or symbolised to those around them (Van der Kolk, 1989). BPD patients are often unable to adequately explain the source of guilt behind their masochistic behaviours, if it is recognised as an emotion at all, and this can often frustrate the clinician as they attempt to persuade such patients against the use of self-harm. In order to survive their traumatic experiences, the BPD patient has utilised a complex process of defence to guard themselves against the affect associated with the subjective experience of their upbringing. As the sense of guilt and where this may stem from will be unconscious to them, the patient will be unable to speak about their trauma but will continue to – or be compelled to – act out their traumatic experience in a process of repetition through their DSH behaviours (McAllister, 2003).

Moral masochism, as a conceptual framework for interpreting behavioural disturbance in BPD, clearly designates that the need for punishment can only be seen or observed during episodes of DSH behaviour, and remains beyond the patient's conscious awareness:

> ...it falls on the ego's own masochism which seeks punishment, whether from the super-ego or from the parental powers outside...what is involved is a need which is satisfied by punishment and suffering...the masochistic trend of the ego remains as a rule concealed from the subject

> and has to be inferred from his behaviour…In order to provoke punishment from this last representative of the parents, the masochist must do what is inexpedient, must act against his own interests, must ruin the prospects which open out to him in the real world and must, perhaps, destroy his own real existence. (Freud, 1924/1961, pp.169-170).

When working with the BPD patient, as clinicians it is imperative to consider that somewhere in the past, pain was connected to the idea of home and comfort (Levenkron, 1998). For those that have come from a secure and loving family background, this idea can be difficult to process. As mentioned above with regard to the masochist, the experience of humiliation and suffering is the status quo for many BPD patients, whether acted out through DSH behaviours or via the unconscious seeking of other circumstances of misfortune, misery of suffering. Freud (1924/1961) acknowledged that the unconscious sense of guilt or need for punishment represents one of the most difficult problems to solve in analysis. As a rule, people will generally seek the familiar or the repetitious, rather than that that could be considered as new or constructive (Levenkron, 1998). This is of importance to consider in the treatment of BPD patients. The therapeutic work can be slow and setbacks should be expected.

> As soon as things could start improving with the patients, a relapse occurs. They cannot tolerate the feeling of no longer having any complaints or bad luck. Their unconscious feelings of guilt are the foundation of a need for punishment, which evokes symptoms or other misfortunes. As a rule, this pattern has to be worked through repeatedly with the patient before the area succumbs. (Derksen, 1995, p.260).

If one looks past the nature and extent of the injury, past the behavioural level, and looks toward understanding the psychical turmoil of the patient who has inflicted the injury through some form of unconscious process, it is argued that the therapeutic relationship may be more easily maintained and the anxiety of the therapist or clinician managed more effectively.

APPLICATION OF THE FREUDIAN CONCEPTUAL FRAMEWORK

The therapeutic treatment through pure behavioural management of the behavioural disturbance, including the presence of DSH behaviours, can be punitive as the patient themselves may not be consciously aware of the motivation within themselves to self-harm. How can the patient stop cutting their body if they are truly unaware of why they are internally compelled to injure themselves in such a way? Having an understanding of this internal conflict, and the motivating factors behind why some patients ‘choose’ to attack themselves in such ways, may provide a therapeutic framework for the clinician that can assist in a reduced experience and manifestation of negativity in the countertransference. Ignorance often leads to intolerance. With appropriate knowledge and increased understanding a level of tolerance can be achieved, thereby reducing the barriers to effective treatment. The realisation of being drawn in to persecute and punish, in the patient’s attempt to maintain the equilibrium in terms of the need for constant pain and suffering, can assist in an improved behavioural response of the clinician. It is imperative that we attempt to disrupt this process, not be engaged within it. The consideration of the moral masochism framework to manage the countertransference response, and allow for an active seeking, investigation, or interpretation of the need for punishment (through identification of the ideational correlate) helps move towards a more therapeutic process in the psychotherapeutic treatment of BPD.

Neutrality in the countertransference response, achieved through greater therapeutic inquiry and a realisation that the observed behaviours may be generated from an unconscious process, should enable the clinician with the theoretical knowledge to help them to avoid reacting with inappropriate behavioural responses that I deem as typically derived from the clinician's rejection or disapproval of the patient (such as discharge from the health service or inpatient hospitalisation). Accepting the patient's distress, and being prepared to stand still[8] during the turmoil by being there to listen to their concerns and inquire about their experience, should equip the clinician with the appropriate knowledge to be able to therapeutically engage their patient, and ultimately unlock the cyclic pattern of the masochistic experience of the patient. In terms of providing psychotherapeutic treatment, this approach is also required in order to discover the ideational correlate that evokes the unconscious feeling of guilt and need to engage in DSH behaviours, allowing interpretations by which to extinguish the patient's need for punishment.

In sum, the everyday triggers to DSH behaviours are indeed variable for each BPD patient however it is argued here that the unconscious masochistic drive remains similar in each patient that intentionally harms him or herself. This is in direct opposition to the earlier position discussed of the Australian Psychological Society (1999), in relation to the shifting nature of intent with regard to DSH episodes. Although each instance of DSH behaviours should be assessed and inferences not be made from previous patterns of behaviour, these individual assessments require adequate exploration in order to reveal the persistent unconscious drive of the self destructive behaviour. Having an understanding of this concept, and the motivation behind why some patients choose to attack themselves in such ways, may help to reduce the frustration experienced by the people who are affected by the DSH behaviours of the BPD patient – the treating clinician, the patient's family, and the emergency medicine staff that are to medically attend to the self injury or poisoning.

> It is important that therapists understand that the masochists' apparent need to suffer is based not in their perverse enjoyment of pain, but rather in their belief that they will experience less of it by doing what they do. (Millon, 1996, p.606).

Although as clinicians we are more able to identify the dysfunction in this belief (that DSH behaviours can reduce the experience of pain rather than generate the experience of this), the BPD patient may not. As discussed, there is a coherent yet unconscious rationale behind the choice of engaging in self-harm for each BPD patient. This is often the cause of great frustration to the treating clinician as they attempt to persuade the BPD patient against using this type of coping mechanism. The presence of DSH behaviours, whereby existentially relief is gained by the act, is a kind of short term and ongoing evidential loop that again leads to great frustration in the treating clinician without knowledge of these structural processes. The persuasion against using DSH behaviour as a form of self punishment or coping mechanism will be perceived as punitive as the patient themself may not be consciously aware of the source of the drive within them to self-harm. As previously discussed, the

[8] A term used by Cohen & Sherwood (1991) to conceptualise the position of the therapist as a constant object, deemed as necessary in the psychotherapy with patients diagnosed with BPD.

theoretical framework of moral masochism contains some consideration of how the self injury episodes are linked to past traumas that become reactivated in the current day; it allows for a greater consideration of the unconscious process of the patient. In this regard, it seems to move beyond the consideration of behavioural disturbance than that explained by some other theoretical frameworks used with BPD.

The theoretical framework of moral masochism allows a greater consideration as to the ability of self injury to appease the patients' distress and angst. The discharge of the sense of guilt that is facilitated via the episodes of self injury, a punishment for the sense of being or doing wrong, allows some consideration as to the function of DSH behaviours. Beyond this simplification, the moral masochism framework also posits the unconscious sense of guilt and need for punishment as a repeated compulsion from the patient's childhood. If we review the childhood experience, where the parental figures are ones that have instilled the sense of guilt or the need for punishment, the current day stressors that appear to activate the behavioural disturbance in BPD patients develop a greater sense of meaning. This is where the issue of the transference can offer us, as clinicians, some meaningful insight into the behavioural responses of the patient.

A lack of understanding of the rationale behind the behavioural disturbance commonly observed in cases of BPD may lead to a greater probability of the clinician's attitude being formed on the basis of the clinician's emotional response to the patient's behaviours. Without adequate theoretical knowledge by which to mediate the clinician's affective experience, the risk of break down in the therapeutic relationship is increased. Typically clinicians have an anxious response to BPD patients when in direct clinical contact with them following DSH behaviour. Unfortunately this can negatively influence clinician attitudes and responses.

Transference and the Unconscious Repetition of Trauma

The transference relationship, a place in which the patient is enabled to enact the grievances of their past relationships with other figures of importance, is of great significance in the consideration of behavioural disturbance and other symptoms of BPD. The response of the clinician to the patient's difficulties requires considered reflection in the workings of the transference relationship. If one considers not only self-harm but the presence of affective instability, transient paranoid ideation, intense expressions of anger, and the pattern of intense interpersonal relationships characteristic of BPD, we can see that they can all be reactions to the transference interactions of previous important figures from the patient's past projected onto the therapist. "…the patient sees in him the return, the reincarnation, of some important figure out of his childhood or past, and consequently transfers on to him feelings and reactions which undoubtedly applied to this prototype" (Freud, 1940/1964, p.174).

The countertransference reaction of the clinician can be instrumental in helping the patient work through past trauma. For those clinicians that respond negatively, again denying our patients acknowledgement and attention, or again denying care and nurturance, the trauma can be repeated and reactivated. Again the need for punishment may be reawakened. A return of the trauma via the countertransference leads to a behavioural response from the patient that is a repetition of the past. They punish themselves, abuse themselves, and deny themselves the care and nurturance in the manner they have become accustomed to. It is hypothesised that they inflict their own punishment to discharge their own idiosyncratic sense of guilt.

It is within the transference relationship that a point of difference does and should exist. When the transference occurs, upon insistence from the patient's unconscious, a repetition occurs. The repetition of the primal identification will occur within the therapeutic context but there is also a need for a dimension of creative difference. It is within this difference that the repetition can be broken. Although the repetition can re-traumatise the patient, particularly when the countertransference response of the clinician is most similar to that of primal figures, the clinician can respond with a therapeutic degree of difference to the projected figure's role to allow for therapeutic processing of this past trauma. To affect this, the transference response of patient towards the clinician must be recognised within the clinical setting. A thorough and detailed exploration of the patient's history is of course required for this recognition.

The psychoanalytic theoretical basis by which behavioural disturbance occurs in BPD postulates a reduced awareness of the motivating force behind the behavioural response of the patient. In order to identify the source of the drive to inflict their own suffering, and to consider that the DSH behaviours of the individual BPD patient occur through an unconscious process, a careful consideration by the clinician is required. An identification of this within the therapeutic relationship and a working through of the unconscious conflict by the patient are the therapeutic aims. Although many instances of DSH behaviours in BPD patients do appear related to a current stressor, or in response to some crisis or interpersonal conflict (between the patient and their social network, or indeed with the health professionals), there appears to be some evidence of a lack of awareness of the unconscious process by the clinicians involved (and also in the patients themselves). The parents, the ones to whom the patient was born, become the first surmountable figures by which to gauge their own existence and the symbolisation of these figures remain present within the patient's psyche long after the physical presence may be terminated. The development of the super-ego, which can continue to provoke punishment and suffering, becomes the unconscious and unforgotten representative of the parental figures that caused pain, suffering, and the sense of guilt.

As seen with many BPD patients, the parental figures are often considered as the inflictors of pain, suffering, and punishment. The parental figures, reported in the histories of these patients, can be hypothesised as the originator of the ongoing trauma and sense of guilt, and unconsciously be the motivators of the behaviours observed in these patients within a current day environment.

> We were able to translate the expression 'unconscious sense of guilt' as meaning a need for punishment at the hands of a parental power…In order to provoke punishment from this last representative of the parents, the masochist must…perhaps, destroy his own real existence…the masochistic trend of the ego remains as a rule concealed from the subject and has to be inferred from his behaviour. (Freud, 1924/1961, pp.169-170).

An Approach of Therapeutic Inquiry Looking Beyond Patient Behaviour

As clearly outlined here by Freud (1924/1961), the unconscious nature of the masochistic drive can only be discovered through a process of considered reflection of the patient's behaviours. Although most clinicians are aware that in clinical contact with BPD patients that the behavioural displays cannot be ignored, it is imperative that the clinician looks beyond the behavioural disturbance to understand the mechanism by which such behaviour occurs. According to the moral masochism framework, the patient cannot simply answer us when we ask the question of why they have acted in such a way[9]. This is where the theoretical framework of moral masochism may provide a greater source of insight into behavioural disturbance in BPD than that of other theoretical frameworks. For example, the psychotherapeutic treatment of BPD patients using DBT targets the affective, cognitive, interpersonal, and behavioural response of the patient. Through developing greater skill in distress tolerance, communication, emotional validation, problem solving, and cognitive modification, the patient is believed to develop the necessary skills by which to reduce their reactive affect and consequent behavioural disturbance, including that of suicidal and DSH behaviours. The theoretical basis of DBT describes the way in which the patient, as an adult, has come to present with such symptoms. This does include interactional difficulties in childhood.

The psychotherapeutic treatment of BPD patients using a psychoanalytic model however can appreciate the aetiological constellations in greater detail than that of DBT, using the patient's history as a mean by which to interpret the use of DSH behaviours in response to current day stressors. Rather than a treatment approach based on altering the patients' behaviours, this conceptual framework posits its interest in the structural realm of the unconscious drive and its connection to past incidents of trauma that compel the patient to behave in such a way. It also makes greater use of the transference responses in order to discover the unconscious material that generates such undeniable guilt and a need for punishment (see Table 1: Summary of key theoretical postulates of the moral masochism framework).

The dialogue with the patient during therapeutic encounter often gives rise to the revelation of traumatic experiences which have led to the development of their masochistic tendencies. Although many clinicians have questioned the truth of patient report, particularly of those diagnosed with BPD, it is within this patient's reality with which we have to work. The subjective patient experience of trauma, which may be discounted in the questioning of other family members or external third party, is the first glimpse by which we can construct the development of the masochistic drive, including the function of their DSH behaviours. The perception of abuse, invalidation, and mistreatment is the central to the patient's existence and therefore objective reality may not often be even relevant within the therapeutic setting.

From the case histories to be presented, it becomes apparent that a considered approach of inquiry can often facilitate a more advanced understanding on behalf of the clinician as to the patient's behavioural difficulties. The need for clinicians to reflect back to the theoretical

[9] Although there will be some aspect in the speech as it will contain a fragmented or mutilated form of truth as to the reasons why.

basis of the development of the behavioural disturbance in their work with each patient with BPD is imperative in the psychotherapeutic treatment of this complex disorder. To assist the clinician, the use of this framework should enable the maintenance of compassion when working with these patients. As provided for by the discussion of the transference and the idiosyncratic significance of past parental figures, it is paramount that the clinician attempts to sit with their own anxiety when in a therapeutic relationship with the BPD patient. The BPD patient will often be able to detect this anxiety in the clinician, which can often lead to repetition of trauma and an exacerbation of their behavioural disturbance.

As suggested in this exploration, for effective therapy with the BPD patient, and throughout the treatment period, the clinician should attempt to replace their anxiety with inquiry. Attempting to understand the development of the DSH behaviours will challenge the treating clinician but ultimately understanding this will help in the maintenance of the therapeutic relationship and assist in the process of achieving structural change to extinguish the drive for punishment and persecution. This is the benefit of viewing the BPD patient from a structural perspective, rather than the behavioural level of self-harm. In approaching the behaviours from the structural viewpoint, the clinician should be more able to maintain empathy and hopefully see past the act of self-harm itself. Ultimately the clinician needs to attempt to empathise with the patient that unconsciously feels the need or drive to inflict such injuries upon themselves, thus keeping neutral in the countertransference. Contrary to popular belief, the prognosis for the BPD patient is often quite good depending on the management of the transference relationship. The work involved, although time consuming and demanding, can be very rewarding for both the clinician and BPD patient.

Table 1. Summary of key theoretical postulates of the moral masochism framework

Key theoretical postulates	Moral masochism
Paradigm of therapy	*Psychoanalytic*
Conceptualisation of BPD symptomatology	*Masochistic actions as manifestations of a process of repetition of trauma*
Theoretical Consideration	*Psychical apparatus; the Unconscious*
Developmental experience of significance	*Presence of trauma, neglect, abuse, or smothering*
Trigger to DSH behaviours	*Reactivation of trauma creates an unconscious sense of guilt*
Function of DSH behaviours	*To achieve constant state of moral pain (humiliation) and achieve punishment*
Mechanism of DSH behaviour to achieve function	*Discharge of unconscious sense of guilt*
Consideration of transference	*Active analysis of the transference response*
Aim of treatment	*Discovery of the ideational correlate to sense of guilt and resolve past conflicts*
Position of clinician / therapist	*Acceptance of figure in transference but with degree of difference*
Treatment strategies	*Use of construction and interpretations; considered therapeutic inquiry*

PART 3: THE CLINICAL ILLUSTRATION OF THE MORAL MASOCHISM FRAMEWORK

These chapters introduce three clinical case studies to illustrate the Freudian theoretical framework in considering the unconscious trigger and function of deliberate self-harm. The case study information for each is presented in rich clinical detail, according to a standard case assessment format. A discussion of how the moral masochism framework can be applied to help interpret the specific function of deliberate self-harm in each case is offered. After considering the aetiology of each case, the required elements of effective psychotherapeutic practice (including appreciation of the transference responses) are suggested. Before moving into recommendations for clinical practice, these chapters also contain specific feedback from the three patients as to how they have experienced clinical care. This feedback has been offered in an attempt to develop a degree of clinical insight into patient perception of care and response, and also a consideration of such feedback in appreciating the transference response.

Chapter 6

THE USE OF CLINICAL INTERVIEWS

The three female adult patients (M age = 42 years) whose cases are presented here were receiving treatment from an area mental health service (AMHS), had actively self-harmed within the preceding 12 months, and were approached to be interviewed to provide some clinical information to assist with the illustration of the moral masochism framework[1]. The AMHS provides psychiatric care and treatment to people in the community with a mental illness or mental disorder, through both inpatient and outpatient treatment modalities (Drake, Green, Mueser, & Goldman, 2003). The presence of a history of DSH behaviour was a prerequisite to the invitation to participate, and all three patients had been given a formal psychiatric diagnosis of BPD. It was made by an AMHS psychiatrist according to the criteria of the Diagnostic and Statistical Manual of Mental Disorders, fourth edition, text revision (DSM-IV-TR) (American Psychiatric Association, 2000). This diagnosis was also given voluntarily by all three patients on interview (who agreed with their diagnostic categorisation).

The three patients involved were all deemed mentally stable[2] at the time they gave their consent to participate by an independent, qualified mental health clinician. This clinician was involved in the ongoing treatment of the patient, and informed their patient of the opportunity to participate as the clinician felt that such patient was mentally stable and therefore able to provide informed consent. The three patients were not advised or educated about the moral masochism (Freud, 1924/1961) framework to be utilised to conceptualise their difficulties.

THE PRESENTATION OF THE CASE ILLUSTRATIONS

The clinical illustration here of how the conceptual or theoretical framework of moral masochism understands behavioural disturbance (specifically DSH behaviours) in patients diagnosed with BPD has been achieved using clinical information provided by three patients

---

[1] Following ethical approval, the interviews of the three patients were conducted between August and December 2005, with all three patients completing the three clinical interview sessions within a one month period. All the interviews were digitally recorded. Routine treatment and contact was provided to all three patients by their treating clinician at the AMHS throughout the full duration of each patient's participation in the clinical interviews.

[2] This included the absence of significant depressive symptomatology (as determined by the independent mental health clinician).

diagnosed with this complex disorder, upon clinical interview only[3]. In considering the unconscious sense of guilt, and appreciating BPD symptomatology as a manifestation of an unconscious process of repetition, we rely purely on creating an honest dialogue with the patient. The clinical interview of patients on initial assessment, about their difficulties and experiences, does hold a surmountable amount of information that can assist the clinician in beginning to conceptualise the presence of the moral masochism drive. It can be common, however, that the clinical interview data is not utilised in this regard. To illustrate how we can move beyond initial assessment procedures to reflect on the unconscious significance of the patient's difficulties[4] the clinical presentation of these three patients has been modified beyond that used in typical clinical practice. The three case illustrations contain the presentation of standard clinical information according to today's clinical case assessment outline, and then provide for a distinct case formulation and conceptualisation of the three patients with BPD according to a moral masochism framework. Although reading this section of text (outlining the process of the clinical interviews) may seem tedious, it is important to reflect on how we obtain and clinically use the information provided to us by the BPD patient.

Further to the extraction of clinical data on DSH behaviour and developmental history, at the time of the clinical interviews feedback was also sought from these patients on their experiences of clinician response and perceived level of clinician understanding of their DSH behaviours. This is common practice in initial assessment procedures – what treatment has been provided previously, and what was the response to this? This has been done here too, however it has been utilised beyond the more typical use of this information. It is important to start to consider the transference response of the patient early in the psychotherapeutic work. Beyond a consideration of the moral masochism framework, this information can also assist in the guidance of clinical response to ensure the therapeutic alliance is maintained and therefore utilised effectively by the clinician.

In compiling the case illustrations, the patients were required to complete three clinical interviews using a semi structured interview format, discussing their DSH behaviours, childhood experiences, and impression of community response to their self-harming behaviours (see Appendix A for a copy of the interview schedule). Beyond this typical clinical assessment procedure, the interviews also included the use of word association techniques (words provided were: self-harm, guilt, punishment, trauma, family, therapy, support, and coping). A technique not commonly used in today's clinical practice, word association can assist in providing some glimpse of the patient's unconscious workings and contribute to the development of the first working hypothesis the clinician can derive about the patient's difficulties, and a means by which to proceed in the clinical care. The third interview in particular was left unstructured to discuss any ideas or matters the patient raised without influence from a predetermined interview schedule. The dialogue offered by the patient, uninfluenced by predetermined questions, can also contribute to the development of the working hypothesis and consideration of the patient's more unconscious conflicts.

[3] In considering the application of the diagnosis of BPD, psychometric assessment tools can be used to improve the accuracy of the diagnostic procedure.

[4] Although there will be pressure from the patient to attempt to manage the more conscious difficulties early in the therapeutic work, from the onset of treatment clinicians should at least start to consider the myriad of unconscious conflicts underlying the patient's more conscious concerns.

Although in this instance, this particular clinical interview format was chosen to allow for the retrieval of particular information relevant to the illustration of the chosen theoretical framework (such as the collection of information on the patient's life history and experiences), it does also provide for a greater consideration of the unconscious workings of the patient. Within clinical practice, it is recommended here that we make much more use of the patient's dialogue and (as to be discussed in part four) consider a different approach to the clinical work with BPD.

THE USE OF CONSTRUCTION IN CONSIDERING THE PATIENT'S HISTORY

As a method to suggest the relationship between BPD, developmental experiences, and the unconscious guilt and need for punishment behind the DSH behaviours exhibited by each patient (according to a moral masochism framework), the use of construction in these illustrations is a standard process utilised when the direct observation of a patient cannot be completed (Wallerstein & Sampson, 1971; Chassan, 1967). The process of construction, whereby the patient's experience was obtained from clinical interview (and therefore patient recall) and the connection is made between the patient experience with the descriptions of the patient's DSH behaviours, is used here to provide a rich illustration of the possible development of the unconscious guilt relating to the presence of the behavioural response of DSH (Wallerstein & Sampson, 1971). This traditional case study method, innovated by psychoanalysis, has been used to infer the relationship between unconscious guilt and DSH behaviour (Wallerstein & Sampson, 1971). The presentation of the clinical information pertaining to each patient here was used to illustrate the theoretical concepts of the moral masochism framework. This was purposely provided in a case assessment format; a format typically used in today's clinical practice (rather than a traditional case history). The conceptualisations or constructions offered here to illustrate the presence of behavioural disturbance in BPD would make similar use of the interview data and comment on the transference relationship as consistent with a more traditional case history reading of the material.

The purpose of such a presentation, using case assessment method with further discussion of case study material with the formulations, is to allow for a particular arrangement of the material in the reading of this text. The readers of this text would be familiar with the case assessment format that is used to present the patient information. The following conceptualisations provided however also allow for the illustration of how the clinical interview can be used beyond the presentation of case material as commonly practiced in today's clinical setting. To guide the reader in this appreciation, the full verbatim interview transcripts for all three patients have been supplied (see Appendix B, C, & D).

The importance of the investment on behalf of the clinician to the transference relationship, and the carefully considered reading of the patient's dialogue about their experiences and responses, will be demonstrated within the next chapters. The three case presentations have been compiled using the interview data only (semistructured questions, word association, and free formats) and pertinent sections of dialogue have been highlighted through the illustrations and case conceptualisations offered here[5].

Although the case study approach may be debated by some on its possible limitations, particularly with regard to generalisation, it does provide for a rich and detailed illustration of the relationship inferred between the variables of interest (Chassan, 1967). Traditionally the singular case study was used to illustrate the universal phenomenon and many may argue that it is from here that the discovery develops meaning:

> If we consider mankind, as a whole and substitute it for the single human individual, we discover that it too has developed delusions which are inaccessible to logical criticism and which contradict reality. If, in spite of this, they are about to exert an extraordinary power over men, investigation leads us to the same explanation as in the case of the single individual. (Freud, 1937/1964, p.269).

As a disclosure, the information that is presented here has been de-identified for each participant. It has also been shown to all three patients prior to its inclusion. They all had a three month period in which to withdraw their consent of the use of their clinical information once they had viewed the material as presented here. No patient took this opportunity. The patients were also given the opportunity to read both the interview transcripts and case presentations as part of the rigorous process of gaining consent and assisting with disguise of the patients' identities. Patients were given the option of altering their case presentations; however none chose to do so.

Following this, the information was collated into a final case assessment for each participant and a process of *Konstruktionen* (construction) (Freud, 1918/1961) was then used to demonstrate the possible interpretation of the behavioural disturbance from the moral masochism conceptual framework – as stemming from an unconscious sense of guilt linked with childhood or early trauma[6]. In lieu of an experimental method of examining the relationship between the variables, which could not have been achieved here, a retrospective method enabled a detailed discussion of the variables through the presentation of three case studies (Wallerstein & Sampson, 1971).

As a further disclosure, Patient 1 (referred to within the text as 'Lisa') was known to me prior to the completion of the clinical interviews, having undergone psychotherapy for BPD when I was employed by the AMHS. I treated this patient at two different intervals; in 2000 upon Lisa's first presentation to the psychiatric service (for a duration of approximately two years), and in 2004 when Lisa was referred back to me for psychotherapy (this second

---

[5] The reader is also able to consider the full interview transcript data prior to the reading of these case assessments. There is much value in developing case conceptualisation skills via reading the interview data prior to the consideration of the cases of Lisa, Helen, and Eve offered here, through a process of allowing for your own non-prejudicial working hypothesis of these patients.

[6] The material collected from the three patients has been disguised using a variety of traditional methods, including the omission and disguise of non critical demographic information (Gabbard, 2000; Tuckett, 2000, 1993). Some of the material has also been actively disguised and similarities to any patient are purely unintentional and coincidental.

episode of psychotherapy was for 12 months duration). Therefore Lisa's case assessment presented here is more detailed in its discussion as it also includes personal information obtained beyond the clinical interview that was already known to me from the prior clinical work. All patients gave their consent to the information presented as it is here.

"We shall begin at the end and attempt to understand by working backwards" (Lacan, 1993, p.106).

Chapter 7

THE CASE FORMULATION OF 'LISA'

HISTORY OF PRESENTING PROBLEM

Lisa was a married woman, living alone and estranged from her husband. She was in her forties and had a diagnosis of BPD, and frequently engaged in severe forms of self mutilation. Throughout her clinical care with the psychiatric service, she has had multiple episodes of self-harm. This had predominately been the cutting of the right arm with a knife at the wrist, forearm, *or* elbow, or the inserting of objects (usually nails) into the soft tissue of this arm at previously cut sites, normally under the dermal layer of the skin. On most instances Lisa was intoxicated with alcohol, however she also engaged in DSH when not intoxicated. Lisa had been known to the psychiatric service for the preceding five years following a referral from a private rehabilitation clinic where, when she was attending there for alcohol detoxification, she cut her wrists with a piece of broken bottle. Lisa reported that this was the first episode of intentional self injury that she had engaged in*: "I got out and bought a bottle of alcohol, I started cutting my wrist. And that was the first time of self-harm".*

Lisa's predominant self-harm activity was the cutting of her right arm with a knife. She had cut her arms with other objects, including broken spoons and mirrors, and had inserted foreign objects into the wounds, usually nails. There had been two attempts at cutting her throat and one attempt at hanging herself with shoelaces. There had also been attempts of overdosing on medication, both paracetamol and psychotropic drugs, and jumping off a bridge onto a railway track. She had attempted running in front of traffic and also burnt her arms and legs with boiling water and a hot iron.

Lisa initially expressed suicidal intent when the self-harm behaviours began to emerge. Lisa later often denied having the intent of suicide. She had become clearer in voicing her intent when self-harming: "I need an instant relief", *"I deserve to hurt myself so then I don't feel so guilty",* and *"it's a release".*

The cathartic consequence of her cutting in particular had often been offered as her motivation to the psychiatric services' staff that were in attendance immediately following her self-harm episodes. Lisa defined "*a good cut*" as one where she felt adequately relieved. Unfortunately Lisa reported that to be adequately relieved, she usually needed to keep cutting her arm until a nerve was either exposed or severed. To reach this point, she had often spent over an hour carefully, and meticulously, cutting at her arm whilst usually suspending the injury over the basin to prevent the spill of blood onto the floor – often producing a sticky mess of coagulated blood in the bottom of the sink[1]. She reported that she did not feel any physical pain whilst cutting herself, and only experienced this during the treatment of the wound by medical staff.

Family History and Structure

There is a history of alcoholism and may be a history of depression in Lisa's family. Her maternal grandfather and indeed Lisa herself had all been noted to have a history of alcoholism; however Lisa reported that her father was only a "*heavy drinker*". Her immediate family did not suffer from any mental illness, however her paternal grandmother was said to be *"strange"* and Lisa suspected from reports by other family members that she may have suffered from depression. This grandmother died when Lisa was only an infant.

Lisa had a difficult relationship with her mother whom she described as emotionally detached and overly critical of her. Throughout her childhood, and even her adult life, Lisa reported that her mother saw Lisa as a difficult child and even referred to her as *"a naughty baby"*. Her father was more nurturing of Lisa in her younger years, providing support to Lisa to pursue her sporting interests. Lisa felt that although her father was also very firm in his discipline, often resorting to severe physical punishments, he showed her more love and attention than her mother. Lisa was however sexually abused by her father on a regular basis from the ages of approximately 9 to 16 years of age.

Lisa had a closer relationship with her brother than older sisters when younger, and attributed this mainly to the age difference between her and her older sisters. Lisa reported that her parents always targeted her during sibling disputes, and therefore she received punishment more often than her siblings. Although Lisa's brother was reported to be as equally as disruptive, Lisa felt that he was often excused for his behaviours as it was seen as more acceptable by her parents for the male child to act in this way. Her brother, however, also received severe physical punishments by their father.

Medical and Educational History

A review of Lisa's medical history revealed that she had her wisdom teeth removed via surgery, she had an emergency caesarean birth in the 1990's, and she suffered from a prolapsed bowel in the preceding few years. No significant illnesses were contracted in childhood, but since puberty she had had continuous difficulties with her menstrual cycle. There was a reported history of bulimia from age fourteen, and a subsequent long term abuse of laxatives, which presented as a dependency at the present time. She reported the development of panic disorder, coinciding with the removal of her wisdom teeth as a young adult.

Academically, Lisa was a poor student who was the receiver of regular discipline at school. She reported that her grade one and two teacher gave her the leather strap every day: "*she picked on me for getting a sum wrong or for poor spelling*". At times her older sisters

[1] The coagulated blood in the bathroom sink was often discovered by staff in the residential unit when Lisa was an inpatient in this facility.

were called into the classroom to be informed of her unruly behaviour or poor academic performance so they could report the information to her parents. She would receive further punishments at home. She felt that although she was not excelling in her grades, she was managing well enough for transition to high school; an all girls' school. She also felt reassured by the presence of her older sisters there. Her best subject was typing and felt that her teacher supported her in this. In form three, Lisa was put into a special class for extra tutoring of mathematics. She reported that she improved in this area and was proud of her own efforts. She could not recall any encouragement offered by her parents in this. Lisa had a small group of friends at this school but was often picked on by the other girls. She recalled being taunted and even physically assaulted on a regular basis. Lisa had no self confidence so she reported that she did not retaliate in any way against these bullying behaviours.

Developmental History

Lisa was born from a multiple birth, with a twin brother. Her mother experienced a difficult pregnancy, feeling sick throughout the gestation period, but gave birth naturally. The twins weighed approximately six pounds each. Lisa was not aware if she was breast fed as a baby. Her mother remained at home to care for the children during their childhood, having four children under the age of five when the twins were born. Her father worked long hours as a manager, and would return home each evening and consume "*a few beers*".

Lisa described herself as a quiet, timid, and shy child who was uncomfortable around people, often keeping her opinions to herself: "*I lacked a lot of self confidence*". Her parents were very firm in their discipline. Her father was the parent who usually dealt out the punishment with his belt; however her mother often punished the children, using a wooden spoon on most days. Lisa vividly remembered witnessing her father beating her brother on the legs with a wire brush to the point of bleeding; a punishment given for her brother returning home late one evening. Lisa could not recall any memory of her older sisters receiving a smack from her mother, or even recall any time that her mother gave her any affection; this was reported however to be given to her other siblings, including her twin brother. When ten years old she asked her father: "*why does mum pick on me?*" He replied to Lisa that her mother was not expecting twins and only wanted to be pregnant again to try and conceive a boy. From this point on, Lisa reported that she considered herself, and still considered at the time of entering psychotherapeutic treatment, that she was a piece of "*afterbirth*"; a by-product to the son the family always wanted. She remembered having thoughts of wanting to run away but never attempted this for fear of the consequences of doing this.

Lisa reported a good peer group in her early years as the neighbouring families all had children her age. She started playing sport in primary school, which her father also had an interest in, and she would spend most of her free time outside the house with her father and brother playing this sport. Because her mother would allocate chores to Lisa if she were inside, as her mother was "*very orderly and obsessive with keeping the house clean*", Lisa would prefer to remain outside with her father and brother.

It was around the age of nine that Lisa's father began sexually abusing her. He would constantly expose his penis to her at any opportunity that they were alone and would often take her down to the wood shed at the back of the house where he would kiss and fondle her, and make Lisa touch his penis with her hand. Although there were no recollections of sexual intercourse, Lisa did report that he would insert his fingers into her vagina. The interludes would occur on average for an hour's duration and approximately three times per week, but her father would take any opportunity to expose himself to her or to walk in on her getting undressed or showering. He would tell her not to tell anyone about this behaviour and that it was "*just part of growing up*". Lisa assumed that her father, in this manner, had educated her older sisters also; but she never inquired.

Lisa began menstruating at the age of 13 years. Her mother had "*very basically*" explained this to her but the topic of sex in the household was very taboo. Lisa approached her sister initially when she first menstruated, and then the sister informed her mother: "*When the time did come, I couldn't approach her and I approached my sister. I said, what is happening here? I am bleeding...I couldn't approach mum about that*". Lisa often felt ill during the time of menstruation and would try to conceal this from her mother. Her older sisters also found menstruation difficult and her mother took both of them to the doctors to receive medical management of this. Her mother never took Lisa: "*I never got pain killers, or Panadol, or anything to help with the pain*". She did not speak to her mother about sex at all, having her education on this topic provided only by the school curriculum.

Lisa reported the emergence of bulimia at the age of 14 years. She was an overweight child, had a poor self image, and often took comfort in food. Whenever she had the chance, Lisa would binge on large amounts of food and then induce vomiting each time. To further control her weight, she would also try to have lengthy periods of starvation. This later developed to the abuse of laxatives at19 years of age, and her dependence on them continued to the present day (time of interview). When she transferred to a commercial college in her mid teens, Lisa recalled that her male teacher picked on her at this school and would often report her poor performance to her parents. At the age of 16 years, in response to a report back to her father by her teacher, Lisa's father told her to pull down her pants and bend over so he could smack her bottom. For the first time Lisa told her father that she was not comfortable doing this, as she felt that she was old enough to have some privacy. The sexual abuse and exhibitionistic behaviour by her father then suddenly stopped.

Once in the workforce, Lisa started drinking alcohol socially with colleagues after work and felt that her self confidence was gradually starting to improve. The partying with friends and consumption of alcohol gradually increased. Lisa would drink most nights, either after work with colleagues or following her sporting games with other friends. Eventually Lisa gave up playing her sports and concentrated on her work, and spent her spare time drinking with friends. It was about this time, when she was typing a report for her employer on a child abuse case, that Lisa reported that she realised that the past actions of her father were not normal. Lisa happened to mention to a colleague, a male social worker, her discovery about her own sexual abuse by her father. She felt that he helped her with this and she felt no need to discuss it further with family. She did not do this until 2000, long after her father's death and the development of her DSH behaviours.

Lisa met her estranged husband when she was in her twenties and they started dating. She had not had a previous boyfriend. The relationship developed quickly and Lisa was engaged to him two years later. Lisa recalled that her fiancée was very domineering in their relationship, making most of the decisions regarding their social activities on her behalf and usually without consultation. In the three months before her marriage, she moved in with her older sister. She was kept busy working and arranging her own wedding. Her father however died five weeks before Lisa's wedding. She reported a feeling of relief when her ill father passed away: "*because of his deterioration I did not wish him to go on*". Lisa felt that this time in her life should have been a happy one for her; however it was "*horrific*".

Lisa's relationship with her mother remained difficult after her father passed away. She felt uncomfortable during one on one contacts with her mother; it was always easier having her husband there with her during visits to help with the flow of conversation. Lisa and her husband enjoyed socialising with friends together but he began to become concerned about the amount of alcohol that Lisa would drink. He started trying to limit her drinking, which was at times as much as three bottles of wine on an occasion. At this time his attempts to do this were unsuccessful; Lisa continued to drink heavily.

There were also difficulties reported in the marriage with regard to the sexual relationship. Lisa had informed her husband before they were married about the sexual abuse she had encountered by her father as a child, and they both waited until after their marriage to become intimate. Lisa reported that it took a long time for her to feel comfortable with sexual intercourse and she was very modest about her body, always undressing in private. Lisa recalled often laying in bed hoping that her husband would not come in wanting to have sex with her. She reported that her only enjoyment in intercourse was in seeing her husband enjoy himself.

After Lisa's thirtieth birthday, her husband again started trying to limit her alcohol intake. He would restrict her access to money but Lisa reported that she could always find a way to get it: "*whenever I got the chance I would buy alcohol*". She started closet drinking. Their arguments were mainly over Lisa's inability to control her drinking problem. In her mid thirties, Lisa and her husband started trying for a baby. It was the first time in her life that she felt at ease with their sexual relationship, as there seemed to be some purpose associated with act of intercourse. Within three months she was pregnant. Lisa reported that she started looking after herself by taking folate, watching her diet, exercising, and she stopped drinking alcohol; although she "*had a glass of wine on occasion*". She felt that at this time she was the fittest she had ever been. She experienced a normal pregnancy and during this time she felt that the relationship with her own mother had improved: "*it's like she had a different respect for me*".

Lisa required an emergency caesarean section to give birth to her child. The baby was not feeding properly and had stopped growing in the womb. The next day after giving birth to her child, she began to be tearful. She had trouble adjusting to the breast feeding and had a hematoma. Lisa remained in hospital for nine days post delivery, tearful every day. Lisa continued to find it difficult when she returned home with the baby. The baby would continue to cry after feeding. After the problem was discovered, that Lisa was not producing enough breast milk, the baby was given additional formula and things started to settle. Lisa reported that her child was "*a good baby*", sleeping six to eight hours per night at four weeks of age.

When her child was approximately two years of age, Lisa started drinking heavily again. She started feeling depressed and anxious, limiting her contact with friends and family. She found that caring for her baby interfered with her usual housework routine. She turned to alcohol to cope. Her husband would not tolerate her drinking behaviour and convinced her to admit herself to a private rehabilitation clinic. Lisa reported that she would continue to drink alcohol during this admission, and one night the staff there found her in the toilet trying to cut her wrists with a piece of the glass bottle. This was the first episode she recalled of DSH behaviour. Lisa spent time in and out of the psychiatric hospital, returning to her family home, until a few years ago (at the time of interview) when her husband refused to allow her to come home. He was concerned about the impact her DSH behaviours and ongoing alcohol abuse was having on the development of their child.

Diagnosis (DSM-IV-TR)

Axis 1: Alcohol dependence (303.90)
Major depressive disorder, recurrent, unspecified (296.30)
Axis 2: Borderline personality disorder (301.83)
Predominant symptoms: frantic efforts to avoid real or imagined abandonment; a pattern of unstable and intense interpersonal relationships; identity disturbance (markedly and persistently unstable self image or sense of self); recurrent suicidal or self mutilating behaviours; affective instability due to marked reactivity of mood
Axis 3: No diagnosis
Axis 4: Problems with primary support group (separation from family) Occupational problems (unemployment)
Axis 5: GAF 45 (current)

Use of the Psychoanalytic Framework in Considering Self-harm

From a psychoanalytic theoretical point of view, the aetiological constellations to the development of the self-harm behaviours can be approximated from careful consideration of the speech and words of the patient. The symptoms of the body, the cutting of the flesh on Lisa's right arm, are hypothesised to be linked with her construction of her childhood experience. If we carefully review her dialogue within the interviews, we can begin to estimate the aetiological constellation related to her deliberate forms of self mutilation[2]. The mapping of Lisa's speech and words used in response to the semi structured questions, word association, and free interview format lead us to consider a history of abuse and persecution, within the subjective context of the early family environment.

As found within the clinical interviews, the first clue considered to the development and purpose of her cutting behaviours was Lisa's continual reference to the family when questioned about her DSH behaviours. When asked about her age when the self-harm behaviour began, she replied "*when I was about...when (daughter) was about three things were really happening*", and again when describing an episode of cutting prior to an appointment at the psychiatric service: "*...and I had an interview with him and, you know, (daughter) was still really little...I didn't want to...it was a review or something*". Further suggestion of the significance of her family in the emergence of her DSH behaviour was the first instance of cutting her wrists in the alcohol detoxification clinic, where Lisa indicated that "*being sent away*" was a significant event in her life, as well as the suicide attempt that

[2] The constructions to be used here are to be considered with much caution; although there is some relativity in the subjective response of the patient, constructions from patient reports are never considered an established truth.

came on Mother's day: "*I just couldn't handle the thought of mother's day and that…the way I had turned out*".

Throughout the dialogue there were aetiological constellations that can be tentatively considered between her own DSH behaviours and the relationship that she reported that she had with both her mother and father. Lisa described her mother as a source of persecution: "*I felt I wasn't being treated fairly by mum*", "*that is how I felt; that mum hated me*". Lisa described her mother as someone that was very orderly and obsessive with house cleaning – this symbolisation of the mother may be suggested to be inherent in Lisa's own attempts to "*control*" her deliberate self mutilation, as well as a sense of guilt when she is unable to function in a domestic role. There are references to such behaviours during her admission to the alcohol detoxification clinic, where she tried to keep busy and assist the staff with the cleaning of the windows, as well as her attempts to be there as a mother for her daughter: "*When you just want to be there, you just want to have a clean house, and cook tea, [daughter] comes home from school and be there for her, or go and pick her up from school*". Lisa associated much of her feelings of guilt surrounding her inability to provide for her husband and daughter in this way; perhaps to function the same as her mother did during her childhood. Her inability to play with her daughter during access visits was described during interview one. "*I try and do what I can even though [daughter] wants me to play, and I would say look I will just fold this washing for daddy, get the washing in for daddy, or do the dishes you know. And she doesn't want me to because she wants me to play…*". Again in interview two, Lisa discussed her contacts with her daughter of a weekend. The angst associated with her contact as a mother was clearly stated here by Lisa, with the need to prepare a plan for contact with her daughter being described: "*And prepare myself for Sunday. I still…to think that I have to do that, to even plan and put a plan in place for Sunday you know, to see my daughter and that…Should just happen naturally but I have to prepare myself for it*". Further discussion of Lisa's struggle with nurturing her daughter emerges in interview three, with comments made: "*I just feel a bit lost. I am trying to get through Sunday and have a good day with [daughter] and everything feels natural and normal*".

The ritualistic sexual abuse and severe physical abuse that she endured by her father were clearly linked by Lisa to her deliberate self mutilation in reporting her own history. She identified feelings of guilt related to the abuse by her father, which would trigger the need to punish: "*…because things would start coming back…between dad and my life. What was happening and my guilt, it would all start coming into one…*", and "*from when I was young, if I did something wrong I was punished. So, I guess as an adult I feel that I have to be punished…for doing what I felt was wrong and doing what I did was wrong, you know that I felt was wrong*". Lisa's response to the sexual behaviour, that she reported that she had thought it was "*a natural thing*" with her father, also may have generated much confusion with Lisa needing to possibly acknowledge that the only parent that showed her any love and affection was actually abusing her through his actions – what I consider as the incompatible idea (that the sense of love and comfort that she found with her father was abusive).

Within the second interview, it is interesting that Lisa clearly made a link between self-harm behaviour and her family: "*the self-harm definitely comes into family, that I'm cut off from them…when I have self-harmed, I don't see my family…I need my family for that stability*". The consequence of her deliberate self mutilation, "*you get cut from your family*", could suggest that the pain associated with the act of mutilation is indeed paralleled by the pain that she experienced, not in regard to being separated from the family, but perhaps from the repeated painful experience that she had in contact with the family. The symbolisation of the mother, the one that rejected, and the father, the one that abused and punished, may have become the internalised figures that generate feelings of guilt and the active seeking of her own punishment. It is hypothesised that regardless of the physical presence of the rejecter or abuser in her life, Lisa may carry these representatives within her psyche, and as such treat herself as her family did; thus becoming her own persecutor and abuser.

"*Sometimes I think that because all my life I have relied on someone, who was going to get me through...like parents, and then [husband] took over the role*". The fear that Lisa expressed about her moving to live on her own, connected to the hypothesised internalised persecutory figure, is interesting when one considers that two of the self-harm incidents that were described by Lisa during the interviews were actually achieved using a broken mirror. "*I got a mirror from my beauty case and started cutting*" whilst in the inpatient psychiatric ward in 2002, and again more recently in 2005: "*I had this big mirror in the bedroom, it was massive. I smashed into it and broke it; all the sharp bits...I could have cut myself to bits...*".

Self-Harm behaviours were reported by Lisa during periods of perceived abuse, persecution, or rejection from those around her, and this provides some evidence as to the lived experience of repeated trauma from her childhood – the father that abused and persecuted, and the mother that rejected. Although Lisa's masochistic tendencies may appear to be triggered by environmental or social stressors, it is hypothesised that the underlying mechanism for the seeking of punishment and for the feelings of guilt remain unconsciously attached to her past traumas. The experience of this need for punishment and feeling of guilt can therefore be considered as a possible reactivation of the past trauma by current (and unconsciously connected) environmental stressors.

A Psychoanalytic Formulation of the Case of Lisa

Lisa had a diagnosis of BPD. This psychiatric disorder is hypothesised to be a result of the marked failure of the oedipal prohibition by both her father and mother; her father who sexually abused her as a child, and her mother who was unavailable to her. If her mother was emotionally available to Lisa during her formative years, this may have provided her with a secure base from which she may have been able to regulate and work through her own emotional experience, and in fact confront her father. It is hypothesised that Lisa lacks an adequate formation of the symbolisation of both the father and the mother in her psyche, and this is associated with her deliberate self mutilation and poor coping with her own role as a mother observed at the time of interview.

The perversion of her father, namely his sexual advances, exhibitionistic exposure of his penis, and voyeuristic thrill of observing his naked daughter may be considered as linked to Lisa's own behaviour of cutting. The pleasure the pervert experiences through causing anxiety in the other person, as Lisa's father experienced as he caused her to be anxious through his abusive acts, appears to be replaying itself through the act of Lisa's cutting. Her ability to terrorise others and generate anxiety through her cutting may be considered as connected to her father's symptom. The abuse of trust that his daughter had in him, and the role that her mother played in the failure of the oedipal prohibition, could be considered as aetiological constellations to Lisa's presenting symptom. Her ongoing self-harm and alcohol abuse is suspected to be related to Lisa's attempt to remain attached to the memory of her father; the only person with whom she felt a true sense of place – even though the place that he created for her was an inappropriate and abusive one.

When old enough, Lisa reported that she found comfort in the use of alcohol to dull the pain of her abusive childhood; a comfort that was originally found through the socialising with friends at her sporting activities. She believed that she found a sense of place in her social world through her active partying, and eventually the playing of sport was overridden by the "*release*"[3] she had found in her alcohol use. The emergence of her cutting and other self abusive behaviours is hypothetically constructed to have perhaps followed the first instance when the only strategy she reported she had to cope with her emotional experience was truly threatened; in a rehabilitation clinic where she was sent by her husband and family to address her ongoing abuse of alcohol.

From her childhood, it is hypothesised that Lisa had developed an intolerance of her own emotional experience, with the only discharge of this emotion being used by her at the time of entering therapy being the cutting or self abuse of her body. When placed under normal levels of daily stress, Lisa was unable to tolerate this; she will regress to the memory of her father[4] – the only person she felt that loved her. Seeking comfort in the memory of her abuser is hypothesised as resulting in the feelings of guilt that she regularly described. This sense of guilt may be associated with the role she may have believed that she had played in the sexual abuse; was she an active participant in the abuse? It is considered that she may have needed to allow the abuse from her father in order to feel loved and have a sense of place in her family, rather than considering herself to be the piece of afterbirth her mother did not want. This idea, although it would be unconscious to her, may be the correlate to Lisa's regularly reported feelings of guilt and subsequent need to punish herself through her DSH behaviours.

The ambivalence toward her father, the one person that she considered loved her but also abused her for his own gratification, is suggested through the predominant attacking of her right arm. It is hypothesised that in doing so, she may have been attempting to severe the same arm that was used to touch and stimulate her father, and in doing so reduced herself to sticky and bloody remnants of "*afterbirth*". When placed under stress or feeling unwanted by those around her, it is suspected that Lisa may have regressed to the memory of her father. Such an idea would be unconscious to Lisa. During daily stress, or when perceived as unwanted, it is reconstructed here that she would resort to self-harm behaviours to reduce this general feeling of guilt. She would not consciously understand the connection between daily stressors in her life, the feelings of guilt that she regularly experienced, and the consequent need for punishment that she achieved through her DSH behaviours.

The following interpretation was offered during the work undertaken with Lisa in a psychotherapeutic context, and interprets the masochistic drive behind Lisa's cutting of her right arm as being related to the sense of guilt she had regarding her role in the sexual abuse she suffered by her father. This possible construction became apparent in a particular session with Lisa:

---

[3] Release is a term that is described by Lisa herself with regard to her self injury and alcohol abuse.

[4] The regression of Lisa to the memory of her father when feeling stressed or in conflict with others is a process by which it is considered that the identification with her aggressor becomes activated, thus leading to an increased probability of DSH behaviours.

Lisa: *"I've been spending some time with another patient who also cuts herself. She doesn't cut her arm though, she cuts her leg. It sounds strange but I can't understand why anyone would want to cut their legs".*

Me: I've noticed some peculiar tendencies actually when it comes to the use of your arms. What hand to do you write with?

Lisa: *"My right".*

Me: What hand do you pick things up with?

Lisa: *"My right".*

Me: What hand do you eat with?

Lisa: *"My left".*

Me: What hand do you wash with?

Lisa: *"My left".*

Me: What hand did your father make you touch him with?

Lisa: *"My right... I see what you're getting at. I've never thought about it like that but you're right, it was always my right hand he used to make me touch him with. I guess that's why I cut that arm I suppose... (long pause)...it was my right hand".*

The predominate attacking of herself by cutting her right arm, which was the same arm that Lisa used to fondle her father's genitals with, was constructed as her response to the sense of guilt that she may have had for her perceived part she played in the sexual abuse. Although her father did this to her, Lisa still loved her father and had not been able to express any anger toward him for this abuse of trust. Over the eight years that she experienced the abuse, she never once protested against his advances, and to please the only parent that gave her any love or attention, she continued to play out the role of her father's lover. This aetiological constellation was considered to be a significant source of the sense of guilt she experienced, and was hypothesised as the major contributor to the development of her masochistic tendencies, and the consequent need to punish herself through her deliberate self injurious behaviours.

Reflections on Issues of Transference: The Unwanted Afterbirth

In appreciating Lisa's feedback on the professional response she has encountered during her clinical contacts, and the way in which we should proceed within the transference relationship, careful consideration of Lisa's perceived treatment by the historical parental figures is needed. Pertinent to Lisa's self concept is the notion of being an unwanted twin – the afterbirth of the desired son. The perceived sense of rejection by those around her, and the active rejection of professional care by Lisa throughout her clinical care, can be considered as a transference response and cause of an unconscious sense of guilt. When the sense of guilt is activated, the need for punishment can only be achieved via the use of self mutilation. To reinforce the inherent belief of being unwanted, Lisa would also cut herself off from her family through the action of her DSH behaviours. She would also attempt to disengage from the psychiatric service. The masochist's need for equilibrium (to remain in a constant state of pain) could be achieved through causing those around her to cut her off from their lives. The symbolisation of her choice of self-harm, to cut herself so severely on her right arm that it was at times almost amputated, is of importance to consider – you can only reach out to those you love if you have your arms to do so.

Within the clinical environment, the repetition can continue[5]. Lisa's intolerance and rejection of care can also activate DSH in a confusing presentation of repeated mutilation – as clinicians, if we reject we can create harm but if we attempt to soothe we can also create harm. The frustration experienced by professionals involved in Lisa's care is understandable when one considers that no matter how they attempt to engage or respond to her distress, the outcome is the same. The juxtaposed position we can adopt, by accepting the need of repetition by adopting the projected figure of the abusive or critical parent or compensating this by becoming the supportive parental figure, will frustratingly result in having the same clinical outcome in initially working with this patient.

The degree of difference required in the transference, to become the figure to Lisa that recognises her value in this world, can only be accepted after a significant period of clinical time where Lisa can start to appreciate the unconscious link between her daily stressors, social interactions, and the underlying imprint[6] bestowed upon her by her parents. The conscious awareness of her actions, and their link to her need for punishment and its connection to her upbringing, can only be achieved when continued attempts are made by the clinician to tolerate her self mutilation and not allow Lisa to cut herself off from the therapeutic relationship. This is a long term active process by which the clinician is required to hold steadfast in their commitment to the therapeutic alliance and consider the frequent attempts to disengage and harm herself as a signal of the intolerance Lisa has of considering herself as being adequate enough to deserve care and recognition[7]. The impact of being either dismissed or critically treated by her mother (even as an adult), and being used as a sexual toy by her father, has reinforced Lisa's intolerance of nurture and support by others (including professionals) – without conscious recognition of the imprint, and acceptance of the 'wrong' inherent in the behaviours of the parental figure/s, Lisa will continue to feel unwanted, reject any attempt to engage or help her, and pursue activities of punishment that reinforce her sense of being unwanted. This behaviour ultimately assists in achieving some sense of discharge in the sense of guilt Lisa has of her own existence – in the end, afterbirth should be discarded following the delivery of the desired male baby.

---

[5] One would also say that the repetition needs to continue to allow for a successful working through of one's conflicts; but with a degree of difference.

[6] Imprint is a term I commonly use in psychotherapy to denote the influence that one's development has had on the patient's concept of themselves, their relationship to and common interactional patterns with others, and their value in this world.

[7] Viewing Lisa's behaviour as an adaptive strategy (albeit a warped adaptive strategy) in opposition to the commonly interpreted maladaptive strategy, particularly in early stages of treatment, could assist in the appropriate management of the countertransference response.

Chapter 8

THE CASE FORMULATION OF 'HELEN'

HISTORY OF PRESENTING PROBLEM

Helen was a single woman in her forties with a diagnosis of BPD, who frequently engaged in multiple active forms of self-harm, such as self poisoning by the deliberate overdosing of medication (usually paracetamol), refusing to take her prescribed medication (required to control her chronic and life-threatening physical condition), and self mutilation by cutting her arms or stabbing herself in the stomach with a knife. She has had multiple admissions to the emergency department, general ward, and psychiatric unit of the hospital over many years.

Helen had been known to the psychiatric services since her young adult years. She reported that the first instance of self-harm behaviours occurred when she was thirteen years of age. At this time, she had suffered a broken leg that was not detected for many days despite her complaints of pain, her grandparent had died, a neighbourhood girl of a similar age had died of a brain tumour, and her cousin had suicided. She had cut her legs with a knife. This injury was not detected by the family until it became septic. Helen explained this cut on her leg as an accident from climbing over a barbed wire fence. There were further periods of self injury; however these were undetected as forms of DSH: "*I always made excuses*".

Despite regular DSH and suicidal gestures, Helen believes the first real instance of attention being paid to her DSH behaviours occurred when she was in her late thirties and was admitted to the psychiatric ward for depression. Whilst on leave from the ward, she had bought a large amount of paracetamol and had ingested this. At this time, Helen felt that her life was out of control as she was sectioned under the *Mental Health Act* as an involuntary patient. Helen described similar feelings of loss of control prior to other self-harm behaviours. She had tried to hang and strangulate herself, cut various parts of her body, stabbed herself repeatedly with a large knife, jumped off a building (resulting in broken legs), and overdosed on various medications. There had been periods of suicidal intent with such behaviours; however this is not always present with her deliberate self injury and self poisoning behaviours. Helen described the need to be punished and general feelings of guilt prior to engaging in self-harm: "*To move the pain. Guilt…I feel really relieved*".

Family History and Structure

Helen was raised by an intact family unit. She was the middle child, with two siblings. Financial strain resulted in limited family and schooling activities. Her father was the main disciplinarian, and would physically "*discipline*" the children in response to what was deemed as inappropriate behaviour. During periods of such punishment, severe bruising would result. Children would also be restricted to their bedrooms "*for a period of a week, only exiting for meals, school, and toileting*". Helen described her childhood as strict but loving. Her father was reported to be emotionally distant and non affectionate; however her mother was described as also strict but loving and affectionate toward the children.

Her parents lived some distance from her. She described an unusual relationship with her father. She described him as "*a closed person*" who does not "*express emotion*". Helen reported a close relationship historically and currently (at time of interview) with her mother: "*she is my best friend*". Her mother however had deteriorated physically and was suffering from poor health. She did not describe a close relationship with her siblings. She felt her brother did not accept her as an equal, due to her psychiatric condition, and her sister, whom she felt somewhat closer to, did not live locally.

Medical and Educational History

Helen was diagnosed with a neurodegenerative metabolic disorder in her late teens. This condition required ongoing medical management and prescription of medication by a specialist. Without treatment, the disorder would result in death in approximately three months.

Helen had also suffered multiple broken bones, from car accidents and whilst playing sport. There have also been medical complications secondary to her metabolic disorder, such as hepatitis, and her DSH behaviours, such as a perforated intestine.

At school, Helen was a popular child and was the school captain. She reported to be a high achiever in school, receiving outstanding grades in subjects such as chemistry. Her grades however started to deteriorate as she became physically unwell, and she felt that she lost her confidence when the teachers informed her that she may fail her high school certificate. Nevertheless, Helen completed her high school certificate and planned to pursue a career in the health care field: "*my ambition when I left school was to be a nurse*". She commenced this training however was unable to complete this due to her medical condition, and despite undertaking six attempts to do so. In her adult years, she had completed other courses to pursue similar work (child care and disability support) but she was not working in these areas. Helen described a desire to care for people to ensure that they receive the care and attention that she herself has not received.

DEVELOPMENTAL HISTORY

Helen reported a difficult upbringing. She described herself as a "*fiercely independent*" and "*defiant*" person, even as a child. Her father suffered a broken leg when she was an infant, and her mother was required to run the family business. This resulted in her father attending to the children. Helen described a lack of tolerance of her by her father, compared to that particularly of her brother. She described feeling unloved in her childhood, and recalled writing letters to her parents at a young age that she knew they did not love her and she was planning to run away.

Her earliest memory was from the age of four. Helen, her brother, and an older neighbourhood boy were smoking cigarettes behind the haystack on the farm. The haystack burnt down and Helen and her brother were strapped until "*black and blue*" by their father with a belt. The two children also had to remain in their rooms for the following week, exiting only for meals and toileting. Helen believed that this incident was the fault of the older neighbourhood boy and felt that he should have been punished for the haystack burning down: "*he got off scot-free*". Helen reported that she and her siblings were regularly strapped by her father to punish them for unruly behaviour: "*He never hit us for any reason but for punishment…it was the formal turn of events*".

Helen described herself however as an outgoing child among her peers. In her teenage years, she began to feel different. Her performance at school deteriorated, and her behaviour became more disorganised. She was flown to the closest capital city to undergo extensive medical examination. She remembered being photographed semi naked by strangers, due to the extensive jaundice that she suffered from, and was to undertake many invasive tests. She was then diagnosed with a metabolic disorder: "*I was told to go home and take these tablets; it won't affect the rest of your life*". She felt she had never received adequate counselling for this debilitating disorder and the changes this had caused to her life. Helen described herself as "*not having her own identity*". She attributed this to growing up in a small town. She was known as "*her father's daughter*" or "*that sick girl*" due to her physical illness. This continued through into her young adult years and it distressed her immensely. Out of exasperation, she would sit in the middle of the road and wish for a car to run her over. During this time, she was under care by the psychiatric service.

Many traumatic losses and abuse by others were reported to be experienced throughout her childhood and adult years, from an orphaned boy who was staying at the family home exposing his penis to her when she was young, to a well respected business man (who was friend of her father's) wanting to touch her. She disclosed these advances to her mother, however due to the social reputation of the man involved, her mother did not confront this man nor inform Helen's father. Instead her mother would just let her know when this man was planning to visit the house so that she could make herself scarce and avoid contact with him. When she moved to a neighbouring town in her twenties, Helen reported further sexual advances by an elderly neighbour: "*because he gave me a job, he thought I owed him something*". The behaviour continued until Helen reported this to the police who confronted the man and asked him not to visit her anymore.

Helen reported that there have not been any significant intimate relationships; although she did wish to have a partner whom "*will love me for me*". Any possible relationship avenues were reported to be quickly severed by her before any substantial connections could be made. Helen reported that her parents never approved of any boyfriends that she started dating and bought home to introduce to the family. However her parents were very fond of her siblings' partners, often raving about her brother-in-law and sister-in-law, and Helen felt that she could not compete with this. She would then terminate the relationship.

A review of Helen's history, from a personal writings book, showed that she had also lost many family members and many friends in tragic circumstances[1]. Further to the loss experienced when she was thirteen, in her twenties her grandfather whom she was close to died and she was unable to see him before his death. She was also required to nurse her dying grandmother's identical twin during her nursing training. Helen also had three close friends die as a result of two car accidents within ten days of each other. During a holiday trip around Australia, one of the fellow passengers suddenly dropped dead in front of the other travellers. Many years later, a male friend committed suicide by shooting himself. Helen was the last person to see him alive before he took his own life. Looking back, she believed that there were signs there of his despair however she did not recognise this at the time. She reported that she could understand his wish to die.

Whilst working in a disability service in her thirties, a client committed suicide; she felt somewhat responsible for this due to her role as this person's carer, so she then resigned from this profession. Another friend died due to stroke in their thirties. When she moved to the town she currently (at time of interview) resided in, she befriended another person that soon after also committed suicide. During this period, Helen was also taken advantage of by an older male in his fifties who proceeded to physically assault her. Soon after this, her mother's health started deteriorating, and this deterioration was continuing. Whilst coming to terms with her mother's failing health, two other friends died from cancer.

Due to her physical illness, Helen was unable to have children and was in receipt of a disability pension. She described this as the source of a lot of her guilt. She attempted to complete her nursing training however she was unable to do so. Six weeks before sitting her finals for completion of this training, Helen was required to withdraw from the course. She recalled her nursing tutor taking her off the hospital ward, telling her that she "*was sicker than the patients*" she was nursing in the hospital!

More recently, Helen had lost another two people whom she knew through tragic circumstances. A friend's daughter was killed in an unusual accident that had not been ruled out as a suicide. Another person within the same week, with whom Helen was an acquaintance of, suddenly died from an unknown medical condition.

DIAGNOSIS (DSM-IV-TR)

Axis 1: Adjustment disorder with mixed anxiety and mood, chronic (309.28)

Axis 2: Borderline personality disorder (301.83)

Predominant symptoms: identity disturbance (markedly and persistently unstable self image or sense of self); a pattern of unstable and intense inter-

[1] Helen produced this personal writings book to me on the first interview, wanting me to read its contents and return it to her on next interview.

personal relationships; recurrent suicidal behaviour, gestures, or threats, or self mutilating behaviour; affective instability due to marked reactivity of mood; chronic feelings of emptiness.

Axis 3: Metabolic disorder

Axis 4: Problems with primary support group (estrangement from family due to geographical distance and poor physical health)
Occupational problems (unemployment)

Axis 5: GAF 30 (current)

Use of the Psychoanalytic Framework in Considering Self-harm

From a Freudian framework of moral masochism, an unconscious sense of guilt and a need for punishment is inherent in the DSH behaviours of many patients. To construct the source of this unconscious guilt and need for punishment, the dialogue of the patient has been reviewed. As outlined earlier, the behavioural response of the patient – in this case DSH behaviours – can be often constructed from careful consideration of the words of the patient. As understood within the clinical interviews, Helen's dialogue leads us to consider a possible ambivalence about the need to be cared for, and in fact whether she indeed deserved to be cared for.

The first indication to consider of the masochistic drive underlying her DSH presentations comes from review of the first instance of self mutilation. Helen reported that this occurred when she was thirteen years of age – she had suffered a broken leg that was not detected for ten days, her grandmother had died, her cousin had suicided, and a neighbouring boy had died from a brain tumour. When asked within the word association task, in response to the word 'trauma', Helen gave the following response: "*Death. Suicide. Sickness. Accidents. Unhappy. It can be physical, emotional…*". What appears to have perhaps been the original trauma was considered to be related to the simultaneous aetiological constellations of *death*, with her grandmother, *suicide*, by her cousin, *sickness*, from the neighbourhood boy dying of a brain tumour, and *accidents*, from her broken leg. With the prior idea that Helen considered herself to not be loved by her parents, it is constructed that she experienced a time where she genuinely required care; however she reported that she was not provided with this. The guilt may then be interpreted as an effect of this trauma, from which she developed the incompatible idea that she was not deserving of care.

Helen's desire to become a nurse, and she indeed attempted the training on many occasions, appears to be related to her efforts to provide care for those around her; in an attempt to address the original trauma. "*I just feel like dirt when I go and see both of them (parents)…I'm very much like dad, I'll give and give and give. But I give at my health's expense and he gives at his family's expense*". Throughout her interviews Helen made reference to poor responses to her requests to provide her with care, claiming the support was "*inconsistent*". It appears from her reports that she was highly sensitive to any forms of perceived dismissal by health professionals, with Helen even taking a friend with her to the emergency department to support her story that the injury she required attention for was an accident. In opposition to this, there was also difficulty expressed with Helen feeling "*very selfish*" about prioritising her own care during times of distress, enacting the same response as that we have been told from her childhood – she does not deserve to be cared for. The development of her metabolic disorder was a significant event in her history, and perhaps in the ongoing behavioural disturbance. She found the investigatory and diagnostic processes to be dismissive, and its presence prevented Helen from becoming the nurse she desired to be in order to care for others in the way that she had not been provided for.

A Psychoanalytic Formulation of the Case of Helen

Helen had a diagnosis of BPD. This psychiatric disorder is hypothesised to be as a result of the inconsistent parenting she received in her childhood and the physical abuse she endured. The physical abuse and emotional distance experienced by Helen from her father, and the role that her mother played in this abuse by remaining the silent observer, is constructed to be an aetiological factor in Helen's presenting symptom. From her earliest memory, Helen reported to have felt unloved and even made to feel intolerable to her family. In order to attract the attention of her family, she reported that she has had to resort to continual complaints about her physical and emotional pain, or demonstrate her existence through defiant behaviours; for which she was further punished. The emergence of her cutting and other self abusive behaviour followed Helen's reported first instance of trauma – at the age of 13 when she suffered a broken leg that was not detected for ten days despite the constant verbal complaints from Helen that she was in pain. This aetiological factor also occurred during a period of bereavement with the death of her cousin, grandmother, and local child the same age as herself.

From her childhood, it is hypothesised that Helen had developed an intolerance of her own need for care and medical attention, and the only discharge of the guilt associated with this intolerance available to her was the physical abuse of her body. During periods that she perceived that people around her did not care about her pain, it is constructed that Helen was unable to tolerate this; she would regress to the memory of the first instance of absolute loneliness and desertion – the age of thirteen years when the pain from a broken leg she was complaining of was disregarded and she therefore first self-harmed. Seeking comfort from those around her may also result in the feelings of guilt that she regularly described, as it is hypothesised that she struggled with the need to accept assistance and help in managing her own medical condition due to the ingrained notion that (historically) she does not deserve to be loved or cared for.

It is suggested that the lack of nurturing by her family had resulted in Helen being unable to adequately accept her own medical condition or grieve the numerous losses in her life. She presented with ambivalence toward the health care system, seen in her desire for empathy, support, and understanding from a source that at times she reported that she felt she did not deserve. This ambivalence is suspected to further contribute to the frustration experienced by those associated with her care as she would continually sabotage attempts to provide her with adequate services to minimise the disability associated with both her physical and mental conditions. It is hypothesised that Helen's childhood experience had resulted in this idea of unworthiness, which then combined with the angry desire to be finally cared for. The fury at her past neglect was also seen in her unrelenting desire to become a nurse; to perhaps seek to care for people in the way that she always wanted but never received.

From her report of possible aetiological constellations, it is hypothesised that the desire to be cared for produced the sense of guilt that Helen described prior to self-harm behaviours. Interestingly, when sectioned under the *Mental Health Act* as an involuntary patient in her thirties, the DSH behaviours actually escalated. This evidence of the inability to accept care when needed or provided also shows us the ambivalence, and the continued activation of trauma from her early experiences. Due to feeling unworthy of care and attention, which she requires to manage her physical condition, Helen often experienced feelings of guilt. This then results in Helen needing to punish herself. The need for punishment was achieved through her DSH behaviours in the same form of punishment she received as a child; the physical assault of her body.

REFLECTIONS ON ISSUES OF TRANSFERENCE: THE UNWORTHY PATIENT

Given Helen's reports of being consistently denied love or care, or made to feel unworthy of care provided to her, careful consideration of the developmental experiences and imprint provided by the parental figures reveals her intolerance but angry desire for love and care. The punishment of the body by her father as a child, and the disregard of complaints of pain due to a broken and septic leg injury, is continuously activated in a process of repetition that is exacerbated by Helen's debilitating and life-threatening metabolic disorder (and by her continued episodes of DSH). When physical or emotional care is required or desired, the sense of guilt is activated – the belief of not being worthy of care conflicts with the desire for help, often activating further DSH (via active self punishment or via more passive denial of access to prescription medications). Her anger towards those that have denied her care, and her attempts to enforce her need for care via her extreme self mutilation episodes, is a complex cyclic pattern that needs to be thoroughly considered – if she felt that she was unworthy of care, why would she often go to such extremes as stabbing herself in the abdomen (requiring ambulance attendance and surgery) in order to ensure that she received some form of care?

Within the clinical environment, the repetition can continue in an active process of causing the need for care (either intentionally or unintentionally) and activating the feelings of intolerance and frustration onto the medical team required to treat her injuries or illness – the medical team (as to be seen in later feedback presented about the professional response to Helen) can easily become the projected parental figure from the past when they express frustration at the repeated presentations of Helen to the emergency department. The reinforcement of unworthiness by being disregarded can be achieved through activating this response in those around her. The punishment of the body can be achieved through Helen's treatment of herself and at times seeking of her own pain and misfortune (explicitly achieved through denial of care and treatment for her metabolic disorder). The response of the clinician, whether one of frustration and disregard or of support and reassurance, ultimately can lead again to the same cyclic pattern of DSH behaviour – by accepting the projected figure or compensating this by responding contrarily will have little impact initially on the occurrence of repeated DSH. Helen is unable to tolerate expressions of care and nurturance as the inherent belief of being undeserving of care remains fixed – the confusion of the professional in their attempt to rectify Helen's angst often only escalates the unconscious sense of guilt (and then only leads to escalating attempts to punish herself to discharge this sense of guilt).

The only means by which Helen can be able to recognise her entitlement to care and nurturance is a lengthy process of psychotherapy where the therapeutic alliance can be maintained adequately enough to allow for some appreciation of the error in the response of the parental figure (as opposed to the held imprint of unworthiness of the self). The lack of conscious awareness of this concept, despite Helen's regular proclamations and demands of being cared for, is more complex that simply telling or reassuring Helen that she needs support or treatment[2]. Helen's frequent demands for support are confusing when one considers the underlying belief that she is not worthy of being cared for or about – she seeks to be disregarded (which then activates further DSH as the sense of guilt is intensified). Confusingly, if reassured and nurtured she also rejects or sabotages these attempts as ultimately the sense of guilt about needing care causes conflict with her feeling that she is not deserving of care (and this sense of guilt requires discharge via her masochistic actions). The inherent belief bestowed upon her by the parental figures is what requires gradual investigation and modification for structural change, and therefore cessation of the self destructive impulse, to occur.

[2] The incongruence in what she seeks or desires, and what she inherently believes, in regard to her entitlement to or worthiness of care requires careful consideration here. The rejection of the incompatible idea will activate the unconscious sense of guilt and escalate the occurrence of DSH episodes (in a process of "I want help"; "yes you need help"; "no I don't deserve your help").

Chapter 9

THE CASE FORMULATION OF 'EVE'

HISTORY OF PRESENTING PROBLEM

Eve was a married woman in her early forties with a diagnosis of BPD, who frequently engaged in active forms of self mutilation by cutting her arm (wrist and elbow joint), usually with razor blades. She has had multiple admissions to the emergency department, general ward, and psychiatric unit of the hospital over the past few years. Eve had been known to the psychiatric services since her early thirties. She reported that the first instance of DSH behaviour occurred when she was 32 years of age. At this time, she had lost a baby through an ectopic pregnancy. She was approximately eight weeks pregnant. She had cut her wrist with a razor blade: "*I am presuming that it is just the stress of the situation that triggered it…I wanted to punish myself for the loss of the baby, I think that it was my fault even though it was ectopic. I felt that I should have died with the baby; rather than aborting the baby…even though the baby would not have survived anyway. I feel that if I was a proper mother I should have died with the baby and been there for the baby in heaven*". There were further periods of self injury following this; however Eve believed that these were undetected as forms of DSH as people saw them purely as attempts at suicide. Eve described a feeling of "*unbelievable depression*" and "*feeling of futility*" prior to engaging in self-harm. These depressive periods were reported to occur approximately every four to five months since she lost the baby, and usually lasted for around eight weeks before receding.

Eve reported that she would cut herself to relieve frustration – although if she ended up dying from her deliberate self mutilation, she did not care about this: "*but that is not my motivation behind it…it is just that I can't cope with this anymore*". She had cut only one other site on her body, a vein on her leg, and this occurred during a time when she was in hospital and her arms were placed in plaster casts to prevent her from continuing to self-harm or remove her sutures. Eve denied any other active forms of self-harm, such as self poisoning or other self injury. She did however suffer from anorexia as a teenager and described a period of being suicidal during this time. She did not however make an attempt on her life. Eve reported that the self mutilation is common during times when daily responsibilities overwhelm her: "*just to relieve the pressure. Just the act of cutting and the pain that is associated with the cutting. Just releases…lets go some of that pressure. I can't explain it any other way than that*".

Family History and Structure

Eve was raised by an intact family unit. She was the youngest child, with an older brother. She described a close relationship with her mother, who has supported her throughout her childhood and adult years. In her later adult years, her mother treated her more like a girlfriend: "*Mum treated me more like a friend than a daughter…she always told me that she and dad had a very active sex life*". Her father was away a significant amount of time during her childhood due to his career, however she recalled periods of molestation from her father from an early age – approximately four years old. Eve reported a general lapse in memory from this age until about ten or eleven years of age, but had recently come to experience "*flashes*" of her father who would touch and fondle her inappropriately: "*I have very little memory for anything up until about the ages of ten or eleven. It is all just blank except for the few instances that I remember*". The remembering of the molestation three months prior to the interviews distressed her immensely and was described as a contributor to her most recent DSH episode and consequent admission to the psychiatric hospital. She reported trying to seek her father's approval for everything that she did "*thinking that if perhaps I could do something right, it would stop*".

Eve had not disclosed the molestation to her mother or brother, not wanting to distress them with this information. She had an affectionate relationship with her mother, however tried to avoid any contact with her father, even verbal communication: "*I feel uncomfortable in his presence. I feel uncomfortable if he does anything toward me…be it physical, emotional, or verbal. I don't want to speak to him or to touch him…anything*". Eve married her first boyfriend and has had two children. She described a close relationship with her husband, who can "*read her moods*" and assist her with the care of the children as needed. He often used a "*problem solving*" approach to assist Eve with managing her urges to self-harm, exploring options of practical support when needed. Eve did not feel that he understood why she self-harmed, preferring to leave him to believe that she has attempted suicide many times.

Medical and Educational History

Eve reported suffering from anorexia at fourteen or fifteen, which continued until approximately twenty years of age. This required a three month period of hospitalisation and she undertook many months of psychological therapy, which was reported to be "*pointless*". With her first pregnancy eight years ago, Eve experienced an ectopic pregnancy requiring the termination of the foetus at approximately eight weeks of gestation. Her second pregnancy was also difficult with Eve experiencing contractions at five months, resulting in hospital admission. When her child was born, he was very ill. The third pregnancy was a "*dream pregnancy*" with no complications. Eve described an "*elevated mood*" during her second and third pregnancies with no periods of self-harm: "*I was pretty happy most of the time…delighted to be pregnant, delighted to be having another child*".

Academically, Eve described herself as being a very conscientious student who "*had this desire to do well…so I studied my guts out. And I did pretty well…it is the only thing that I can do well*". She had attended university and held qualifications in science. At the time of interview, Eve was also completing her Master's degree. Eve reported having some good friends from primary school, but "*they dropped off*" when she developed anorexia in her teens. Due to the extended hospital admission, and her health in general, Eve deferred her schooling for a year. When she returned, her previous friendships became estranged as they were then in the year level above her: "*It was really hard when I went back because I didn't have any friends and I was really skinny. Shy and reserved, lacking in confidence and all that stuff*".

Developmental History

Eve reported a difficult upbringing. Her mother was emotionally supportive of her however the relationship with her father was always estranged: "*I was always seeking approval for what I did...I was always trying to please him and never seemed to achieve that*". There were no extended family close by; they were all living in other states of the country.

Eve described very little memory of growing up. She had an older brother who she deemed as having more worth to her father as he was a male: "*He acknowledged my brother and my brother's intelligence...my brother won a full scholarship to [college] and I just didn't seem to be in the same league as my brother in my parents', no my father's, eyes. I just didn't seem to be worth what my brother was worth*". She described the impression that her father only saw the worth of a woman in her domestic capacity and as a source of sex: "*women should be doing all the work and the men should sit back and put their feet up*". She reported a general feeling of unease around her father as a child that until the flashbacks started to occur was reported to be unknown to her: "*I always felt sexually uncomfortable around dad...I always felt so uncomfortable in the house with him growing up. I never felt safe with him....I felt safe as a human being but not as a female around him. There was always that feeling that it just wasn't right*". Eve was very uncomfortable with her father near her or even if he was anywhere in the house. She reported that she would dread the time that he would come home at five o'clock every day, and as soon as she heard his car in the driveway, she would go straight to her bedroom and shut the door. She would come out to have the evening meal and then return back to her bedroom.

In her teenage years, approximately 15 or 16 years of age, Eve developed anorexia and was hospitalised for three months. She described being suicidal at this time: "*they assumed that I was trying to get my father's love. And that he wasn't noticing me. And as hard as I tried that I did not want dad to notice me, that is all that they assumed it was...I was a child crying out for their father's love. To me, it was more a case of starving yourself so he won't notice you, rather than a case of starving yourself so that he will notice you*".

Whilst studying a science degree at University, Eve met her first boyfriend whom she later married. She was still recovering from anorexia but reported that the support from her boyfriend helped her through that. She described a continuation of that solid support from her husband over the past 18 years of marriage: "*[He] has been the best supporter of all...when I say hey I am feeling really down and I just can't cope today, he will say 'what do you need from me? Do you need me to come home right now? I will come home now if you need me. Do you want me to grab some tea on the way home? Do you need me to pick the kids up?*

What do you need from me?' and that is really good because he just knows the right questions to say. I guess he has been there long enough".

Eve described an estranged relationship with her husband's family, and she preferred to keep them "*at arm's length*". She reported that her mother-in-law was "*very condemning*" of her. Following a two year remission in her depressive cycles and self-harm behaviours, Eve attempted to return to full time work (in 2005) but described a feeling of being unable to cope with the demands of work, managing the household, and caring for the children. In order to "*cope with these demands*", she cut her wrists. Eve also reported the occurrence of "*flashes*" of memory about the relationship with her father; memories of her father "*touching and fondling her*" when she was a child. Eve then believed that her father "*molested*" her from a young age: "*I have only flashes. I just know that I was not happy. I can remember a few instances with dad. That distressed me greatly... When I was pretty young. Starting at about three and a half, four and I am not sure how far it goes*".

Eve had not disclosed this to her mother or brother but suspected that her mother knew of the abuse but did not protect her for fear of her father: "*I don't know how mum could not have noticed...whether she chose not to...mum has always been totally dominated by dad and I guess this is another case of mum being totally dominated by dad...even if it was the welfare of her child, she would not have been able to say anything*". This caused Eve to "*pity*" her mother. Although Eve had an intact family system with her supportive husband and two children, she continued to fluctuate in her moods and engage in self mutilation. She described a poor sense of self worth: "*I don't deserve to have a husband who is as good as the one I have got; I don't deserve to have such great kids*".

Diagnosis (DSM-IV-TR)

Axis 1: Major depressive disorder, recurrent, unspecified (296.30)

Axis 2: Borderline personality disorder (301.83)

Predominant symptoms: identity disturbance (markedly and persistently unstable self image or sense of self); recurrent suicidal behaviour, gestures, or threats, or self mutilating behaviour; impulsivity; affective instability due to marked reactivity of mood; chronic feelings of emptiness.

Axis 3: No diagnosis

Axis 4: Problems with primary support group (estrangement from family)

Axis 5: GAF 60 (current)

Use of the Psychoanalytic Framework in Considering Self-harm

The words by which Eve described her own self mutilation, and the conscious idea of "*futility*" that she described prior to engaging in DSH, lead us to consider the possible source of guilt and need for punishment. As evident within the clinical interviews, there were many aetiological connections that could be made between her current self mutilating behaviour and her childhood, where the original trauma is considered to be posited. Eve had been cutting herself since the loss of her first pregnancy, and continued to do so when she was unable to function domestically. Her report of her childhood history demonstrated a deep sense of unworthiness as a female, and this leads us to consider an unconscious connection between a source of guilt and the idea of futility.

Eve described herself as "*a pretty useless person*" who did not "*deserve to be on this planet at all*". She was able to consciously connect this idea to her father, however the hypothesised connection to the sense of futility that she experiences when unable to function in her domestic capacity, or by which to bear children, remained unconscious: "*Not so much things in the past coming back to me, more current day stressors are too much*". In the first interview, Eve identified that her father molested her: "*well, dad molested me…and I was always seeking approval for what I did. Thinking that if perhaps I could do something right, it would stop. But it was all my fault anyway*". In the subsequent second interview, Eve discussed the chauvinistic approach of her father and recalled being "*sexually uncomfortable*" and not safe "*as a female around him*". The active sex life between her parents that her mother disclosed to Eve and the way in which her father treated her mother (as a servant) may have lead to the symbolisation of the wife and mother; a consideration of the sense of worth of a woman is only in her domestic capacity and her ability to sexually pleasure a man.

If we consider that Eve reported that she improved in her anorexia when she met her husband, and found a sense of worth in her function of housewife to him, we suspect that Eve had carried this idea of worth from her childhood. The instance where the feelings of futility returned was when she was required to terminate a pregnancy, possibly reawakening the original trauma of uselessness from her childhood: "*I wanted to punish myself for the loss of the baby, I think that is was my fault even though it was ectopic. I felt that I should have died with the baby; rather than aborting the baby…even though the baby would not have survived anyway. I feel that if I was a proper mother I should have died with the baby and been there for the baby in heaven…rather than leaving her alone, I pretend it is a girl even though I don't know, I pretend it is a girl*". Despite being able to later bear two children, Eve reported that she continually struggled with acknowledging her own sense of worth. The feeling of futility was a persistent affect when Eve continually struggled with her role of a mother and wife: "*I also feel like I don't deserve what I have got. I don't deserve to have a husband who is as good as the one I have got; I don't deserve to have such great kids*".

The cyclic nature of her depression she reported, being every four to five months in its pattern but lasting for an eight week period, can be hypothesised as related to the eight week period of gestation from her first pregnancy. Due to the termination of pregnancy at eight weeks, Eve failed as a woman to bear children, possibly leading to a reactivation of the sense of futility. "*I am big on punishing myself. I guess that partially that is what the cutting is about too. That I do not deserve to be a mother and I don't deserve to have children. Don't deserve to be living…that sort of thing*". During times where Eve struggled to provide for her family (when juggling fulltime work, study, and managing the children and household chores), it is hypothesised that the unconscious idea of futility from her childhood returned. Such an idea of "*I am not good enough*" is considered to perhaps lead to the drive to engage in self destructive behaviours, and thus destroy her own existence.

A PSYCHOANALYTIC FORMULATION OF THE CASE OF EVE

Eve had a diagnosis of BPD. This psychiatric disorder is hypothesised to be a direct result of the marked failure of the oedipal prohibition by both her father and mother; as was seen in the case of Lisa, her father sexually abused her as a child, and her mother was unavailable to protect her from his advances. It is hypothesised that the molestation Eve reported that she had endured from her father was a punishment for failing to achieve her father's attention: "*if perhaps I could do something right, it would stop*". It could also be seen as a reinforcement of the sense of worth of a woman is in her ability to sexually satisfy the man. The only attention given to Eve by her father was in a sexual form. The molestation that Eve reported from her childhood, memories that have recently been raised to her conscious awareness and no longer repressed, could also be considered by Eve as a punishment she had to endure for not being of worth as a daughter to her parents. This may further be inferred by the expressed ideas from Eve that she, to be a worthy mother to her deceased baby, should have died to go to heaven with the ectopic foetus.

Such aetiological constellations are considered to have been unconscious to Eve until the partial recovery of these memories through flashbacks over the preceding three months to the completion of the clinical interviews. During domestic difficulty, Eve is again faced with the idea of being unworthy. It is hypothesised that she would resort to DSH behaviours to reduce general feelings of being overwhelmed, however only in the last day of interviews was the feeling of guilt in relation to the molestation by her father recognised: "*I guess that [guilt] is more associated with dad. I don't feel guilty for cutting myself. Or for even trying to have killed myself in the past. I don't want to feel guilty for any of my actions that I have done. I feel guilty that I must have done something as a little girl [to deserve the molestation]*". At the time of her research participation, Eve had not yet come to understand the connection between her domestic capacity, the sense of futility or unworthiness, the feelings of guilt that she recently recognised that she experiences, and the consequent need for punishment that she achieves through her deliberate self mutilation behaviours.

REFLECTIONS ON ISSUES OF TRANSFERENCE: THE FUTILE WOMAN

Upon consideration of the insurmountable parental figures, the development of the feeling of futility (as aptly described by her on interview) that underlies Eve's masochistic actions in the current day begins to take on greater meaning. It would be straightforward to view her DSH behaviours and poor self esteem as a result of feeling overwhelmed by the pressures of her life, frequently balancing the home, work, and her family needs. In fact, the most helpful response by her husband that Eve reported was his suggestion and attempts to assist her domestically. The uncomplicated view of not coping and its connection to her behavioural disturbance however does not appreciate the psychically significant release that her self injury enables, or the implications of the therapeutic response in managing the continued eight week cycles of despair and harm. The sense of guilt associated with feeling unable to perform domestically as a mother (whether with regards to carrying a successful pregnancy or manage the daily household routine) that underlies the action of punishment through her cutting behaviours, is connected to the imprint imparted upon her by her mother and her father. The woman's sense of worth domestically and sexually, reinforced by both Eve's father and mother, presents itself as a dominant measure by which to gauge her own existence. The trivial nature of the conscious triggers to her DSH episodes, such as not being able to keep her home in a neat and orderly fashion due to competing work demands, can result in a negative countertransference response in the clinician – we all have these pressures in our lives and we don't decide to purchase razor blades to cut ourselves.

Although successful in her occupational field, generally competent in bringing up her two children, and capable of maintaining a long marriage, Eve's acceptance of her own worth was most challenged by the incapacity to carry her first pregnancy to full term. The symbolisation of her choice of self-harm, to cut herself on her wrists and arms, is significant when one considers that you hold a baby in your arms. The need for repetition in her self injury episodes, every four months, demonstrates the constant influence that the sense of futility has on Eve's life. The aim for psychotherapeutic invention, beyond keeping her safe and reducing the occurrence of DSH behaviours, is to uncover the unconscious significance of the feelings of guilt and its connection to her need for regular punishment. Eve's attempts to have her husband, or attempts to have her clinician, reinforce that she is not capable domestically by offering or arranging increased support at home only enable the process of repetition to continually reinforce the sense of futility stemming from her childhood experience.

Through attempting to respond to Eve, either via counselling to improve motivation to attend to daily tasks or by providing reassurance that she can capably manage tasks at home, the clinician is again adopting the projected figure that gauges her sense of worth in terms of how capably she can perform domestically. The need for a degree of difference in the transference, to enable a working through of the past, is clearly evident. It is significant that not only did Eve's father instill the sense of worth via a woman's domestic and sexual capacity, but her mother also reinforced this via her over-inclusive reports to her daughter about the parents' sex life. The resistance to being able to accept the error in the inherent sense of her futile existence is problematic due to the grief associated with needing to terminate the ectopic pregnancy[1].

[1] As indicated in the interviews, Eve felt that her basic role as a person was to become a mother – and she failed to be able to achieve this with her first pregnancy.

Chapter 10

The Patient's Feedback on the Professional Response

Although much research has been dedicated to reviewing the attitudes of health professionals toward this patient group, in comparison minimal time has been dedicated to collecting patient perspectives of the mental health and emergency medicine service provision. Of the patient outcome studies and qualitative interviews with BPD patients that have been completed within the current literature, it is feared that very little time has been dedicated by health professionals to reviewing the patient perspectives of the provision of care across the mental health and emergency medicine sectors. As discussed earlier, this information is clinically useful to the therapeutic work and does require careful consideration upon entering into an alliance with each individual patient. It is the first glimpse we can see of the transference at work.

Many BPD patients that engage in DSH, particularly repeated episodes, feel that the health professionals are not willing or interested in their perspectives. Upon review of such feedback, it becomes apparent that "service users describe contact with health services as often difficult, characterised by ignorance, negative attitudes and, sometimes, punitive behaviour" (National Collaborating Centre for Mental Health, 2004, p.28). As discussed earlier with the three case illustrations, this can unwittingly result in an exacerbation of DSH behaviours (whether contacts are difficult and judgemental, or whether they are supportive and nurturing). Upon completion of the clinical interviews, the three patients presented here were also given the opportunity to provide feedback on the typical contacts they have had with service providers. The result of the clinical interviews demonstrate that these patients have found their contacts with emergency medicine and mental health staff to be problematic, and at times judgemental. This information has been utilised to assist with the development of the hypotheses relating to the unconscious sense of guilt inherent in all three case presentations.

Further to this, suggestions were elicited from Lisa, Helen, and Eve to assist health professionals who are involved in the treatment of BPD in understanding the behavioural presentation and the transference-countertransference reactions with this patient group. In reflecting on this dialogue it is hoped that clinicians will consider the clinical contact that they themselves have had with patients with BPD, resulting in a greater consideration of how the professional community can start to mend the gap between the current level of care the patient receives and the level of investment that is required on the part of the clinician to enable effective psychotherapeutic treatment. Further recommendations of how to respond to behavioural disturbance in BPD patients are then offered in the next chapters of this text.

Reflections on the Response from Emergency Medicine Clinicians

All three patients reported problematic responses from the health professionals in the emergency medicine department of their local health service, with explicit expressions of intolerance being described:

"I have had experiences where I have had to go into emergency…different doctors or nurses give me the short shift…'oh, she's done it again'…they sort of just wipe me…very arrogant and rude in their response to me…". (Lisa)[1].

"Instead of saying 'look I don't know how to help you', they cover up. I stabbed myself…I had to call an ambulance and they said 'oh hurry up it can't be all that bad', and I knew I was sick, very sick…They took me up to the hospital and one of the first comments was that I looked very pale. They didn't do any observations, put any blankets on me or anything and I have put in a formal complaint about it… [Why do you think they've responded to you that way?] Because most of them know me and most of them know I self-harm". (Helen)[2].

"The only people I have had any negative [responses] from are the doctors in emergency, who do not understand why I have done it and who chastise me for doing it. Maybe they are just frustrated. I don't know but I have had that a fair few times… I feel like I am wasting their time and that I am just a nuisance". (Eve).

The patients reported that they have also found that the level of understanding of why they have engaged in DSH behaviours is limited. This had been, at times, candidly expressed to the patients themselves upon presentation to the emergency medicine department.

"I was coming in so often and I was coming in so many times that they couldn't understand why…There was a registrar that kept coming, he was very arrogant and I explained to him that I am trying not to do this. I am trying not to, but he was very rude and arrogant and didn't have any understanding of it. I don't ever want to see him again. They get quite annoyed by us, 'you are a nuisance'…". (Lisa).

"I would treat each patient with respect and empathy. Now, that's not taught. It's all out of a book. You can't get out of a book how to treat or how to sit with patients. When I went to hospital, I went to Triage. They said 'what did you do that for?'…then another nurse comes in 'what did you do that for?' and started". (Helen).

"Comments like 'what did you need to do that for?' or 'why did you do this?' or 'whatever possessed you to do this?' or 'what are we going to do so you do not do this again?' I wish they would understand, they just see it as attention seeking and a waste of their

[1] This response would again reinforce the concept of being unwanted, reactivating the sense of guilt and need for punishment (and greater likelihood of self mutilation) – see earlier comments of transference reactions in Lisa's case illustration.

[2] This response would again reinforce the concept of being not deserving of care, reactivating the sense of guilt of requiring some treatment, and therefore exacerbate the need for punishment (and greater likelihood of further self injury) – see earlier comments of transference reactions in Helen's case illustration.

time...They need to understand that it is not attention seeking, the person is in real trouble, and needs their help – not their chastisement". (Eve).

It was also reported from one of the patients that the form of medical treatment applied to the injury was often inconsistent, feeling that it was based on the attitude of the treating medical practitioner not in response to an examination of the wound.

"I have had different doctors say 'no we are not suturing' and then you get other doctors say 'yeah, I will fix this'". (Lisa).

REFLECTIONS ON THE RESPONSE FROM MENTAL HEALTH CLINICIANS

A lack of understanding from the mental health services regarding the impetus to self-harm was also reported. The lack of understanding of the behaviour was evident as shown in the following patient comments:

[Have they have understood you?] "*...Not really, I think that they are a bit scared by it...I felt they were anxious and really didn't know what was happening. And even when I cut superficially, they would come in and find me cutting, there was anxiety there...I think that seeing blood and how far I have gone – not really knowing me, how far have I gone? It does cause concern for people who do not understand self-harm. You know yourself how far you have gone, although a couple of times this year I had gone a bit far. But you can't blame them for not understanding just how far you have gone or why it is happening; they don't understand why you are doing it"*. (Lisa).

"One night I rang up Triage, and it was hopeless and I gave up. I felt rejected because I was being passed from pillar to post. I was in the too hard basket". (Helen).

[Did any of them ask you why to try to understand?]... *"No. No I have never had that...I don't know if I might have been able to explain that to them but it may have been useful instead of 'what have you done?' You never get 'why?' or 'what's happened?' or anything like that*". (Lisa).

All three patients also reported problematic responses from the mental health professionals in the inpatient and triage department of the health service, with explicit expressions of intolerance being described:

"I have been told to behave myself like a grown woman, I have been told to grow up, act my age – things like that....More of a frustration that they are having to...sit in the room with me or expend all this energy on me". (Eve)[3].

"When I was in [town], they queried schizophrenia and I was self-harming and I remember one of the psych nurses, he was my case manager, he was really arrogant and seemed out of touch... He said he is just sick of me ...Even with my last admission, they didn't listen. It wasn't pleasant to stay with them". (Helen).

[3] This response would again reinforce the concept of being futile in a domestic capacity (especially with direct reference to being a woman), reactivating the sense of guilt and need for punishment (and greater likelihood of further cutting behaviours) – see earlier comments of transference reactions in Eve's case illustration.

Suggestions Offered to Improve the Professional Response

There were some instances reported of helpful responses being provided to these patients, particularly with regard to adequate time being given to the patients when in distress. Suggestions were also made regarding the need for more specialised care and understanding when it comes to the treatment of BPD, as well as a need to recognise that often the patient is just as confused as to the reasons behind the DSH behaviours as the clinician is[4].

> [In general, from mental health staff, what responses from them, after your self-harm, were helpful?] *"I just wanted to talk to someone who knew, or I knew that cared and I kept saying "you don't want to listen to this garbage" and she said "Yes I do, you need help". I spoke for ¾ of an hour."* [Is showing some form of caring or empathy is really important in getting you to open up and accepting help?] *"Yeah, and that's my first step of hopping off the merry-go-round....It's that someone actually genuinely cared".* (Helen).
>
> *"There needs to be a special section cordoned off [in the emergency department] for mental health".* (Lisa).
>
> *"They will never understand because being a patient yourself, you do not understand yourself why you do it.* [So talking about what creates the stress can help reduce the stress?] *"Yeah. Like it really helps – I had the problem for years that I could not really express what was going wrong or what was happening. I probably know myself – I had to learn what was happening and what had happened.* [You had to learn to create a dialogue with someone else?] *Yeah. I had never been taught how to talk – that sounds silly but you have to be taught to be able to talk about things you know?".* (Lisa).
>
> *"I don't like people feeling sorry for me because people feeling sorry for me doesn't get me anywhere, empathy and understanding does".* (Helen).
>
> *"I think the general population find it easier to see it (self-harming) as suicide attempt rather than a coping strategy. Because I think that if they saw it as different from a suicide attempt they would call it attention seeking...you feel like you are all alone because no one understands. They think you are just doing it for attention and that is it".* (Eve).

Considering the Transference in the Patient Experience of Care

It is evident from the feedback presented here that these three patients with BPD have often found their contacts with emergency medicine and mental health services to be pejorative and dismissive. The lack of consideration of the distress that the patients were presenting with is shown by the reports of inconsistent attempts to engage the patients in their treatment, and by comments offered regarding the patients' perceived frustration by health professionals in direct clinical contact following self injury or self poisoning. With these

[4] This is significant to consider when one can appreciate the presence of the unconscious in the therapeutic work with BPD patients.

perceptions, the engagement of the patient to a suitable therapeutic relationship becomes difficult. The consideration of the transference, and the presence of critical primal figures in the developmental years, is essential – from the critical approach, trauma can be reactivated. The importance of this therapeutic relationship is paramount, providing a place where the patient's turmoil and distress can be analysed and understood. It is well recognised that BPD patients will continue to self-harm until they receive appropriate and sufficient psychotherapeutic interventions and support (Strong, 1998), and persuading such patients against using self-harm will be futile until the meaning or purpose of such behaviours can be recognised.

In an attempt to bridge the gap between the levels of insight that can be developed when two parties allow dialogue regarding the need for medical and therapeutic assistance, as well as the form of assistance available, the patients here have provided feedback on the problematic responses that they have received from health professionals involved in their care. They have also suggested a more tolerant and empathetic approach by health clinicians. It is imperative that this feedback is considered carefully and deliberately by health professionals that regularly come into contact with BPD patients (on an individual level). Although the patient cannot express themselves well about the unconscious conflicts they possess, we can begin to approximate the workings of their psyche through careful and considered appreciation of their childhood experience and their feedback as to how they have been responded to (and reacted to that response). "Engaging service users in a therapeutic alliance and promoting joint clinical decision making on the basis of understanding and compassion is essential, especially is further help and treatment are to be offered" (National Collaborating Centre for Mental Health, 2004, p.28). As shown by the patient feedback presented here, often the assessment of self-harm intent is neglected, which results in the patient perceiving intolerance and neglect from health providers.

> In attempting to prevent a person from hurting him or herself, rather than looking at the underlying causes of such behaviour, or indeed the function such behaviour serves a particular individual, services can inadvertently either exacerbate the behaviour or 'drive it underground'. (National Collaborating Centre for Mental Health, 2004, p.73).

Negative responses, whether unconsciously or consciously communicated to the patient, have significant impact on the engagement of the patient in psychotherapeutic treatment and can trigger further behavioural disturbance. Patience and empathy were both identified from the patients' perspectives as areas that require greater consideration by today's health professionals. It is important to give all patients the opportunity to voice their perceptions. As health professionals however it is essential that we do take the time to consider patient feedback with open minds to reflect on and improve our clinical practice, as well in the consideration of the unconscious process of repetition of trauma that occurs for the patient in their interactions with us. Although all three patients desired an empathetic approach, if we consider their histories we can see an intolerance of this – they themselves did not feel deserving of our empathy and in fact in some cases this only activated further DSH behaviour. As clinicians it is important to consider that although the dismissive and uncaring approach exacerbates the behaviour, and the empathetic and caring response can also exacerbate the original trauma but it does move towards developing a sense of resolve for the patient (and therefore an extinguish of the drive to injure themselves). In time, and over the course of the psychotherapeutic treatment, it is important to realise that the empathetic response will yield results, where considered efforts are made to understand the source and function of the DSH behaviour. The initial rejection of our attempts to empathise with our patient must be considered in terms of the strong intolerance they will have for this response – it is not what they know. The patient's resolve of their trauma can only be celebrated by a conscious, and *unconscious*, acceptance of their worth to themselves, the people around them, and the world in general. The sense of guilt (as seen in Lisa through her thoughts of being afterbirth, as seen in Helen in her belief of being not worthy, and as seen in Eve in her consideration of being futile) can only be addressed if we, as clinicians, can continually allow these patients to use us as a vehicle of repetition until this trauma can be resolved. We cannot allow ourselves to become the persecutor in the transference that reinforces the sense of guilt and need for punishment in our patient. Furthermore, we also need to be patient in our attempts to address the unconscious conflicts of the patient as they continually reject our initial attempts to nurture and care for them. The resolve of the patient's unconscious conflict can happen in time with a strong and enduring commitment to the therapeutic alliance, where a degree of difference within the transference is provided and eventually permitted by the patient.

PART 4: CLINICAL PRACTICE AND TREATMENT RECOMMENDATIONS

These final chapters aim to provide discussion on clinical practice and treatment recommendations. Necessary clinical training experiences, the good practice of applying theoretical frameworks to consideration of symptomologic patterns of specific patients, of obtaining detailed developmental information from patients in terms of understanding individual aetiology constellations, the active consideration of transference responses (both patient and clinician), and using clinical frameworks to guide clinical thinking and practice responses to individual patients are discussed in detail. The discussion offered further builds on the recommended practice of considering theoretical frameworks by providing some specific strategy recommendations to clinicians in emergency medicine, crisis response, and ongoing mental health or psychotherapeutic treatment sectors. Final comments are made regarding the importance of building and maintenance of an active therapeutic alliance with the patient.

Chapter 11

Important Considerations in Working with Borderline Patients

For those readers who have eagerly flashed forward to these chapters, seeking a ready remedy in their work for patients diagnosed with BPD, or those that engage in DSH behaviour, your enthusiasm is commended. Although the reading of this part of the text can be only fully appreciated following consideration of the earlier discussion on the moral masochism framework, there are some more 'generic' strategies discussed here that can be used successfully with regards to risk management, issues of engagement, treatment of patients with other diagnoses, or in consideration of our own approach to clinical practice.

The Predominance of Behavioural Observation in Psychiatry

To successfully appreciate these clinical practice issues, it is important to attempt to shift our thinking from the dominant behavioural focus (of the patient's actions and in our response to these actions). The behavioural governance of clinical practice, which has been entrenched in the therapeutic setting and often enforced by the patient in their contact with us following DSH behaviour, is reinforced by the requirements of diagnostic procedures, conceptualisation of the patient's 'symptom', and the pressure to act to help the patient change their behaviour. The ready response of risk management plans and distress tolerance strategies is understandable given what our BPD patients bring to us in terms of their need for clinical treatment – they present with thoughts of acting on urges to harm themselves and this can often be the way in which they have learned to communicate their distress and activate some sense of support. Of paramount importance is what is underneath the surface of the behavioural disturbance we see in our patient – before looking at what we should do, or how to respond to the patient, we need to stop to reflect on the why of the behaviour, and consider the influence of what we cannot see – the patient's (and our own) unconscious.

As discussed earlier, the basis of psychiatric diagnostic categorisation is delineated by the *Diagnostic and Statistical Manual of Mental Disorders,* fifth edition (*DSM-V*) (American Psychiatric Association, 2013). A review of the history of this classification system in diagnosing mental disorders shows a predominance of using behavioural observations, with criteria sets listed to help guide our understanding of what we see and how to treat this. The difficulty is that in recording observable or reported symptoms, our focus becomes fixated on the *outcome* of the patient's inner or more unconscious struggles. Indeed Wilson (1993) suggested that the concept of the unconscious was marginalised by the American Psychiatric Association (1980) in the *DSM-III* as there was a loss of the concept of the unconscious in general psychiatric thinking, and a preference made for brief interview screening procedures than the unfolding of the patient's history over time in the therapeutic work. This has been further supported by other researchers:

> Psychiatry's medical basis required evidence of a visible entity or pathology that could be constructed as a symptom...a lack of empirical evidence for brain abnormality led to psychiatry turning its attention to the observation of behavioural manifestations of disorder...The invisibility of the unconscious excluded it from scientific research that was dependent upon the detection of visible abnormality and its translation into statistical analysis. (Crowe, 2004, pp.3-4).

The ongoing chase for evidence-based practice, efficacy via empirical studies, and standardised assessment and treatment practices in the clinical setting has perhaps led to a heavy reliance on the observable and more objective consideration of not only BPD but other psychiatric and medical disorders. Psychiatry aside, other clinical professions have also experienced a shift in the historical view of the patient-clinician relationship. The original view of nursing by Peplau (1952), which described nursing practice as central to the facilitation of the development of the patient's personality, has been shifted to now being focused on the alleviation and prevention of symptomatology. The loss of traditional practice in treating psychopathology in particular is disappointing, in terms of historical conceptualisation and nosology. "Psychiatric interventions are not concerned with the underlying cause of distress rather with the amelioration of symptoms" (Crowe, 2004, p.6).

The preference for the health system to become purely an advisor to the patient on the management of their symptom is again cautioned here as the sense of suffering (and the recognition of the patient's history in the development of this suffering) often becomes lost in the prescription of pharmacology and in the instruction of behavioural strategies to reduce the severity or frequency of the patient's symptoms. Developing insight into suffering often becomes the secondary process to symptom reduction. In the recognition of the development or history of the patient's symptom, providing generic insight[1] (through the provision of psychoeducational practice) is not considered adequate. Indeed this can even be experienced as patronising or demoralising to some patients who then consider themselves only in the general terms of the diagnosis of which they have been given following this education.

[1] An insight by which the patient is informed as to the general (not specific) development of certain symptommatology (i.e., using population statistics on aetiology).

The numerous patients I have seen who then begin to see themselves as a diagnosis require much more clinical intervention in terms of reconstructing their self concept – in the clinical work, I treat *individuals* with mental health disorders and require the patient to be able to reflect on the unique experiences they have encountered in order to understand the development (and consequent treatment) of their particular symptom.

Recognising the Unconscious in Considering Behavioural Disturbance

In terms of treating BPD, to understand the patient's suffering and make sense of what is beyond the behavioural presentation of DSH, a consideration of the unconscious is required. "...a return to an emphasis on unconscious processes...could provide mental health nurses a basis on which to establish psychotherapeutic relationships that may provide a more comprehensive understanding of the patient's needs" (Crowe, 2004, p.2). The unconscious was recognised by Freud (1915c/1957) as an entity that could be used to further understand the conscious processes of the patient that defied rationalisation in consideration of their affective and behavioural presentation. Indeed the somewhat trivial account of some patient's reason to engage in DSH behaviour (such as a minor argument with a neighbour over a barking dog) can only take on its full meaning if we attempt to appreciate the unconscious cause of this reaction, as opposed to accepting the face-value in the patient's attempts to consciously explain their actions[2]. As considered by Freud (1915c/1957), the cause of the patient's symptom was determined by an underlying unconscious process that was not directly retrievable by conscious process. The content of the unconscious was only successfully revealed through the analysis and interpretation of the patient's thoughts, dreams, behaviours, symptoms, and interpersonal interactions and relationships[3]. It became the missing link between the confusing conscious level of determining cause and effect in the development of symptomatology. The resurrection of the concept of the unconscious in today's health system may be of some use in the provision of health care to patients diagnosed with BPD, as well as in the education of health clinicians about this disorder (Mintz, 2103; Commons Treloar, 2009a). Recognition of the unconscious may also assist in the establishment and maintenance of a psychotherapeutic relationship between patient and clinician that can have more significant and enduring effect for the patient (Crowe, 2004).

In terms of 'deliberate' self-harm presentations to the emergency medicine department, and consequent referral to the mental health services, the consideration of the unconscious workings of the patient indeed lead us to a contemplation of 'accident' and 'emergency', as earlier defined by Finch (1956) as unforeseen mishap or injury. Is this not just as apt in its description of DSH behaviours in BPD when one provides adequate recognition of the unconscious workings underlying the behavioural presentation of self mutilation and self poisoning?

[2] The trivial account of triggers to DSH by some patients can unfortunately only contribute to the frustration experienced by the clinician in their attempts to assist the patient to work through more adaptive strategies to managing interpersonal stress.

[3] And this could only be detected or considered by a clinician who was tolerant and open to the possibility of the unconscious and its influence it was having on the patient's development and maintenance of their symptom.

There is value in viewing the presentation of DSH behaviours from this conceptualisation of the unconscious. I believe that this has helped in the provision of psychotherapeutic treatment within my own clinical practice. With the unconscious 'in mind', how do we then work effectively with the BPD patient? In order to successfully engage and maintain a therapeutic alliance, the foundations lie not only in the therapy room but also outside the clinical session – being open to the prospect that there is more to what we can observe in our patient, and in ourselves, is essential. Prior to interacting with the patient in session, it is imperative that we consider what we need in terms of our clinical knowledge, practice approach, and our own personal response to the patient. In the end, it is who we are to the patient that makes all the difference to their prognosis.

Chapter 12

Issues to Consider Outside of the Therapeutic Session

The clinical practice and treatment recommendations presented here are considered in two broad senses: as a clinician working *for* BPD patients and as a clinician working *with* BPD patients[1]. There are distinct differences with these two considerations. This chapter will focus on techniques and therapeutic considerations we, as clinicians, need to reflect on in our work with BPD outside of the therapy room. It is important that we consider this basic foundation prior to reflecting on what we can do with our patients in the clinical work. The next chapter on clinical practice and treatment recommendations will present strategies with regards to how we interact and work with our BPD patients in the therapeutic session.

Having a Basic Knowledge of the Disorder

What do we do with the patient and how we respond to the distress of the BPD patient who engages in DSH behaviour has its origins prior to the initial clinical contact we have with them. Our preconceived notions of the disorder, our past clinical experiences, and our past personal experiences all make the difference to who we are in the clinical setting. Our knowledge and experience ultimately directs not only our choice of profession but how we respond and empathise with each individual patient we encounter. As earlier discussed, many clinicians however engage in the treatment of BPD without prior formal training in this disorder. Without this basic knowledge or premise, the clinical encounter can be highly influenced by our conceptions from past personal and professional experience (including the feedback[2] from other clinicians).

---

[1] In this sense, I refer to these differently in terms of strategies for the clinician, and then strategies with the patient. For successful treatment, the clinician requires just as much clinical focus outside of the session as the patient may require within the session. Unfortunately professional burnout rates are higher when working with BPD patients, and these chapters hope to address some of these problems.

[2] This feedback can be both positive and negative, derived from their experience with BPD patients. Typically though, clinicians tend to forewarn other professionals about working with BPD (Potter, 2006).

Once open to the acceptance of the unconscious[3], a grounded theoretical knowledge of the disorder (for both diagnostic and treatment purposes) should be the first starting point to considering in preparing ourselves for the clinical work with these patients. The consideration of the theoretical frameworks can assist in the accurate identification of the diagnostic categorisation, beyond the presence of behavioural disturbance such as DSH or suicidal gestures. As suggested here, the use of theoretical frameworks in their consideration of aetiology appears to also be a missing yet integral part of the work with BPD. "Clinician are expected to offer understanding, explanations for treatment interventions, undistracted attention, and respectful, compassionate attitudes, with judicious feedback to patients that can help them to attain their goals" (Oldham et al., 2001, p.7). In order to be able to provide such responses, the clinician is required to have developed sufficient insight into the development of the borderline pathology, as well as a thorough working knowledge of the treatment interventions in their ability to target particular symptomatology. The generic basis of this information can assist in the accurate diagnosis of the patient but also in the required understanding of possible aetiology of the disorder to more successfully guide our exploration of the patient's history in the therapeutic work with BPD.

As seen in the electrical wiring of a house, serious damage can be caused if, in the urgency to connect power, fundamental connections between appliance and power source are not adequately considered. The aim here of using theoretical models of BPD is to equip the clinician in the understanding of the patient's 'wiring', before attempting to connect them into psychotherapeutic treatment. As seen within the literature, the provision of psychotherapy can produce a lowering of risk of suicide and self-harm attempts in BPD (Weinberg & Maltsberger, 2007). The anxiety associated with working with patients that engage in such behaviours is often obvious, and therefore it is understandable that the clinician often reacts to such anxiety with the urgent need to solve the problem. The complexity of this disorder also has great significance and often impacts on the clinician's ability to adequately conceptualise the patient's difficulties and history. The psychotherapeutic treatment can often therefore be influenced by the complexity and instability of the patient, creating difficulties for the countertransference response of the clinician. Given that the BPD patient can make extortionate demands for extraordinary caring and love, which expose the clinician to risks of boundary subversion and loss of clinical balance (Weinberg & Maltsberger, 2007), a solid theoretical grounding in this disorder is recommended for all clinicians in order to understand the necessary therapeutic position required for its treatment.

> Overall, what is important to remember in treating and understanding borderlines is that combined with their extreme difficulties in experiencing and expressing anger and anxiety, there are major issues that are the result of their faulty attempts at engagement. These difficulties in interpersonal engagement lead to the difficulties of maintaining the participant-observer position with these patients. (Watson, 1996, p.84).

I feel that consideration of the transference response with patients diagnosed with BPD appears to be lacking within the state of current health care provision. It is considered here

[3] Acceptance of the presence of the patient's unconscious, AND an acceptance of our own unconscious, in the clinical work is needed. The ability to stop and reflect on the patient's and our own behaviours and responses is highly fruitful. In my early training, one of the most valued comments made by a supervisor I had was that a psychologist's greatest skill to have and master is the ability to do nothing – not to act or respond or instruct on strategies but to just sit and think about what they have just seen in front of them and how they feel about that.

that the evidence-based practice models, such as DBT and indeed even the newer breed of mentalization-based treatment (MBT)(Fonagy & Bateman, 2004), do not systematically address the issue of transference as a diagnostic tool or psychotherapeutic instrument, often appearing to lack the consideration of the patient and their history and how this can impact not only on the patient's development of the disorder but also in their response to the psychotherapeutic relationship. In contemplation of the other symptoms of BPD outside of the present examination of DSH behaviours – issues of real or imagined abandonment, intense and unstable interpersonal relationships, unstable self image, impulsive and reckless behaviours that are self damaging, affective instability due to markedly reactive mood, chronic feelings of emptiness, inappropriate and intense anger, transient paranoid ideation, and severe dissociative symptoms (delineated as symptoms characteristic of BPD by the *DSM-IV-TR*) – every one of these can be considered psychotherapeutically beyond the application of the diagnosis of BPD. The development of all the symptomatologic issues of BPD can be traced back through the patient's history and in contemplation of the transference response with the BPD patient.

As discussed here, the consideration of the aetiology of the BPD pattern is deemed necessary within the therapeutic relationship and in the provision of psychotherapeutic treatment. The consideration of the childhood experience in general personality development (as well as in the development of 'disordered' forms of personality) is viewed as fundamental to the characteristics and responses of the adult person to the environment around them. The difficulty is however that consideration of aetiology appears to be perhaps the missed component in the screening of the diagnosis BPD (with behavioural observation procedures being more dominant) and in the therapeutic work (with behavioural management of self-harm tendencies being prioritised in treatment models).

Further to this basic foundation, and particularly in light of the ongoing challenge for us in maintaining an adequate therapeutic alliance in the clinical work with this disorder, *continued education* and *ongoing clinical supervision* (from a theoretical and practical grounding) is also recommended for clinicians who work with patients with BPD that engage in DSH behaviours. The impact of continued work with this patient group can unfortunately distract us from our theoretical appreciation of the disorder – therefore continued reinforcement can be beneficial. There is a distinct advantage of using theoretical frameworks in the consideration of the symptomatologic interpretation of each patient[4]. The use of theoretical frameworks to develop an understanding of the individual patients and their suffering appears necessary to guide treatment practice with BPD and to also mediate the countertransference responses evoked from working with such patients – we need continuous reminder of what they do and regular pausing to reflect on why they do this; there is a logical or coherent rationale underneath all of the unpredictable reactions to themselves and others (although we may not initially be able to appreciate this). There are many treatment options with regard to the provision of psychotherapy with BPD, however it is feared that little time has been spent in comparison on conceptualising the *development* of the symptomatology observed in the patient that then becomes diagnosed with BPD. This is where suitable clinical supervision throughout the clinical care of each patient can be advantageous.

[4] Despite earlier caution of considering diagnostic categories of patients, much can be achieved via the application of the generic principles of the disorder as long as it is considered in relation to the individual presentation of each patient.

The Need for Ongoing Clinical Supervision

One of the most important things to consider outside of the treatment room when working with BPD patients is ourselves – as mentioned above, who we are to our patient affects their progression through treatment and their general prognosis. Taking the time for adequate reflection on ourselves and our experiences in the treatment room, outside the clinical setting, and in life in general is really imperative but unfortunately its one of the most missed components of working in mental health[5]. We exist before our patient comes along – we are already something to ourselves and someone else, and this does have some sort of influence on how we interact with our BPD patient. The recognition and monitoring of the counter-transference can be central to the therapeutic work – by nature of the BPD diagnosis, these patients will require so much from us with regards to who we are, how we feel about them, and how we respond (not just behaviourally) to their crises. The advantage of continued supervision and monitoring of the countertransference is in the development of a personal understanding of our unconscious and our personal response to the patient – emotionally, interpersonally, cognitively, and behaviourally. A restrained consideration of the unconscious can ultimately assist in the conceptualisation and interpretation of the patient's behaviour and their intrapsychic conflicts. In order to provide some form of framework around the consideration of the countertransference in the supervision process, discussed here are the key elements of the supervision encounter that require discussion: the clinician's emotional reaction to the patient, a consideration of why this emotional reaction has come to be (on reflection of the clinician's personal background and past clinical experience), and how the patient may respond to the presence of this.

Paramount within the clinical supervision is the concept of emotion identification – not just the emotion of the patient but the emotional response or reaction of the clinician; the 'how am I feeling about is this?' reflection[6]. There is no right or wrong emotion that should or will be evoked in the treatment of BPD patients – what becomes important is being able to identify what this is. Within the supervision session, allowing time for reflection on resemblances to other times in the clinician's personal and professional life where similar emotions may have also been experienced, and the identification of our experiences which contribute to how we feel, is required. There needs to be a measured and balanced reflection as to how we feel about our patient, and this needs to be done regularly as this will often change and fluctuate. Who we are within the patient's transference and what they require from us in this regard through the various stages of treatment will impact on our counter-transference response.

Once identified, it is also important to consider how the patient would view this in us. Within the therapeutic alliance, emotional reactions cannot be disguised or manipulated by either the patient or the clinician. The genuineness of who we are in the therapeutic relationship, and how authentic we are in response to the patient, is central to the working

[5] Although most professions have continued professional development requirements with regards to the annual completion of supervision hours, as to be explained, the supervision recommended here in terms of treating BPD patients is something that has its own unique element in terms of reflecting on the clinician's personal response to the patient.

[6] This includes how am I feeling about the patient in general, how am I feeling about their response to treatment, how I am feeling about the concerns they express, and how am I feeling about their response to us as a clinician and a person in general.

through of the patient's unconscious conflicts. The legitimacy of our reaction, understood as an activation of the transference and/or as a countertransference response, will make the difference to the therapeutic work. Outside of the session if time can be spent reflecting on what we can and do bring (as well as why) to the therapy room, the treatment of the BPD patient can have greater therapeutic benefit. The pollution of the unrecognised and unmanaged countertransference to the therapeutic work will impact on the need of the patient to work through their inner conflicts in a safe and non-judgmental environment. Consideration of what the patient is requiring from me, not what are they trying to enact with me or have caused in me, is paramount.

The selfless sacrifice of the clinician, allowing the patient to use us in a way they need for clinical and therapeutic benefit, requires ongoing attention and management via the supervision process. "The role of supervision and the importance of its guidance as balancing, ameliorating factors of the possibly destructive impact of negative countertransference feelings, has not received the attention it deserves…" (Aviv & Springmann, 1990, p.693). The BPD patient group is typically highly complex in terms of its therapeutic need, with patients often presenting with a multitude of symptoms and complaints. Unfortunately many clinicians may need to engage these patients without adequate theoretical grounding or clinical support (Moran & Mason, 1996). In working with BPD patients, and indeed with each individual patient with this diagnosis, it is important early in the clinical work that there is the reflection on behalf of the clinician as to whether they can and are prepared to do this. Ultimately it is important to remember that you cannot be drawn into conflict with the BPD patient, despite their possible attempts to enact this in us. Issues of abandonment, the previous experience of critical and/or abusive parental figures in formative years, and the restrictions within the clinical work (in terms of ensuring ethical response and maintaining professional boundaries) will all accumulate and then be tested early in the psychotherapeutic treatment, shown by the engagement of the BPD patient in treatment[7]. Given the extremes of the often disturbed behaviour towards themselves and to others, it is important to recognise that as a clinician you cannot go 'toe-to-toe' with the BPD patient as unfortunately they can often be prepared step outside the expectations of society norms to communicate their distress to us. It is better to not to engage with the BPD patient if we feel that we may be manipulated into this form of interaction[8]. At the end of the day it is important to understand the provision of mental health services in terms of people working with people[9] – therefore the development of a therapeutic alliance or counter-therapeutic alliance can occur depending upon the alignment of different clinicians to different patients. Within the supervision process, the use of open and honest discussion about your personal and professional ability to work with each patient with BPD should be encouraged. If feeling unable or unwilling to do so, the transfer of the patient's care to another clinician prepared to work with the patient would be

[7] In consideration of the prior damage to these patients, the initial testing of our commitment to them and their treatment is quite rationale and can form the basis of the development of a good working alliance (if in the process of supervision, the countertransference can be restrained and appropriately understood).

[8] And this can be a generic decision. I have worked with clinicians who feel that they are not able or willing to work with this group of patients, or this could be a decision made in consideration of each presentable case of BPD. I have worked with some clinicians that can work so successfully with some patients with BPD, but also so unsuccessfully with other patients with the diagnosis. This furthermore substantiates the need to consider the patient in individual terms as opposed to a diagnostic category.

[9] Everyone possibly has a preference for a particular doctor, dentist, teacher, or even hairdresser so why should we expect that mental health treatment should be any different (especially where you are expected to divulge such personal information to another)?

recommended. Ultimately the transfer of care will be (and should be) for the benefit of the patient, and this does need to be honestly but cautiously explained to the patient.

"Countertransference is an especially important clinical tool with these difficult patients" (Watson, 1996, p.81). This is an area of the psychotherapeutic treatment of BPD that many clinicians may fail to recognise with adequate significance. Countertransference is of paramount concern in the understanding of the patient's behaviours and in their response to the therapeutic alliance. The awareness of our response in the transference is considered imperative as we can often continue to traumatise the patient by becoming the projected figure of the original abuse, trauma, and/or neglect. Our countertransference responses can often trigger particular behavioural responses, unconsciously, in the patient. If we consider the aetiology of abuse and emotional denial that may have aetiological significance to the development of this disorder, the cynical abandoner who is hardened and sceptical of prognosis can too easily become the projected figure within the transference. The flustered rescuer who is panicked and reactive to the distress of the BPD patient can also be a repetition of the transference held by the patient with primal figures that were considered over involved and protective. Pressure by the patient to adopt the projected figure in the transference often can occur; thus re-traumatising the patient and possibly activating further DSH behaviours (Sbaih, 1993).

Returning to a point raised earlier with regard to the presence of the unconscious in the clinician in the provision of psychotherapy, one can consider these sceptical or panicked clinician responses as an outcome of a countertransference response that may have been projected onto us by the patient. It could be however also considered that these responses may be indeed induced from the unconscious of the clinician, due to the clinician's history. Aviv and Springmann (1990) outlined three possible and distinct categories of countertransference: therapist-induced (direct expression of the therapist's personality), patient-induced (generated by the patient), and combined countertransference (as is the case in most situations met within therapy where therapist-induced and patient-induced countertransference reactions are intimately intertwined). The transference relationship with the patient diagnosed with BPD is considered as imperative to the psychotherapeutic treatment of patients with this disorder and, given that the therapist's or clinician's response to this treatment can reactivate the patient's trauma, we must take some clinical responsibility for the reaction of the patient. An active reflection of the BPD patient's history, in consideration of the clinician's response to the interactions with the patient (achieved through regular clinical supervision), is deemed a necessary feature of the psychotherapeutic treatment of this disorder.

The Development of a Working Risk Management Plan

Further to obtaining an initial theoretical knowledge of BPD, and engaging in regular clinical supervision where the countertransference can be recognised and monitored, there will inevitably be the times where a patient does require an immediate response from us – particularly in regards to the management of their risk to themselves. The regular consideration of good practice and clinical guidelines can assist with guiding the professional response to patients under these circumstances[10], where prolonged reflection cannot (and

[10] And discussion of these are provided for in Chapter 14.

should not) be the first reaction. In the immediate aftermath of DSH or suicide attempt, having a clear idea of how you should respond is imperative – the patient's life may depend on this. Many clinicians, by way of good clinical practice, proceed with devising risk management plans for their BPD patients. This can assist in providing for a more consistent response by other professionals also involved in the patient's care (such as emergency medicine clinicians), but also in the guiding of the primary therapist's response to the BPD patient in periods of crisis. The way in which the risk management plan is devised and then utilised however is of significant importance.

Unfortunately I have seen risk management plans placed into patient files without the signature of the patient involved – explaining the concept of the risk management process and why risk management plans are used in crisis circumstances is really valuable to the therapeutic work. They should definitely be devised with the patient's input[11]. Thorough explanation as to why it is used, and what it contains, in terms of helping us keep our patient safe is really important and can assist in the active maintenance of the therapeutic alliance. It is paramount that we ask the patient about how they feel about our responses in the clinical treatment, and this can have benefits beyond the crisis period for the therapeutic relationship with the patient – it is within this feedback about our response that we can begin to appreciate the transference of the patient. As we are treating individual patients, each risk management plan should have its own idiosyncrasies in terms of clinician response during crisis. Sadly there has been one occasion I have encountered recently where a patient of mine requested a copy of a risk management plan from a local psychiatric service only to discover that in some parts of the plan the name of another patient was written; obviously an error in the editing of a very generic and previous patient's risk management plan! Furthermore this patient (although not diagnosed with BPD) had not even been involved in the actual development of the risk management plan for her suicidal behaviour. She was told it was done and inquisitively requested a copy. In terms of the therapeutic *alliance*[12], the consideration of the patient's choice with regards to their treatment is important. If this choice is not possible for some reason, the patient should be counselled with regards to why this is so. The initial assessment of the borderline pathology is central to the conceptualisation of the patient's clinical presentation, but also to the formulation and implementation of an appropriate treatment plan. Once the risk management plan is completed and agreed upon, it is also vital to regularly review and edit its contents (in conjunction with the patient). This will allow the patient to be able to see some evolution in their psychopathology and reinforce our commitment to the therapeutic treatment of their symptom.

---

[11] Although it is recognised that there are some BPD patients who do not wish to be engaged in completing these types of plans, the opportunity to participate should be offered (along with a thorough explanation as to why we would feel their participation would be of benefit).

[12] It is important for clinicians to really consider the idea of the alliance in working with BPD patients.

Chapter 13

Strategies to Consider in the Therapy Room

Establishing and Maintaining Patient Engagement

Within the clinical session, one of the first considerations is the issue of engagement with the patient. It is important to recognise (particularly with the BPD patient group) that establishing a rapport and developing engagement of the patient in the therapeutic alliance is not just an initial part of the clinical work. This is an active and ongoing process in the treatment of such 'damaged' people that come to be diagnosed with BPD. Their pre-existing issues with fear of abandonment from earlier periods in their life, as well as their sometimes often behaviours of splitting (determined by their perception of whether we gratify or frustrate them) and manipulation, will all impact on the initial engagement in treatment *and* throughout the process of treatment. It is important to recognise that instability in their relationship is a primary issue for BPD patients and, in consideration of their histories, why they have come to develop this disorder. The therapeutic relationship is not immune to this instability.

A transparent regard for the patient's engagement in treatment and the clinical relationship (as well as a transparent regard our own fluctuations in engagement within the countertransference) can be valuable in the therapeutic work in terms of maintaining a working alliance with the patient, and in allowing some recognition and appreciation of their history, their trauma, and attempts to discover their unconscious conflicts. Throughout the clinical work, their varied levels of engagement, and what can trigger these fluctuations, signals another working observation of the transference. The degree of difference in our response within the transference, required for a working through of their trauma, can only be achieved if we continually encourage and allow for mending with the patient and a reuniting within the therapeutic alliance. As previously discussed, although some patients desire an empathetic approach, if we consider their histories we can see an intolerance of this – they themselves can feel not deserving of our empathy (and in fact in some cases this can activated further DSH behaviour in earlier stages of the treatment). As clinicians it is important to consider that although the dismissive and uncaring approach exacerbates the behaviour, and the empathetic and caring response can also exacerbate the original trauma but it does move towards developing a sense of resolve for the patient. The continued attempts to re-engage the patient in the treatment, to show them their worth to us, is a means by which we can allow for that required sense of resolve. It is important to view the continued rejection of our attempts to empathise with our patient in terms of the strong intolerance they will have for this response. Unfortunately I have seen many clinicians not actively attempt to re-engage their patient, possibly out of response of their own exhaustion in the clinical treatment. The difficulty with this response is that no attempt to re-engage the patient in the therapeutic treatment only reinforces the sense of their trauma and the unconscious feeling of guilt that may underlie their DSH behaviours. In undertaking the clinical work, it is imperative that we continually allow these patients to use us as a vehicle of repetition until this trauma can be resolved. Any intermissions in treatment, such as a clinician's absence for holidays, need to honestly and openly discuss with the patient as not a response to their presence in our lives, but as a means by which we can be of more value to them. The issue of engagement is complex and ultimately requires adequate recognition.

In terms of the initial assessment of the BPD patient on their entry to the service, or on referral to our clinic, it is recognised that the clinician would not have the opportunity to fully appreciate the patient and their complexities as they sit before us. Using an open mind to consider the more generic experiences or aetiology constellations of the disorder is the only foundation that may assist you in undertaking this assessment. Of paramount concern within this initial stage is the concept of neutrality – the need to maintain neutrality in the activation of transference relationship that begins as soon as the patient takes their seat. The influence of the primal figures (which may not necessarily have been abusive but more so emotionally inconsistent) will impact on how the patient interacts with us and we cannot blindly activate the process of repetition of the trauma if we attempt to remain neutral in the earlier stages of the work[1]. The concept of neutrality is a complex position to hold – we cannot afford to be perceived as distant and cold, nor can we afford to be perceived as arrogant and disinterested. It is the position of being fair minded, impartial, non-prejudicial, or balanced that is of primary importance during the initial assessment process.

Investigating the Patient's Knowledge and Experiences

In terms of discussion of diagnosis, it is recommended to make inquiry about whether the patient has any ideas of their classification or diagnosis (only in terms of what they feel they may be suffering from). I have had many patients present to the initial assessment stating that they have BPD – in such cases, the patients have usually already spent much time in researching this diagnosis and the internet can be a pragmatic source of information. In such cases, I have placed a block on self-initiated psychoeducation by asking patients to refrain from investigating this diagnosis. Simply explained, I tell the patient that I am not concerned per se with diagnostic labels as I am focused on the treatment of the individual person in front of me. The assessment can then proceed to discussion about the individual patient's history and experiences; our first consideration of the aetiology of the patient's symptom. It also allows for the first glimpse of the transference, not only in the discussion on their childhood and upbringing but also in their reports of the response to previous treatment. It is imperative to investigate the patient's experience of prior care, not as a way to critique our peers or to see how the patient has responded to past clinical intervention, but to allow for some

[1] It is important to consider here that if the patient's early experience was of the smothering or overprotective parental figure, our enthusiasm to be compassionate and affectively engage the patient can be perceived very differently to that which we intend. In such cases, the patient would be more likely to repel or become traumatised by the eager clinician than that possibly caused by a more critical or detached one.

consideration of the patient's transference and unconscious workings. The consideration of the transference and the unconscious working of the patient should also become part of the treatment focus as at some stage surely the patient will want to understand and make sense of their suffering. "...therapists must have a clear expectation of change as they help patients understand the origins of their suffering...to offer interpretations of unconscious patterns that help the patient develop insight" (Oldham et al., 2001, p.12).

The development of insight in the patient is dependent upon the conceptualisation of the suffering of the patient from the clinician's investigation. This requires intensive focus and lays the foundation for the provision of appropriate psychotherapeutic work. The psychotherapeutic treatment cannot (and should not) proceed without an in depth qualitative investigation of the patient's history. Through the investigation of the patient's history from the onset of clinical contact in the assessment phase, engaging the patient in meaningful dialogue about their life is considered a means by which to facilitate a more accurate assessment of the applicable diagnostic categorisation. It also sets the foundations for a working relationship with the patient. "Recognising trauma-related aspects of the patient's affective instability, damaged self image, relationship problems, fears of abandonment, self injurious behaviours, and impulsiveness is important and can facilitate psychotherapy in a variety of ways" (Oldham et al., 2001, p.20).

Coping Skills Training for the Management of Risk

Following the initial assessment phase, where the patient's knowledge of the disorder is investigated and the development of a working hypothesis with regards to the aetiology of the disorder is derived, the next phase of the clinical work should be centred on considering the management of both deliberate self-harm and suicide risk. As previously discussed, we cannot afford to become complacent about the risk of suicide in patients with BPD – the mortality rates of this patient group support this. As seen within the clinical case illustrations presented here, attempts at suicide and periods of suicidality can occur at various times in the patient's life despite how often or regularly they injure themselves.

The manner in which this is executed however is highly delicate – we do not want to run the risk of becoming preoccupied by the behavioural disturbance, particularly in these early stages of treatment. This can possibly erode the patient's confidence in the therapeutic alliance, rather than be used as a process to assist in the maintenance of this alliance. The way in which we instruct our patient in the widely recognised use of strategies of harm minimisation[2], distress tolerance, mindfulness, relaxation, diversion, and distraction needs to consider the basic premise of why we are doing this. I have heard patients describe a sense of being dismissed in the process of coping skills training. Reassurance of the patient, in terms of the process by which we are committing to the therapeutic relationship in the long term, should be a priority and it is important to inform them of our need to attempt to ensure or assist with the management of their safety. Coping skills training following the detailed

[2] Of note, harm minimisation strategies should only be used for self-injury and not for poisoning. The use of ice burns as an alternative to cutting, burning, or bruising of the skin is the primary harm minimisation strategy that I find most effective in my clinical practice to reduce the risk associated with DSH behaviours.

consideration of risk is an important phase of the treatment prior to opening up 'Pandora's Box', where much of the patient's hurt and pain is exposed and relived.

CONSIDERATION OF THE PATIENT'S UNCONSCIOUS CONFLICTS

Following the initial assessment, establishment of the therapeutic alliance, development of a working risk management plan, and the instruction of coping skills training, we can then move towards allowing the clinical time appreciating the patient's conflicts. At the core of the behavioural and interpersonal presentation of the individual patient is the idiosyncratic response to the environment – both the external and the internal environment. To appreciate the patient's development and experience, and consider the aetiological constellations that underlie the behavioural presentation, it is imperative to spend the time (in the session and outside the session) considering the patient's dialogue in much detail. The patient cannot adequately explain why the act as they do; as previously mentioned, the patient may attempt to explain their act of DSH in response to an immediate stressor in the environment but we need to appreciate how or why the masochistic drive has come to be.

As seen within the clinical illustrations, and upon reflection of the clinical interview data supplied for these three patient (within the Appendices), the patient's dialogue can hold much valuable information for us as clinicians to consider. The use of words, the subjective accounts of their experiences (present and historically), and their response to our questions all contain an approximate truth as to why they behave in such ways. Recording session notes verbatim (with the patient's permission), and using traditional strategies such as word association, can allow for a greater approximation of the unconscious conflicts of the patient that require working through in the clinical work. A consideration of the patient's perception of their childhood experience, without polluting this reality with the influence of a third party[3], is imperative in beginning to appreciate the patient's difficulties.

The development of the working hypothesis, of the patient's experience and the unconscious conflicts they have, is needed to enable our constructions in our attempts to understand the patient. The development of a construction, upon deliberation of the patient's experience and a detailed consideration of their dialogue, should be an infinite process throughout the clinical work. Our working hypotheses will often be influenced by the countertransference (hence the need for ongoing supervision) and the level of engagement of the patient on each clinical encounter. In our attempts to alleviate the patient of their need to injure themselves, it is important to not be rigid in our consideration of the patient. The working hypothesis will evolve with each clinical contact with have with the patient, and with each attempt we make to offer possible interpretations to test its validity.

The discovery of the ideational correlate, the unconscious ideation from which the guilt stems (that is associated with the need for punishment), is one of the fundamental aims of the psychotherapeutic treatment. The unconscious feeling of guilt and the consequent need for punishment is only satisfied through the use of DSH behaviours in the patient with BPD. The

[3] I have worked with clinicians who feel the need to interview the family members of their patients to attempt to verify the patient's account of their childhood experience. At the end of the day, it is the patient's subjective reality that is all that matters and it should be the primary focus of our interventions – whether this reality can be objectively ratified is completely irrelevant and any attempts to do so will often prove to be toxic to the therapeutic alliance.

patient's description of a sense of guilt (although this can often also be an unconscious process) prior to, during, and often following their engagement in self-harm only reinforces the ideational correlate that many BPD patients have in that they are bad and deserve to be punished (Rosenthal et al., 2006). Identification of the ideational correlate that is unconsciously motivating the cyclic pattern of DSH is required.

THE TIME-LINE INTERVIEW PROCEDURE

The time-line interview procedure is something that I use in my clinical practice to attempt to engage the patient in a meaningful consideration of their developmental history. It is a strategy to also assist in the evolution of my working hypothesis in relation to the ideational correlate that underlies the unconscious sense of guilt and need of the patient to engage (consciously and unconsciously) in forms of punishment. It is a form of revision of the initial assessment procedure when the therapeutic alliance has developed greater strength, and the patient has been forearmed with coping skills training and learned strategies by which to regulate the distress that can be experienced by the slow deliberation on the patient's history. It is something that I recommend strongly, but only after the management of risk and assistance of the patient to attempt alternate strategies to sooth themselves more effectively (or actually more safely).

The use of the clinical session to enable a detailed consideration of the patient's formative years can be achieved using a clear differentiation of the time-line, according to the patient's age. Using at least three session[4], where the patient is asked to reflect on the events of each decade of their life (in terms of events, relationships, and experiences), the clinician can begin to appreciate more about the patient's development of BPD than that which can be achieved when the initial assessment procedures only allow for the acknowledgement of what the patient is ready to, or aware of the influence of in reporting their history. Interestingly, many patients attempt to move quickly through this process, whether due to avoidance of discussing some early experience or more simply because they do not understand the significance of the events and interactions that occurred during these phases of life. Gentle redirection to the time-line of focus during the clinical session may often be required to ensure that the clinician can appreciate the less recognised influence of the patient's experience.

Further to the clinician's attempt to gather more detailed information about the patient's history, the time-line interview procedure also allows for the consideration of the patient's conceptualisation of their history and experience. Investigating the patient's interactions with their parents and siblings, inquiring about their experience within the friendship groups throughout school and beyond, and appreciating other people of significance (including any professionals) can all assist in the clinician's approximation of the transference that will come into play within the clinical work. Understanding the influence of these figures in the patient's life, particularly in terms of the development and function of the super-ego that can continue to provoke punishment and suffering, becomes important within the clinical session.

[4] For patients in their twenties, the time-line interview procedure is typically completed over three sessions where each session is dedicated to considering their experiences in 7-9 year blocks. For patients in their thirties, three sessions are allocated to understanding the patient's history in 10-13 year blocks; and consequent numbers of sessions per rates of years for older patients.

The significance of the patient's unconscious requires great acknowledgement in the consideration of their behavioural disturbance, as does the influence of the unforgotten representative of the primal figures that caused pain, suffering, and guilt in terms of ongoing and repetitive DSH behaviour.

Recognition of the Patient's Transference Response

Throughout the clinical work, the patient's varied levels of engagement (and what can trigger these fluctuations) demonstrate the clinical working of the transference. With the detailed knowledge of our patient's experiences, we can begin to approximate, understand, and then make use of the patient's transference in the clinical work. A consideration of the transference needs to be a primary focus of initial stages of the clinical work, as it is imperative to the patient's continued engagement, but also throughout the entire duration of the psychotherapeutic treatment. The impact of the patient's transference in terms of the presence of repetitive DSH behaviour, and their response to us within the therapy room, cannot be clinically disregarded and requires constant monitoring in each clinical contact. We cannot appreciate the unconscious conflict resulting in DSH behaviour if the repetition of trauma within the transference continues – this is the biggest obstacle to prognosis. We, as clinicians, need to identify and collect information about the influence of primal figures to fully appreciate how the patient may project the same feelings they evoked for the patient onto us in the clinical work.

Of central importance in understanding the transference is again the concept of the patient's subjective reality – what were the responses of the primal figures *perceived* to be by the patient? What was the patient's historical response to them? Based on our working hypothesis of the ideational correlate stemming from the patient's encounter with the early attachment figures, what is the degree of difference needed from me to allow for a block of repetition and the resolve of trauma for the patient? It is important to consider that we cannot become these figures within the transference or else we can re-traumatise the patient, particularly when the countertransference response of the clinician is most similar to that of projected figures of the past. A degree of difference *must* be present in the transference. As discussed earlier, it is within this difference that the repetition can be broken.

The degree of difference in our response within the transference, required for a working through of their trauma, can only be achieved if we continually encourage and allow for mending with the patient as they attempt to disengage with us or act out against our clinical interventions and approaches. As previously mentioned, although some patients desire an empathetic approach (as this is the degree of difference required in the transference relationship to resolve the patient's origin trauma) we can see an intolerance of this in the clinical setting; our attempts to support or reassure them can be often rejected. They themselves can feel not deserving of our empathy, and in some cases the empathetic response can actually activate further DSH behaviour in earlier stages of the treatment. As clinicians it is important to consider that although the dismissive and indifferent approach exacerbates the repetition of DSH, and the empathetic and compassionate response can also *initially* exacerbate the original trauma. The degree of difference however does move towards developing a sense of resolve for the patient. Our persistent attempts to re-engage the patient in the treatment when they disengage or act out (in order to show them their worth to us) is a means by which we can allow for that required sense of resolve.

In undertaking the clinical work, it is imperative that we continually allow these patients to use us as a vehicle of repetition until this trauma can be resolved. The clinician can respond with a therapeutic degree of difference to allow for a working through of this past trauma. It is important for the clinician to appreciate this clinical need in undertaking the clinical work with BPD. Managing the countertransference and understanding the patient's transference response (enabled via an appreciation of the unconscious workings of the patient) is fundamental to the efficacy of our clinical interventions. As previously suggested, any intermissions in the patient's treatment (or in our availability to them) need to honestly and openly discussed with the patient.

The degree of difference required in the transference can only be accepted after a significant period of clinical time where the patient can start to appreciate the unconscious link between their daily stressors, social interactions, and the underlying imprint bestowed upon them by the parental figures. The conscious awareness of their actions, and making the link to the patient's need for punishment (in terms of its connection to the developmental experience) can only be achieved when continued attempts are made by the clinician to tolerate the patient's behaviours – behaviours that also serve to verify the notion that they are deserving of punishment due to the way they behave. The working through of the trauma, using the transference relationship, is a long term but constantly active process in which the clinician is required to hold steadfast in their commitment to the therapeutic alliance. The impact of being either dismissed or critically treated by the primal figures has ultimately reinforced the patient's intolerance of nurture and support by others (and this includes health professionals).

Chapter 14

GENERAL GUIDELINES OF GOOD PRACTICE

Further to the theoretical consideration of the disorder, recognition of the unconscious, acceptance and management of the transference and countertransference, and the consideration of the use of the framework of moral masochism in working with BPD, it is imperative to consider general guidelines of good practice in working with this patient group. The below recommended list of therapeutic responses in relation to the assessment and continued engagement of patients with BPD is not by any means considered exhaustive. The recommendations listed here however should assist in enabling the clinician to develop a greater sense of clarity in terms of their clinical response to BPD. Further to the development of a more nuanced and empathic understanding of self-harm behaviours, and the consequent levels of risk within the context of personality disorder (in order to facilitate a more enhanced therapeutic engagement with these challenging patients), a reminder of the general direction of how to proceed in the clinical work can also assist in the management of the clinician's insecurities that the psychotherapeutic work with BPD patients can create in us.

RECOMMENDATIONS FOR THE EMERGENCY MEDICINE SETTING

- Patients with BPD who present to emergency departments following DSH should not be denied access to any form of medical response or treatment that would have been provided for the same injury that was not self-inflicted.
- Clinicians in the emergency department should have ready access to guidelines in the treatment of DSH by emergency medicine. There are existing practice guidelines available within the existing literature base (such as National Collaborating Centre for Mental Health, 2004; Oldham et al., 2001; Work Group on Borderline Personality Disorder, 2001; Mitchell, 2000).
- Emergency medicine clinicians should be readily aware of, and actively acknowledge, the level of distress that the patient is experiencing following instances of self injury.
- Attempts should be made to provide greater privacy within the emergency department for patients following their presentation to the health service.

- Medical treatment should be a collaborative process between patient and clinician, where the patient is offered adequate explanation and provided choice (where available) in the decision of how to medically attend to the patient's injury.
- Referral to appropriate mental health services should occur following the patient's presentation to the emergency medicine department. The explanation as to the purpose of this referral should be offered to the patient, with discussion as to the need for psychotherapeutic care.

SUGGESTIONS FOR MENTAL HEALTH CLINICIANS

- Upon presentation of patients with BPD to mental health services, adequate assessment, including that of the indications of risk to self and others, and recognition of the level of distress endured, should be provided regardless of diagnostic labelling.
- A detailed consideration of the patient's history should be obtained by the clinician prior to the attempt to diagnose and instigate psychotherapeutic treatment for this disorder. Understanding and investigating the possible aetiological constellations to the development of this disorder is imperative at the commencement of (and throughout) the psychotherapeutic work.
- Creation of a dialogue with the patient regarding DSH behaviours can result in the patient feeling more comfortable and respected within the assessment procedures. It also allows a platform by which to understand the purpose and development of DSH behaviours.
- Where applicable, the patient should have some input into the allocation of clinicians to the patient's psychotherapeutic care. Given that the psychotherapeutic relationship requires appropriate levels of engagement by the patient and the clinician[1], some choice as to the people involved should be attempted to be provided.
- BPD patients should be invited to participate in the development of their risk management plans. These plans should also be regularly reviewed throughout the treatment period.
- Careful and deliberate consideration of the patient's dialogue can be extremely valuable to appreciating the patient's conflicts. The use of word association and time-line interview procedures can assist in the discovery of the unconscious sense of guilt.

GENERAL ISSUES OF DIAGNOSTIC PRACTICE

- Consideration of the diagnostic principles (including the pervasive and enduring pattern of instability that is the foundation to the disorder) is paramount in the assessment of the disorder.

[1] As note earlier, the therapist-induced countertransference (Aviv & Springmann, 1990) is of need for consideration – as a clinician, am I able to manage my responses to the patient upon reflection of my own personality and experiences?

- Delay the application of diagnostic categorisation until developmental histories are investigated and discussed in detail with the patient. It is important to demonstrate an active process of listening and sharing with the patient to assist in the development of a comfortable dialogue by which to examine the significance and development of self-harm. This will also assist in the maintenance of the therapeutic relationship as a demonstration of one's commitment to this relationship can assist the patient in feeling more supported, and therefore more likely to actively participate in therapy.
- Each episode of DSH or suicidal gesture must be assessed as a separate event, and inferences from previous patterns of self-harm behaviour must not be used to determine suicide risk. Do not become complacent – there is no evidence to support the view that patients who repeatedly self-harm as less likely to die by suicide (National Collaborating Centre for Mental Health, 2004).
- The presence of self-harm behaviour is not in itself an indicator of BPD; a further four diagnostic criteria are required to be met for the diagnosis of BPD to be made. A detailed assessment procedure to examine the presence of these additional symptoms is needed.
- The use of both quantitative and qualitative assessment measures should be employed in the screening of the applicability of the BPD diagnosis. There are psychometric assessment tools, such as the McLean Screening Instrument for Borderline Personality Disorder (MSI-BPD) (Zanarini et al., 2003), available to assist in the assessment of the disorder. A detailed patient history should also be collected and considered in conjunction with such measures.
- Techniques such as confrontation, or the offering interpretations, must be avoided in the earlier stages of psychotherapeutic treatment until an appropriate therapeutic alliance has been established, and an adequate working hypothesis or construction has been considered.
- Recognition of the patient's subjective experiences of trauma should be provided by the clinician. It is not necessary during the assessment phase to corroborate the patient's reports, as it is the subjective reality, or the patient's construction of their history, which is important to the therapeutic aims.

Ongoing Educational Opportunities and Clinical Supervision

- Completion of targeted education in personality disorders should be compulsory for clinicians (across all service settings) who come into contact with patients diagnosed with BPD. All health clinicians should be enabled access to training opportunities and regular clinical supervision by their employer in the speciality area of working with this difficult but interesting patient group. This should include the consideration of the development of the disorder, not just treatment pathways, from an appropriate theoretical grounding.

- Theoretical and clinical support via regular supervision must be instigated for the clinician during their psychotherapeutic work with BPD patients. The recognition of the transference relationship (and the countertransference response of the clinician) requires careful consideration.
- Outside of the therapy session, the use of supervision to appreciate the clinician's past professional and personal experience, and how this relates to their response to their patient is essential. Recognition of this will be beneficial in terms of reducing clinician burnout and also in the effective maintenance of the therapeutic alliance.

Establishing, Maintaining, and Nurturing a Therapeutic Alliance

- Discounting a trauma history has the potential to undermine the therapeutic relationship with the patient, and therefore impact on the patient's progress in treatment (Oldham et al., 2001). Throughout the psychotherapeutic work, validation of the patient's history and experience must be provided.
- A therapeutic alliance between the clinician and the patient must exist and be *actively maintained* within the psychotherapeutic work. It is within this relationship that the patient's past trauma can be considered, and the clinician must allow for a degree of difference within the countertransference to prevent unnecessarily re-traumatising the patient. We should appreciate the perceived experience encountered with the parental figures, and actively attempt to manage the distinction between them, us, and what is projected upon us by the patient.
- The clinician should actively acknowledge their presence in the therapeutic alliance, and as such accept some responsibility for the distress of the patient in the provision of the psychotherapeutic work. In the event of behavioural disturbance, reflecting upon our possible influence on this (and offering some comment of these hypothetical reflections to our patient) may assist in managing the therapeutic alliance.
- Although exacerbation of the patient's behaviour is commonly observed due to the instigation of the psychotherapeutic work, it is important to consider that the patient will only begin to discover their symptom when feeling safe within the confines of this therapeutic alliance. During such exacerbation, the therapy must continue.

Chapter 15

FINAL COMMENTS ON WORKING WITH BORDERLINE PATIENTS

As identified throughout this text, the transference relationship (and the clinician's commitment to the therapeutic alliance) is of significant importance to the psychotherapeutic treatment of BPD. Unfortunately many clinicians may avoid clinical contact with such patients (which can result in further trauma for the patient when reasonable feedback for this is not provided) or not adequately recognise the significance of their role in the presentation of the patient's symptom. As discussed earlier, patients may sense the rejection in the clinician's demeanour, and this can trigger further behavioural disturbance (Hemmings, 1999). This is the risk with the patient's encounter with the clinician considered as the 'cynical abandoner' – of course there are also further problems with the patient's encounter with the 'flustered rescuer'. The risk of boundary violations and problematic counter-transference reactions to patients with BPD is well documented (Oldham et al., 2001). The repetition of grievances with significant figures of the past, and providing awareness as to the presence and need for resolve of these grievances, is considered of central importance in many psychoanalytic and psychodynamic models of treatment for BPD.

CONSIDERING THE REPETITION OF TRAUMA

The need to reduce the ready consideration of the BPD diagnosis in terms of the behavioural presentation of DSH and other 'observable' symptoms is evident. The need to also understand that this behaviour may be a repeated representation of historic trauma of the patient is also considered as imperative.

> Discounting a trauma history has the potential to undermine the therapeutic alliance and the progress of treatment. It can also hamper patients' ability to integrate and comes to terms with trauma. Not integrating traumatic material into the treatment can lead patients to experience the therapy as a form of collusion with the abuser. (Oldham et al., 2001, p.20).

From a consideration of the unconscious and its connection to past history, we can further understand the presence of DSH behaviours as a hypothesised link to past trauma. According to the moral masochism framework, DSH behaviours can be a way that past trauma is repeated, and the trauma can become reactivated in the present day through the transference relationship. What is important for clinicians to remember is that the patient's symptom, and the unconscious process by which the symptom has developed, can only be discovered when the patient feels safe within the therapeutic relationship. It is in the psychotherapeutic work that the patient often discovers that they have a symptom and therefore an exacerbation of DSH behaviours can occur in the early stages of treatment. Contrary to the belief of some clinicians[1], this exacerbation does not indicate that the psychotherapeutic work is making the patient feel worse – it may be an indication of patient's emerging commitment and acceptance of the therapy. It is important to consider that the transference reactivates the patient's trauma (which is also pathological) and therefore the repetition of trauma is painful and difficult. As clinicians, we should take some responsibility for this.

Unfortunately, the unconscious connection between past experiences and present behaviours remains mostly concealed, and many clinicians often struggle to empathise with the ongoing trauma experienced by patients from their distant pasts. DSH behaviour after a rape attack is more easily understood and empathised with than a person who engages in the same DSH behaviours and has been the victim of childhood abuse many, many years ago. The differentiation is often more narrow than one may think – the abuse becomes activated in the present through a complex and often unconscious process of interacting with others in the environment. Although abuse does not adequately or sufficiently explain the development of the BPD symptomatology and use of DSH behaviours observed in such patients (as not all patients with past trauma come to develop BPD), it is important to attempt to consider why the patient has become pathological. Aetiology is not easy to construct (particularly with BPD) and such construction requires a cautious process of using moral, ethical, and clinical judgements. To achieve this, the clinician needs to be actively engaged (as does the patient) to carefully inquire and investigate these hypothetical connections. It is important that the construction of aetiological constellations occurs as a 'work in progress' (as is considered in the presentation here of the case formulations of Lisa, Helen, and Eve), as the subjective significance of past events in one's life varies across time. The patient's report of their history starts with such a construction, and from this our hypothesis can be formed. Over time, through the continued dialogue with the patient, and in the patient's response to the offering of interpretations within the psychotherapy, our hypothesis or construction should be actively modified. It is important to remember that as clinicians, we can only begin to approximate the truth of the patient's trauma (as can the patient).

Recognising the Concept of Individuality

The focus of this text has been on the mental disorder known as BPD. Although a classification system used to categorise patients with similar symptomatology, what has been

[1] I have worked with some clinicians who have expressed their frustration at the apparent worsening of the patient's behaviours when commencing psychotherapeutic work – indeed this was the case in the treatment of the first patient of this text, Lisa, where staff at the residential facility often complained about her escalating behaviours following initial psychotherapy sessions.

argued here is that we need to recognise the individual experience of each patient (both the childhood developmental experience and the occurrence or presents of certain symptomatology). The stereotypic views of BPD often seem to lose this concept of individuality, and in fact the application of the diagnosis based on purely behavioural symptomatology is common. It is feared that little therapeutic time is used to inquire about the patient's history or experience. Although in my clinical practice the preference is for the minimising of diagnostic labelling or categorisation, obviously the use of diagnosis can assist in varying degrees in the conceptualisation of the patient's suffering.

As previously highlighted, the terms 'borderline', 'personality', and 'disorder' remain problematic to the clinical consideration of such patient presentations. The link of personality to disorder is probably more correct as a reflection of the patient's typical presentation – as a disordered individual. The addition of borderline however is awkward and nonsensical to the clinical presentation of these patients. Although retained from historical perspectives, it appears that this terminology is not only problematic in its ability to influence clinician attitudes, but it also does not describe these patients adequately. "This diagnosis continues to present considerable conceptual and therapeutic challenges for all those involved...and it remains a categorical label that evokes a wide range of conscious and unconscious responses" (Warne & McAndrew, 2007, p.155).

Appreciation of the Patient's Unconscious

Within the DBT theoretical model, we can consider that BPD patients are compelled to injure or engage in other means of DSH behaviours in order to modulate their intense and overwhelming affective experiences (albeit it temporarily). Moral masochism however takes the conceptualisation of this behaviour further in that it considers why the DSH behaviours can make the patient feel somewhat more in control of their affective responses. It is cautioned that moral masochism is by no means considered a 'treatment model' for BPD symptomatology, as moral masochism is a theoretical construct by which to understand the patient's unconscious response – it is used here in its conceptual form by which to understand these behaviours.

The realisation that the patient themselves may not understand their need or drive to self injure, due to the underlying unconscious processes associated with such actions, also lends us to a consideration of the transference relationship with these patients. The history of the patient, and who they have come to be, is considered to be intertwined into the feelings of guilt and the consequent need for punishment and in their active seeking of misfortune and suffering. Ongoing examination of the history of the patient's suffering, and the acknowledgement and consideration of the transference, may also assist us in the interpretation of the ongoing attempts often seen in the treatment of BPD patients to evoke ongoing disappointment and rejection in us.

We must remember that the transference relationship can also be a source by which to evoke punishment and misfortune (in addition to the patient engaging in DSH behaviours). The response of the clinician to the patient can reactivate the past trauma where, within the transference, we become the parental figure from whom the need for punishment was instilled. As hypothesised here for Lisa, the rejection of the clinician may reactive the feelings of being the unwanted afterbirth; for Helen, the rejection of the clinician can reactivate the feelings of not being deserving of care; for Eve, the rejection of the clinician can reactivate the feelings of futility. It is important to consider that we cannot become these figures within the transference or else we can re-traumatise the patient. A degree of difference must be present in the transference. As discussed earlier, it is within this difference that the repetition can be broken. The repetition within the transference relationship can re-traumatise the patient, particularly when the countertransference response of the clinician is most similar to that of projected figures of the past. The clinician however can respond with a therapeutic degree of difference to allow for a working through of this past trauma.

The Importance of a Considered Approach of Inquiry

Deliberate forms of self-harm in the BPD patient are considered by some as a way that earlier trauma is repeated, communicated, or symbolised to those around them (e.g., Van der Kolk, 1989). BPD patients are often unable to adequately explain the source of guilt behind their masochistic behaviours (even if the guilt is recognised as an emotion), and this can often frustrate the clinician as they attempt to persuade such patients against the use of self-harm. It is important to consider the structural view of the patient, where both the conscious and unconscious workings are considered. The BPD patient has utilised a complex process of defence to guard themselves from the affect associated with their history and "these defence mechanisms operate at an unconscious level to mediate intrapsychic anxiety for the individual" (Crowe, 2004, p.4). As the sense of guilt and need for punishment, and where these may stem from, will be unconscious to the patient, it is important to consider that often these patients may be unable to speak about their trauma. It is common however that they will continue to act out their traumatic experience through their DSH behaviours (McAllister, 2003). It is from a consideration of this behaviour that the unconscious process (including the sense of guilt and need for punishment) can be discovered.

When working with the BPD patient as clinicians or therapists, to understand the self-harm behaviours of this patient we need to not just look at the act or episode of self-harm behaviours as this can cause a negative countertransference. This will ultimately affect the treatment provided. The recognition of the unconscious process, and presence of masochistic tendencies in the patient, requires a greater consideration in the psychotherapeutic treatment of BPD. As offered by Millon (1996), it is important that clinicians recognise that the DSH behaviour is not based on the patient's perverse enjoyment of pain – the use of DSH behaviour is a means by which many patients believe that they can experience less pain.

As discussed earlier, there is often a coherent rationale behind the choice of self-harm for the BPD patient. The patient often treats themselves as their family did; history indeed leaves traces and marks in everyone. Being unable to consciously describe these connections, the DSH behavioural response of the patient then appears trivial and nonsensical to the presenting social or environmental stressors that seem to activate these extreme behavioural responses. This is often the cause of great frustration to the treating clinician as they attempt to persuade the BPD patient against the use of these behaviours. The persuasion against using self-harm will often be futile if the patient themselves is not consciously aware of the source of the motivation within themselves to engage in self-harm. The frustration that is commonly experienced by clinicians when dealing with patients that deliberately self-harm is understandable if the conceptualisation of such patient responses lack a theoretical framework by which to interpret such behaviours. Many BPD patients are indeed also frustrated by their own behaviours. Increasing professional understanding of why patients may 'deliberately' self-harm is highly needed.

What has been illustrated here is that the BPD patient's awareness of their masochistic actions may be reduced due to the unconscious nature of these behaviours, as their 'choice' to behave in certain ways can be considered as requiring a process of conscious and deliberate thought. It is hoped that an awareness of this unconscious process may be able increase the tolerance by clinicians when these behaviours occur, and ultimately promote a greater support for the BPD who does not consciously understand their own behaviours. "An understanding of the unconscious and its defensive functioning processes provides a basis for addressing the source of distress and its symptom" (Crowe, 2004, p.6). To uncover the source, the clinician should attempt to replace their negative countertransference reaction with active therapeutic inquiry in order to identify and understand the development and unconscious significance of the self-harm behaviours. What is concluded here is that clinicians should look past the act of self-harm itself, and attempt to understand the history of the patients and the consequent development of the self-harm behaviours, rather than purely react to the behavioural display themselves.

Using Moral Masochism to Understand the Function of Self-harm

As a platform to reduce anxiety, moral masochism as a theoretical framework can enable a consideration of the unconscious response through providing a basis by which to being to interpret and understand the unconscious workings of the patient's behaviour. An unconscious sense of guilt and a need for punishment may not be reflected at all in the clinical contact with the patient; it is in the destructive presentations of DSH behaviour that we can see that it is there. Much as grief can result in remorse and mood change, current and ongoing repetition of trauma may be linked unconsciously to a source of guilt and an original grief response. The recognition of the experience of trauma in the psychotherapeutic work with the BPD patient is considered necessary in the context of unconscious processes that underlie the presentation of behavioural, affective, cognitive, and interpersonal manifestations of BPD. The concept of moral masochism as a theoretical framework by which to understand the presence of DSH behaviours in BPD is considered central to the hypothesis here of the notion of trauma history and the reactivation of guilt through interactions with environmental and social stressors within the present day.

The unconscious feelings of guilt, and the unconscious need for punishment, which have been suggested here as a precursor to the patient's engagement in masochistic behaviours such as DSH, are best understood within the historical context of the patient's trauma and suffering. Whether from the active participation in abuse or the fundamental concept of futility and worthlessness that has been ingrained from childhood (as seen with the three case presentations here), the reactivation of trauma in response to typical stressors appears to develop more sufficient therapeutic meaning from a consideration of the unconscious connections between the need for punishment and the patient's history.

The theoretical context of moral masochism provides some basis by which clinicians can consider the presence of behavioural disturbance in BPD, thus possibly reducing frustration and rejection. The suggestion of a reduced awareness of the motivating force behind their behaviours, due to the recognition of the unconscious processes, is considered to be of greater assistance in the maintenance of the therapeutic alliance. It is imperative to appreciate that it is who we are to our patient that affects their progression through treatment, and of course their general prognosis.

REFERENCES

Alston, M., & Robinson, B. (1992). Nurses attitudes toward suicide. *Omega*, *25*, 205-215.

Anderson, M. (1997). Nurses' attitudes toward suicidal behaviour – a comparative study of community mental health nurses and nurses working in an accident and emergency department. *Journal of Advanced Nursing*, *25*, 1283–1291.

American Psychiatric Association. (1980). *Diagnostic and statistical manual of mental disorders.* (3rd Ed.). Washington: American Psychiatric Association.

American Psychiatric Association. (2000). *Diagnostic and statistical manual of mental disorders. Text revision.* (4th Ed.). Washington: American Psychiatric Association.

American Psychiatric Association. (2013). *Diagnostic and statistical manual of mental disorders.* (5th Ed.). Washington: American Psychiatric Association.

Auditor General Victoria. (2002). *Mental health services for people in crisis*. Melbourne: Government Printer for State of Victoria.

Australian Bureau of Statistics. (2013). 3309.0 – Suicides, Australia, 2010. Retrieval November 29, 2013, from http://www.abs.gov.au/ausstats/abs@.nsf/Products/3309.0~2010~Chapter~Suicide+in+Australia?OpenDocument. Australian Psychological Society. (1999). *Suicide: An Australian Psychological Society discussion paper.* Melbourne: Australian Psychological Society.

Aviv, A., & Springmann, R. R. (1990). Negative countertransference and negative therapeutic reaction: Prognostic indicators in the analysis of severe psychopathology. *Contemporary Psychoanalysis*, *26*, 692-715.

Barbe, R. P., Rubovszky, G., Venturini-Andreoli, A., & Andreoli, A. (2005). The treatment of borderline personality disorder patients with current suicidal behaviour. *Clinical neuropsychiatry*, *2*(5), 283-291.

Bateman, A., & Fonagy, P. (2004). *Psychotherapy for Borderline Personality Disorder: Mentalization-based treatment.* New York: Oxford University Press.

Becker, D. (1997). *Through the looking glass: Women and borderline personality disorder.* Colorado: Westview Press.

Bowers, L., & Allan, T. (2006). The attitudes to personality disorder questionnaire: psychometric properties and results. *Journal of Personality Disorders*, *20*(3), 281-293.

Boyes, A. (1994). Repetition of overdose: a retrospective five year study. *Journal of Advanced Nursing*, *20*, 462-468.

Briere, J., & Gill, E. (1998). Self-mutilation in clinical and general population samples: prevalence, correlates, and functions. *American Journal of Orthopsychiatry*, *68*, 609-620.

Carveth, D. (2001). The unconscious need for punishment: expression or evasion of the sense of guilt? *Psychoanalytic Studies*, *3*(1), 9-21.

Chassan, J. B. (1967). *Research design in clinical psychology and psychiatry*. New York: Appleton-Century-Crofts.

Chatham, P. M. (1985). *Treatment of the borderline personality*. New York: Jason Aronson.

Clarkin, J. F., Levy, K. N., Lenzenweger, M. F., & Kernberg, O. F. (2007). Evaluating three treatments for borderline personality disorder: A multiwave study. *The American Journal of Psychiatry*, *164*(6), 922-928.

Clarkin, J. F., Yeomans, F. E., & Kernberg, O. F. (1999). *Psychotherapy for borderline personality*. New York: John Wiley & Sons, Inc.

Cleary, M., Siegfield, N., & Walter, G. (2002). Experience, knowledge and attitudes of mental health staff regarding clients with a borderline personality disorder. *International Journal of Mental Health Nursing*, *11*, 186-191.

Cohen, C., & Sherwood, V. (1991). *Becoming a constant object in psychotherapy with the borderline patient*. New Jersey: Jason Aronson Inc.

Commons Treloar, A. J., & Lewis, A. J. (2008a). Professional attitudes towards deliberate self-harm in patients with borderline personality disorder. *Australian and New Zealand Journal of Psychiatry*, *42*(7), 578-584.

Commons Treloar, A.J., & Lewis, A. (2008b). Targeted clinical education for staff attitudes towards deliberate self-harm in borderline personality disorder: randomised controlled trial. *Australian and New Zealand Journal of Psychiatry*, *42*(11), 981-988.

Commons Treloar, A. J., & Lewis, A. J. (2009). Diagnosing borderline personality disorder: An examination of how clinical indicators are used by professionals in the health setting. *Clinical Psychologist*, *13*(1), 21-27.

Commons Treloar, A. J. (2009a). Effectiveness of education programs in changing clinicians' attitudes toward treating borderline personality disorder. *Psychiatric Services*, *60*(8), 1128-1131.

Commons Treloar, A. J. (2009b). A qualitative investigation of the clinician experience of working with borderline personality disorder. *New Zealand Journal of Psychology*, *38*(2), 31-35.

Commons Treloar, A. J. (2009c). *Guilt, masochism, and self-harm in the borderline patient: Using educational interventions to improve clinician attitudes and diagnostic practices with borderline personality disorder*. Unpublished doctoral dissertation, Monash University, Melbourne, Australia.

Costa, P. T., & Widiger, T. A.(1994). *Personality Disorders and the five-factor model of personality*. Washington: American Psychological Association.

Crowe, M. (2004). The place of the unconscious in mental health nursing. *International Journal of Mental Health Nursing*, *13*, 2-8.

Deans, C., & Meocevic, E. (2006). Attitudes of registered psychiatric nurses toward patients diagnosed with borderline personality disorder. *Contemporary Nurse*, *21*, 43-49.

Derksen, J. (1995). *Personality disorders: clinical and social perspectives*. New York: John Wiley & Sons, Inc.

Domino, G., Westlake, L., & Gibson, L. (1982). Attitudes toward suicide. A factor analysis approach. *Journal of Clinical Psychology*, *38*, 257-262.

Drake, R. E., Green, A. I., Mueser, K. T., & Goldman, H. H. (2003). The history of community mental health treatment and rehabilitation for persons with severe mental illness. *Community Mental Health Journal, 39*, 110-136.

Finch, P. (1956). The new Elizabethan reference dictionary. Sydney: George Newnes Pty Ltd.

Fishbein, M., & Ajzen, I. (1975). *Belief, attitude, intention, and behaviour: An introduction to theory and research*. Pennsylvania: Addison-Wesley.

Fonagy, P., Leigh, T., Steele, M., Steele, H., Kennedy, R., Mattoon, G., Target, M., & Gerber, A. (1996). The relation of attachment status, psychiatric classification and response to psychotherapy. *Journal of Consulting and Clinical Psychology, 64*(1), 22-31.

Freud, S. (1957). Instincts and their vicissitudes. In J. Strachey (Ed. and Trans.), *The standard edition of the complete psychological works of Sigmund Freud* (Vol. 14, pp.109-140). London: Hogarth Press. (Original work published 1915a)

Freud, S. (1957). The unconscious. In J. Strachey (Ed. and Trans.), *The standard edition of the complete psychological works of Sigmund Freud* (Vol. 14, pp.161-215). London: Hogarth Press. (Original work published 1915c)

Freud, S. (1961). From the history of an infantile neurosis [The 'Wolfman']. In J. Strachey (Ed. and Trans.), *The standard edition of the complete psychological works of Sigmund Freud* (Vol. 17, pp.3-123). London: Hogarth Press. (Original work published 1918)

Freud, S. (1961). The ego and the id. In J. Strachey (Ed. and Trans.), *The standard edition of the complete psychological works of Sigmund Freud* (Vol. 19, pp.3-66). London: Hogarth Press. (Original work published 1923)

Freud, S. (1961). The economic problem of masochism. In J. Strachey (Ed. and Trans.), *The standard edition of the complete psychological works of Sigmund Freud* (Vol. 19, pp.157-170). London: Hogarth Press. (Original work published 1924)

Freud, S. (1964). Constructions in analysis. In J. Strachey (Ed. and Trans.), *The standard edition of the complete psychological works of Sigmund Freud* (Vol. 23, pp.257-269). London: Hogarth Press. (Original work published 1937)

Freud, S. (1964). An outline of psycho-analysis. In J. Strachey (Ed. and Trans.), *The standard edition of the complete psychological works of Sigmund Freud* (Vol. 23, pp.144-208). London: Hogarth Press. (Original work published 1940)

Gabbard, G. O. (2000). Disguise or consent. *International Journal of Psychoanalysis, 81*, 1071-1086.

Goin, M. K. (2001). Practical psychotherapy: Borderline personality disorder: The importance of establishing a treatment framework. *Psychiatric Services, 52*, 167-168.

Green, C. A., Knysz, W., & Tsuang, M. T. (2000). A homeless person with bipolar disorder and a history of serious self mutilation. *The American Journal of Psychiatry, 157*(9), 1392-1397.

Gunderson, J. G. (2001). *Borderline personality disorder: A clinical guide*. Washington: American Psychiatric Publishing Inc.

Gunderson, J. G., & Kolb, J. E., & Austin, V. (1981). The diagnostic interview for borderline patients. *American Journal of Psychiatry, 138*, 896-903.

Harris Jr., J. M., Kutob, R. M., Surprenant, Z. J., Maiuro, R. D., & Delate, T. A. (2002). Can internet-based education improve physician confidence in dealing with domestic violence? *Family Medicine, 34*(4), 287-292.

Haswell, D., & Graham, M. (1996). Selfinflicted injuries: Challenging knowledge, skill, and compassion. *Canadian Family Physician, 42*, 1756-1764.

Hawton, K., Rodham, K., & Evans, E. (2002). Deliberate self-harm in adolescents: self report survey in schools in England. *British Medical Journal*, *325*, 1207-1211.

Hawton, K., Zahl, D., & Weatherall, R. (2003). Suicide following deliberate self-harm: long-term follow-up of patients who presented to a general hospital. *British Journal of Psychiatry*, *182*, 537-542.

Hayes, S. C., Wilson, K., & Difford, E. (1996). Experiential avoidance and behavioural disorders: a functional dimensional approach to diagnosis and treatment. *Journal of Consulting Clinical and Psychology*, *64*, 1152-1168.

Hazelton, M., Rossiter, R., & Milner, J. (2006). Managing the 'unmanageable': Training staff in the use of dialectical behavior therapy for borderline personality disorder. *Contemporary Nurse*, *21*(1), 120-130.

Hemmings, A. (1999). Attitudes to deliberate self-harm among staff in an accident and emergency team. *Mental Health Care*, *2*, 300–302.

Henley, N. M. (1977). *Body politics: Power, sex and nonverbal communication.* New Jersey: Prentice Hall.

Hill, J., Swales, M., & Byatt, M. (2005). Personality disorders. In C. Gillerg, R. Harrington, & H-C. Steinhausen (Eds.), *A clinician's handbook of child and adolescent psychiatry*, (pp.330-363). New York: Cambridge University Press.

Hodges, S (2003). Borderline personality disorder and posttraumatic stress disorder: Time for integration? *Journal of Counseling and Development*, *81*(4), 409-417.

Hormbrey, P., Todd, B. B., Mansfield, C. D., & Skinner, D. V. (1996). A survey of teaching and the use of clinical guidelines in accident and emergency departments. *Journal of Accident and Emergency Medicine*, *13*(2), 129-133.

Horrocks, J., Price, S., & House, A. (2003). Self injury attendances in the accident and emergency department: a clinical database study. *British Journal of Psychiatry*, *183*, 34-39.

Huband, N., & Tantam, D. (2000). Attitudes toward self injury within a group of mental health staff. *British Journal of Medical Psychology*, *73*, 495-504.

Johnstone, L. (1997). Self injury and the psychiatric response. *Feminism and Psychology*, *7*, 421-426.

Karam-Hage, M., Nerenberg, L., & Brower, K. J. (2001). Modifying residents' professional attitudes about substance abuse treatment and training. *American Journal of Addictions*, *10*(1), 40-47.

Kernberg, O. (1967). Borderline personality organisation. *Journal of the American Psychoanalytic Association*, *15*, 641-685.

Klonsky, E. D., Oltmanns, T. F., & Turkheimer, E. (2003). Deliberate self-harm in a nonclinical population: prevalence and psychological correlates. *American Journal of Psychiatry*, *160*, 1501-1508.

Knight, R. (1953). Borderline states. *Bulletin of the Menninger Clinic*, *17*, 1-12.

Kochanek, K. D., Xu J., Murphy, S. L, Miniño, A. M., & Kung, H. (2011). *Deaths: Final data for 2009. National vital statistics reports; vol 60 no 3.* Maryland: National Center for Health Statistics.

Krawitz, R. (2000). Borderline personality disorder: Clinician attitude change following brief training. *Australian and New Zealand Journal of Psychiatry*, *34*, A40.

Krawitz, R. (2004). Borderline personality disorder: attitudinal change following training. *Australian and New Zealand Journal of Psychiatry*, *38*, 554-559.

Lacan, J. (1993). *The Seminar, Book III, 1955-1956, The Psychoses.* London: Routledge.

Lacan, J. (2004). *Le Séminaire, Livre X, L'angoisse.* Paris: Seuil.

Laplanche, J., & Pontalis, J. B. (1988). *The language of psychoanalysis.* London: Karnac Books.

Leichsenring, F., & Leibing, E. (2003). The effectiveness of psychodynamic therapy and cognitive behaviour therapy in the treatment of personality disorders: A meta-analysis. *American Journal of Psychiatry, 160*(7), 1223-1232.

Levenkron, S. (1998). *Cutting: Understanding and overcoming self mutilation.* New York: W. W. Norton & Company.

Lewis, G., & Appleby, L. (1988). Personality disorder: the patients psychiatrists dislike. *British Journal of Psychiatry, 153*, 44-49.

Linehan, M. M. (1993). *Cognitive-behavioral treatment of borderline personality disorder.* New York: The Guilford Press.

Livesley, W. J., Jackson, D., & Schroeder, M. (1989). A study of the factorial structure of personality pathology. *Journal of Personality Disorders, 3*, 292-306.

Lyons, J. (1999). Reflective education for professional practice: discovering knowledge from experience. *Nurse Education Today, 19*(1), 29-34.

Main, M., & Goldwyn, R. (1991). *Adult attachment classification system; version 5.* Unpublished manuscript, University of California at Berkley.

McAllister, M. (2003). Multiple meanings of self-harm: A critical review. *International Journal of Mental Health Nursing, 12*, 177-185.

McAllister, M., Creedy, D., Moyle, W., & Farrugia, C. (2002). Nurses' attitudes toward clients who self-harm. *Journal of Advanced Nursing*. 40(5), 578-586.

McLaughlin, C. (1995). Counselling the overdose patient in casualty. *British Journal of Nursing, 4*, 688-708.

Mental Health Foundation. (1997). *Suicide and deliberate self-harm: The fundamental facts.* Mental Health Foundation. Retrieved 5th September, 2006, from http://www. mentalhealth.org.uk/page.cfm?pagecode=PBBZ0101

Middleton, W., & Butler, J. (1998). Dissociative identity disorder: An Australian series. *Australian and New Zealand Journal of Psychiatry, 32*, 794-804.

Miller, S. A., & Davenport, N. C. (1996). Increasing staff knowledge of and improving attitudes toward patients with borderline personality disorder. *Psychiatric Services, 47*, 533-535.

Millon, T. (1996). *Disorders of personality: DSM-IV and beyond.* (2nd Ed.). New York: John Wiley & Sons, Inc.

Mintz, D. (2013). Teaching psychoanalytical concepts, skills, and attitudes to medical students. *Journal of the American Psychoanalytic Association, 61*, 751-770.

Mitchell, P. (2000). *Crisis intervention and primary care: Evaluation of the national youth suicide prevention strategy: Technical report Volume 3.* Melbourne: Australian Institute of Family Studies.

Moran, T., & Mason, T. (1996). Revisiting the nursing management of the psychopath. *Journal of Psychiatric and Mental Health Nursing, 3*(3):189-194.

National Collaborating Centre for Mental Health. (2004). *Self-harm: The short-term physical and psychological management and secondary prevention of self-harm in primary and secondary care. National Clinical Practice Guideline Number 16.* Leicester: The British Psychological Society. Office for National Statistics. (2012). Suicide rates in the United

Kingdom, 2006 to 2010. Retrieval April 14, 2013, from http://www.ons.gov.uk/ons/dcp171778_254113.pdf

Oldham, J. M., Gabbard, G. O., Goin, M. K., Gunderson, J., Soloff, P., Spiegel, D., Stone, M., & Phillips, K. A. (2001). Practice guidelines for the treatment of patients with borderline disorder. *The American Journal of Psychiatry, 158*(10), 1-52.

Owens, D., & House, A. (1994). General hospital services for deliberate self-harm. *Journal of the Royal College of Physicians, 28*(1), 370-371.

Paul, T., Schroefer, K., Dahme, B., & Nutzinger, D. O. (2002). Self-injurious behavior in women with eating disorders. *American Journal of Psychiatry, 159*, 408-411.

Peplau, H. E. (1952). *Interpersonal relations in nursing*. New York: G. P. Putnam's Sons.

Perry, J., & Klerman, G. (1980). Clinical features of the borderline personality disorder. *American Journal of Psychiatry, 137*, 165-173.

Platt, S., Bille-Brahe, U., & Kerkhof, A. (1992). Parasuicide in Europe: the WHO/EURO multi-centre study on parasuicide. I. Introduction and preliminary analysis for 1989. *Acta Psychiatrica Scandinavica, 85*(2), 97-104.

Platt, S., & Salter, D. (1987). A comparison of health workers attitudes toward parasuicide. *Social Psychiatry*, 22, 202-208.

Potter, N. N. (2006). What is manipulative behaviour, anyway? *Journal of Personality Disorders, 20*(2), 139-156.

Racker, H. (2001). Transference and countertransference. Connecticut: International Universities Press Incorporated.

Rosenthal, M. Z., Cukrowicz, K. C., Cheavens, J. S., & Lynch, T. R. (2006). Self punishment as a regulation strategy in borderline personality disorder. *Journal of Personality Disorders, 20*(3), 232- 246.

Ryle, A., Leighton, T., & Pollock, P. (1997). *Cognitive analytic therapy of borderline personality disorder*. Chichester: John Wiley.

Sacher-Masoch, L. R. V. (1870). Venus im pelz (Venus in furs). In J. Neugroschel (Trans.), *Leopold Von Sacher-Masoch: Venus in Furs*. New York: Penguin Group.

Sansone, R. A., Weiderman, M. W., & Sansone, L. A. (1998). The self-harm inventory (SHI): Development of a scale for identifying self-destructive behaviors and borderline personality disorder. *Journal of Clinical Psychology, 54*(7), 973-983.

Saretsky, T. (1976). Masochism and ego identity in borderline states. *Contemporary Psychoanalysis*, 12, 433-445.

Sbaih, L. (1993). Accident and emergency work: a review of some of the literature. *Journal of Advanced Nursing, 18*, 957–962.

Sharry, J., Darmody, M., & Madden, B. (2002). A solution-focused approach to working with clients who are suicidal. *British Journal of Guidance and Counselling, 30*(4), 383-399.

Silburn, S. R., & Zubrick, S. R. (1995). Attempted suicide among Perth youth. In D. Kenney & R.F. Soames (Eds.), *Australia's adolescents: A health psychology perspective* (pp. 96-102). Armidale: University of New England Press.

Simpson, E. B., Pistorello, J., Begin, A., Costello, E., Levinson, J., Mulberry, S., Pearlstein, T., Rosen, K., & Stevens, M. (1998). Focus on women: Use of dialectical behavior therapy in a partial hospital program for women with borderline personality disorder. *Psychiatric Services, 49*, 669-673.

Skodol, A. E., Gunderson, J. G., Pfohl, B., Widiger, T. A., Livesley, W. J., & Siever, L. J. (2002). The borderline diagnosis I: psychopathology, comorbidity, and personality and personality structure. *Biological Psychiatry*, *51*, 951-961.

Spitzer, R., & Endicott, J. (1979). Justification for separating schizotypal and borderline personality disorders. *Schizophrenia Bulletin*, *5*, 95-104.

Stern, A. (1938). Psychoanalytic investigation and therapy in the borderline group of neuroses. *Psychoanalytic Quarterly*, *7*, 467-489.

Strong, M. (1998). *A bright red scream*. New York: Viking.

Suokas, J., & Lonnqvist, J. (1989). Work stress has negative effects on the attitudes of emergency personnel towards patients who attempt suicide. *Acta Psychiatrica Scandinavica*, *79*, 474-480.

Swartz, M., Blazer, D., George, L., & Winfield, I. (1990). Estimating the prevalence of borderline personality disorder in the community. *Journal of Personality Disorders*, *4*, 257-272.

Torgersen, S., Kringlen, E., & Cramer, V. (2001). The prevalence of personality disorders in a community sample. *Archives or General Psychiatry*, *58*, 590-596.

Tredget, J. E. (2001). The aetiology, presentation and treatment of personality disorders. *Journal of Psychiatric and Mental Health Nursing*, *8*, 347-356.

Tuckett, D. (1993). Some thoughts on the presentation and discussion of the clinical material of psychoanalysis. *International Journal of Psychoanalysis*, *74*, 1175-1189.

Tuckett, D. (2000). Reporting clinical events in the journal. *International Journal of Psychoanalysis*, *81*, 1065-1069.

Van der Kolk, B. (1989). The compulsion to repeat the trauma: Reenactment, re-victimisation, and masochism. *Psychiatric Clinics of North America*, *12*, 389-411.

Van der Kolk, B., McFarlane, A., & Weisaeth, L. (1996). *Traumatic stress: the effects of overwhelming experience on mind, body, and society*. New York: Guilford Press.

Victorian Suicide Prevention Task Force. (1997). *Suicide prevention: victorian task force report*. Melbourne: Information Victoria.

Vivekananda, K. (2000). Integrating models for understanding self injury. *Psychotherapy in Australia*, *7*, 18-25.

Wallerstein, R. S., & Sampson, H. (1971). Issues in research in the psychoanalytic process. *International Journal of Psychoanalysis*, *52*, 11-50.

Walsh, F. (1977). The family of the borderline patient. In R. Grinkler & B.

Werble, *The borderline patient*, (pp.149-177). New York: Aronson.

Warne, T., & McAndrew, S. (2006). Transferring anonymity for a few choice words. *Nurse Education in Practice*, *6*, 63-68.

Warne, T., & McAndrew, S. (2007). Bordering on insanity: misnomer, reviewing the case of condemned women. *Journal of Psychiatric and Mental Health Nursing*, *14*, 155-162.

Watson, R. I., Jr. (1996). The discovery of the borderline patients through countertransference. *Contemporary Psychoanalysis*, *32*, 80-84.

Weinberg, I., & Maltsberger, J. T. (2007). Suicidal behaviours in borderline personality disorder. In R. Tatarelli, M. Pompili & P. Girardi (Eds.), *Suicide in psychiatric disorders*, (pp.333-370). New York: Nova Science Publishers Inc.

Widiger, T., & Trull, T. (1992). Borderline and narcissistic personality disorders. In P. Surker & H. Adams, *Comprehensive Handbook of Psychopathology,* (pp.467-573). New York: Plenum Press.

Wilson, M. (1993). DSM-III and the transformation of American psychiatry: a history. *The American Journal of Psychiatry*, *150*, 399-410.

Wirth-Cauchon, J. (2001). *Women and borderline personality disorder: Symptoms and stories*. New York: Perseus Books.

Woollcott, P., Jr. (1985). Prognostic indicators in the psychotherapy of borderline patients. *American Journal of Psychotherapy*, *39*(1), 17-29.

Work Group on Borderline Personality Disorder. (2001). Practice guideline for the treatment of patients with borderline personality disorder. *The American Journal of Psychiatry*, *158*, 1-52.

World Health Organization. (2004). *International statistical classification of disease and health related problems. The ICD-10.* (10th Ed.). Geneva: World Health Organization.

Zanarini, M. C., & Frankenburg, F. R. (1997). Pathways to the development of borderline personality disorder. *Journal of Personality Disorders*, *11*, 93-104.

Zanarini, M. C., Frankenburg, F. R., Dubo, E. D., Sickel, A. E., Trikha, A., Levin, A., & Reynolds, V. (1998). Axis I comorbidity of borderline personality disorder. *The American Journal of Psychiatry*, 155, 1733-1739.

Zanarini, M. C., Vujanovic, A., Parachini, E. A., Boulanger, J. L., Frankenburg, F. R., & Hennen, J. (2003). A screening measure for BPD: The McLean Screening Instrument for Borderline Personality Disorder (MSI-BPD). *Journal of Personality Disorders*, *17*(6), 568-573.

Zisook, S., Goff, A., Sledge, P., & Shuchter, S. R. (1994). Reported suicidal behaviour and current suicidal ideation in a psychiatric outpatient clinic. *Annals of Clinical Psychiatry*, *6*(1), 27-31.

APPENDICES

APPENDIX A: INTERVIEW SCHEDULE

Session one: Use and development of self-harm behaviours.

1. What age were you when you first used self-harm?
2. What age were you when other people realised that you self-harm?
3. What forms of self-harm have you and do you engage in?
4. In what circumstances do you use self-harm? Examples?
5. Why do you think you use self-harm? What does it do for you?
6. Do you use self-harm as a form of punishment? What for?
7. Do you experience a sense of guilt prior, during, and/or after you self-harm?
8. Do you think that you deserve to harm yourself?
9. Have you ever punished yourself in other ways, such as depriving yourself of anything that you need?
10. Has anyone else ever seriously harmed you?
11. What was your childhood like? Can you briefly describe it?
12. Have you experienced any form of neglect, assault, abuse, or trauma in your life?
13. If yes, who was this by?
14. If yes, do you think that this is connected to your current self-harm behaviours?
15. What is your family's usual response to your self-harm? Do you think they understand why you self-harm? Do you think that they give you enough support? Do you openly discuss it with them? Why/why not?
16. What is your treating clinician/therapist/counsellor's usual response to your self-harm? Do you think that they understand why you self-harm? Do you think that they give you enough support? Do you openly discuss it with them? Why/why not?
17. Have you ever required to attend the emergency department for medical treatment following an episode of self-harm? Do you think that they understood why you had self-harmed? Do you think that they gave you enough support? Did you openly discuss it with them? Why/why not?
18. Is there anything you think that your family needs to know about why you self-harm?
19. Is there anything you think that your treating clinician /therapist /counsellor needs to know about why you self-harm?
20. Do you agree that treating clinicians, emergency department staff, and families need education about why people self-harm? What do you think this will achieve?

Session two: Unstructured session; Word association			
Self-harm	Guilt	Punishment	Trauma
Family	Therapy	Support	Coping
Session three: Unstructured session			
Invitation to make any comments or ask questions; elaboration from earlier interviews			

Appendix B: Interview Transcripts for Patient 1, Lisa

Interview 1

What age do you think you were when you first used self-harm?

I remember going through this this morning actually…and it was when I went to [omit] clinic, which was my first start of all this. That was 2000, the year 2000 so…would have been 37. Probably 37.

So you don't recall any previous instances of any forms of self-harm or even self punishment?

No, no nothing like that. Probably I exercised a lot and probably took it out on myself that way. I worked 9 to 5, ran a house, kept really busy so…and I remember when I went to the [omit] clinic, I looked for things to do and asked them 'what can I do to help?' Used to wipe down windows, do this, do that because I just had to keep active. I was on the treadmill, I was on the go the whole time. But at that time I was there for 3 weeks and somehow I got out and bought a bottle of alcohol and ended up in a toilet somewhere and started cutting with the lid of the alcohol, I started cutting my wrist. And that was the first time of self-harm.

So you found it difficult to keep busy in that type of environment then?

No, they always gave something to do. They allowed me to sort of clean and do things that I was used to doing at home. So I did keep busy and that, but at the same time I received ECT treatment in that 3 weeks and that played an effect on me.

With confusion do you mean?

Yeah, forgetfulness, and it had a physical effect on me. I remember having to stop it because I had the shakes and wasn't coping with it very well at that time so…they ended up stopping the ECT treatment. That was my memory of what was happening.

Do you recall any particular thoughts on your mind at that particular time when…

Oh naturally I was worried about (daughter) because she was only 2, and (husband). Being sent away for 3 weeks was a really big thing. The family came and visited…that was really good, they were supportive. And then things changed at the end of the 3 weeks…well why it ended was I felt like self-harming more, and I explained that to the psychiatrist that was there at the time that I had these thoughts of self-harming and that's where it was all starting to head. They felt they couldn't deal with that…they were a different clinic…it was detox, um…just getting your life back on track because I think that…it was a really nice place and everything and they took on only a certain number of patients and that was it. You were specially cared for and that but I got to the stage at the end of the 3 weeks that something was changing and I wanted to self-harm…I had thoughts of self-harm and I didn't know how to go about it or whatever but the thoughts were there…and they sent me back to (town) and to psych services.

So your family were aware of that first episode of cutting?

Um...I am not sure if they know about that …I'm sure they finally did but there was no open discussion from the family about it. I think it was only very superficial but it was the start.

What age do you think you were when other people realised that you were self-harming?

Would have been when I was back here…when I was about…when (daughter) was about 3 things were really happening then…so 2001…about a year later.

Was there any periods of self-harming between the first episode and when the family finally found out?

I can't remember...I remember going to psych services back here in (town) and it was shock…and then I don't know how long after that that I really started cutting. I can remember being in…I was in for a certain time and I got a mirror from my beauty case and started cutting…and cut my wrist pretty badly. But I can't remember how long that was.

What was your family's response initially when they first found out?

Oh they were pretty worried…yeah

Was it openly discussed though?

No. It was just actually…there were times when I went back home that I started cutting too…I can't remember when that was…I think I transferred here from [town] and then I am not sure if I was ok here and then they let me home; I started cutting at home. Then things got out of hand and they brought me back in here and I cut and everything…I think that might have been what happened. Trying to think…I think I had a certain time in here and they let me home but then I started cutting at home.

Was it superficial?

No, I needed to have stitches. (Husband) would have to bring me in and get the stitches done. I would be in a bit of shock…that I had done it. And we would get through that and then I think that it came to the stage that I needed to come back in to psych services and spend time in here and then I would trying anything…I had my beauty case, and I had glass in there, so I broke that and I was trying anything I could to cut.

Why do you think you were cutting at that stage?

It just got to a point and I couldn't sort of stop it…like it was…it was giving me…giving me relief.

So at the time of cutting, you would be highly distressed and almost agitated?

Oh yeah, very agitated. And stressed and that sort of thing…and depressed and…that sort of thing…and by cutting, it…I felt like I was losing control, so I would cut and then felt like I had control.

So that was your way of stopping that episode of agitation? So you could control the agitation that way?

Mmmm….even though it meant going and getting stitches and suffering the consequences afterwards but it was my way of seeing that I had control and…and I had to do it, it was my relief. Well, I had to cut and I know there was one time I had to see (clinician) from the MST team, and I had an interview with him and, you know (daughter) was still really little…I didn't want to…it was a review or something, I didn't want to go to it so I cut, so I ended up in hospital…had to have stitches, and that sort of thing

Did you do that in those instances so you did not have to go?

Yeah, didn't have to go to the review, yeah…

Because of the distress associated with…?

Yeah, it was just one of those things that I did. I still remember it and you know, I can remember the knife that I used…and everything and…

Predominately, to self-harm you have cut. But you have tried other methods along the way?

Yeah, like I mean I have been through sessions with you…relaxation and that sort of thing. Tried keeping busy…tried talking with professionals and that sort of thing…but ultimately it's still there in my system…so, it's a matter of time heals I suppose and accepting what's going on in your life, what's happening so…

In terms of the self-harm you have also tried overdose with medication?

Yeah, yeah

Was that a self-harming thing or more a suicide attempt?

No, that was …never thought of it as suicide, but trying to get through…not even self-harming, just trying to get me through the day, sort of thing, so the times that I took the medication and that sort of thing I thought this is making me feel better that…I don't need to use alcohol, (husband) is not going to know, but of course it had its effect on me

So the overdosing was more of an escape? To block out whatever was going on?

Yeah, yeah, it was just my way of coping with day to day life…getting through the day…if you could get through the day using medications that would be good. I had access to them, and I did that so...but some of them didn't have a good effect on me and I suffered the consequences of that. And then it got to the stage where (husband) locked away them medications so that I could only have…he had the key to the lock and that, and that was good I felt safer with that. But it was the same as money with alcohol…you know, if I need alcohol to get me through, he would only give me so many dollars and that would be it. So, you just…even though you are working, earning a wage and everything like that, you get a few dollars…but whenever I got the chance I would buy alcohol. That was my way of getting through.

You have also had some periods of burning yourself?

I have done that…I burnt myself on the oven and everything like that but that was a natural thing…but when I was at (CCU) I had a night of drinking and had gone up the bush, not knowing where I was really…hurt my leg and came back and they had to dress it and all that stuff. They thought that I had burnt it…I said no I haven't because I hadn't, but then that gave me the idea and yeah…I did put some burns into it as well…with hot, boiling water, and…don't know why, I just had to do it…they gave me the idea so I had to do it. Initially I rub, I don't know I found…where I ended up, I found rocks and that sort of thing and I rubbed them into my leg until it bled…self-harming, self-harming sort of thing…

Was it a punishment thing or a release?

At the time, like when I felt like I had done a good enough job, I was happy to leave it and get back. I just wanted to get back to (CCU) then. But when they saw my leg…they wondered what was going on, and that sort of thing…I had just; when they said that I had burnt it, and I said I hadn't, you know, I knew I hadn't…

Do you then use it because they accused you of using it?

Yeah, yeah. I guess that's why I ended up burning myself with it as well, because…I did it with the iron as well…yeah, because they accused me of that, so it was like a "I'll get back and you and I'll do it", you know?

So, if you are going to accuse me of it, I am going to do it anyway?

Yeah. They weren't prepared to believe me when I said that it wasn't a burn.

So there have been the cutting, the burning, the overdosing...

I jumped off a bridge...in [omit] street.

Was that a suicide attempt?

I don't know, I was very distressed. I don't think it mattered at the time. I had drunk a bottle of port. Which gave me the courage to sort of do it.

Is there often that anxiety before you are going to do it and sometimes the alcohol...

Oh yeah...I had an argument and all that sort of thing. That was it, I just headed off. And ended up climbing the bridge, thought that this is what I wanted to do. I have never considered it before...it was just that one off. I did my ankle on it a bit...I don't know how I didn't hurt myself more so...I guess I went to not the deeper end of it...sort of the side of it. Still it was a fair drop and yeah, I was prepared to jump off it.

Was there that feeling that (husband) did not understand how distressed you were?

Yeah, he used to get angry with me...he couldn't understand why I was drinking or why I was like I was. He couldn't understand. And he has admitted now that he still doesn't understand...but he doesn't get so angry. He realises there is an illness there, I guess I was someone who always kept fit and worked, around the house. I did everything and then all of a sudden, I...well probably not all of a sudden, I just fell in a heap.

Were there any other forms of self-harm that you tried?

When I was living in the flat in [omit] street before I went into (rehabilitation unit), 2 years ago, I one night laid on the railway tracks. And I reckon I laid there for what seemed like hours. Just waiting for a train to come...I just wanted the train to come. And that was it.

Was that more a suicide attempt though?

Yeah, it was, yeah. I was...it was the night before mother's day. And I just couldn't handle mother's day being like I was, you know around (daughter).

Was there a lot of guilt?

Yeah, and I just couldn't handle the thought of mother's day and that...the way I had turned out. Yeah, I laid on the tracks. I lost my bag that night. So I had no key to get in. I had to go in next door and ring my sister. I was dirty and I had been on the railway tracks. I was just a mess and she just came. She gave me a bit of money and that and the next day I got a phone call from the police station. Someone had handed in my bag and everything was in it....you just couldn't credit...everything was there. I didn't have much money in the wallet but all the cards and everything was in it....everything. It was such a relief. That was a bit of a turning point...to think that somebody had done that. But I went through a really low point at that time. I was prepared to...to just go.

And often that can be a commonly held myth that if you self-harm, you are not going to kill yourself, but lots of people that self-harm do have those times where they do attempt suicide. It is not about self-harm, it is an actual suicide attempt.

There was a time when I was in psych services, in the high dependency area, and I had shoelaces still. And I tied the shoelaces and tied them onto the trap...and I was prepared to choke myself. And I had the marks around (neck). The only thing really that stopped me basically was that I accidentally hit the button, which sent them (staff) coming in. But at that time I already had the rope burn...from string around my neck. Again, I was prepared to go.

What sort of circumstances in general led you to self-harm? What sort of events would trigger that need in you or release to self-harm?

Guilt.

Guilt over what sort of things?

Being sent to (clinic) and not being there to see my daughter and husband. And then, things that happened in the past which we hit on…with my right arm…Dad. It would just happen anytime. I think that I was feeling low, I think I was feeling depressed lots of the time. When I was feeling really low I would do it…and because things would start coming back…between dad and my life. What was happening and my guilt, it would all start coming into one. I would self-harm to think that well I deserve this, you know.

So would you store it up and as you mood got low, and that would be the last straw?

Yeah.

Could that just be a small insignificant event?

Oh, even if (husband) and I argued, I felt guilty. It was my fault. You know, it's because of my drinking and that sort of thing.

But would there be more underneath all that?

Mmmm. Well it was everything else coming as well. It was all stored up and I needed to let it out. About dad, about my guilt with things…my feelings…my relationship with mum…everything was just…not being there with (husband and daughter). Not being there as the mum each day…getting her ready for school. Seeing her to bed of a night. Cooking tea, looking after the house, looking after (husband)…and I still have that. That is still there. I go around there every Sunday and I try to do what I can even though (daughter) wants me to play, and I would say look I will just fold this washing for daddy, get the washing in for daddy, or do the dishes you know. And she doesn't want me to because she wants me to play – but we have all day playing anyway. But I will say to her, look I have to help daddy a bit too. Their life…at least I am contributing something…looking after her as well…it goes towards helping her as well and that…it is just my way of doing things…(husband) and I are getting along really well, we have accepted a lot of what has happened now. And we want to keep things amenable. We want to do things as a family for (daughter's) sake and that. And we have to be amicable between each other and I have got no animosity towards him. For what he is doing, or what he has done. I just have to put my best foot forward and do what I can. Try and keep up…I can't financially and that kind of thing I can't. I can do the best I can.

Overall, when you were self-harming, it was more a release strategy or a punishment?

Punishment. From when I was young, if I did something wrong I was punished. So, I guess as an adult I feel that I have to be punished…for doing what I felt was wrong and doing what I did was wrong, you know that I felt was wrong.

Connecting those two ideas together there, would you feel guilty, and then think you need to be punished?

Yeah.

With the guilt came that low mood and agitation because you felt really bad, and then of course the cutting would be a release because you were punished?

Yeah, like I would punish myself.

Is that where that release comes from because you have got what you deserved and now it is a fresh start?

Yeah, it is also a bit of a mystery. When I self-harm, I go into like a tunnel vision…it is like a tunnel vision…and you don't see outside of it, or the consequences, or…you can't see outside of it. It is tunnel vision and this is one thing…you have to do; until you do it you won't relax…you just have to do it. It is a shut down. It is like everything else is blacked out.

It happened there a few weeks ago…I went into the tunnel vision, and I just didn't see any consequences or anything, I just went into shutdown mode and did it.

You cut your leg in that instance?

Yeah. Which I have never done before. I guess now that I have had my skin graft on my arm.

Given that it usually was your arm, do you think that you thought that I can't do this again to my arm, I need to cut somewhere else?

Mmmm. Yeah, I couldn't do it to my arm but I had to do it, and I chose the top of my leg…and I needed to get staples and stitches and that sort of thing.

Do you remember what triggered that?

I think that it has just been all the…well, (husband) and I have been sorting out a lot of the stuff. Also, just shifting out of (rehabilitation unit) and going into a place of my own and all of a sudden I am responsible for this, and getting used to that. Just my whole life, so…lots of change. I had stressful times with (husband)…he wasn't really good with me. But the last 3 weeks or so he has been really good and we have been actually able to talk and that, so…which is wonderful.

Do you think that there is more empathy there?

Yeah, he admitted on Sunday…I don't blame you for what has happened. But he said he doesn't understand it. I don't understand why you did what you did, or why you do what you do…I don't understand but…he still cares for me and that made a big difference.

Does it help you more with him to talk directly about it?

Yeah, I prefer to talk about it. I am at that stage where I want to talk about it, and be open about it.

Initially the family would not have known what to do or what to say?

No, and they still don't know about this recent episode. I just don't want them to know. I am hoping that just was a one off thing that happened months later. I think that it was just the stress of moving.

It may also be a sign that you need to remain vigilant about the chance that it may still be there as a coping strategy?

Yeah, so it made me aware that this is still possible and that night I…I had this big mirror in the bedroom, it was massive. I smashed into it and broke it; all the sharp bits. I obviously cut my leg with the glass. But the bits that were there…I don't know how I didn't cut myself to bits. The way it was broken.

That shows you that there is some sort of awareness of control in you with regard to the self-harming?

Well, now…that night, I could have cut myself to bits. I could have, and it didn't happen. My tracksuit pants were all cut in different places and my jumper and everything…and yet I only had a few cuts up here (top of leg) where I had cut myself. I could have gone head first into that. And you know, cut myself to bits. I don't know how that just didn't happen and I am thankful for that…it gave me a scare.

Was the thought there to break the mirror and cut, or you broke the mirror and then cut?

I was drunk and I obviously fell into it. And there was little shard bit there, and big shard bits. It was just…I had to clean it up and that sort of thing. I am glad it is gone now but it gave me a scare….that I could have cut myself to bits. I easily could have.

It does sound as if, as you said it has been months since you did it, it doesn't sound like a normal cutting episode?

I don't know why, I think that as I said, it was the shifting…getting used to the idea of not being with (husband and daughter) and being on my own…this is reality and that sort of thing. And it all just got to me; I turned back to that type release/guilt…not being there with (husband and daughter) and being a family and being a mum and a wife and a daughter and all that sort of thing…it just all got to me. I have had friends that are not well, and that has put stress on me as well.

There are definitely stressors there?

Yeah, so you are trying to deal with the whole lot, and I just can't believe I cut myself like I did. But it was a warning sign, which is a good thing I think, because when you have been warned like that you are more wary and scared of it…I really have to watch myself, and as (case worker) says, you don't intentionally want to die but it may happen by accident because of the things I do. I could have easily cut an artery that night…I need to be a bit more wary of what my actions are now.

The understanding that I have seen from you today is remarkable. You have been very good at putting things together, having that conscious awareness there that it could happen, and 'I am aware that it could happen', you understanding is remarkable.

I have come to understand a lot of things. Sometimes it doesn't go into practice but I am trying to put it into practice, and put it into perspective.

We have talked about you hurting yourself, but now I want to talk about others hurting you in your life. Who in your lifetime has seriously hurt you?

Well dad. Sexual abuse and that. I think mum, emotionally…like there were 4 children, and I always got blamed for everything. And mum couldn't talk to me like mother and daughter…we never had that. And when it came time to talk about your periods and that sort of thing, she very bluntly put things to me in the kitchen, took 5 minutes and that was it. When the time did come, I couldn't approach her and I approached by sister. I said, what is happening here? I am bleeding. You know, so I couldn't approach mum about that.

Was she more approachable to your brother and sisters?

Yeah, to my sisters…especially. And I never got pain killers, or Panadol or anything to help with the pain, and the stress of what was happening with dad affected the way my periods were…like I would be down the street and nearly faint from the pain. I was too scared to ask for Panadol and that sort of thing.

Would your dad's abuse reduce during the time you had your period, or would it not matter to him?

Oh no, it wouldn't matter to him. It used to just happen each week, there was a set time, especially the [omit] night when mum was at table tennis, brother at cubs, sisters were out…one may have been married then.

Do you think that your mum didn't acknowledge or give you any support, and that was obviously a difficult time with the pain, do you think you dad should have…?

No, I think he only had one thing in mind. And I was a girl growing up and maturing and a virgin and obviously that is what men like…that is what I get the impression of.

That happened over many years?

Yeah, I reckon up till I was about 16, from when I was at least 10…about 6 to 7 years. It was at different times, not just the Thursday night, it was whenever he could, get me down to the wood shed…touching…show himself at different times. When mum was at hospital I was in bed and had a bad night; I went up to his room and dad called me into the bed, and he touched me.

Can you see how about of those could be related to the self-harm?

I don't really know…it is still a bit of a mystery how the self-harm came into it. Because I can remember before all that happened…I would cut myself and think 'argh! Oh now I have cut myself'…it was terrible. So I don't know…like it was self punishment that way I see it, it happened more with my time away from (daughter and husband). I would punish myself for having done that to them. But I don't know how it happened…why cutting, why not something else? But then, when I think about it, when we were young, we were always belted and everything, used to get the strap all the time…one of those things.

If you have a look at, as you said, you mum was someone that had the household running in a certain way, and she was very cold towards yourself, can you see or relate that in any way to the guilt that you experience when you are away from (daughter or husband)?

Oh yeah, like all that…and it still goes through my head! Mum sort of, every now and again gives a little hint on things…not as bad, but still gives a little hint on things. I know that that I am trying to work towards that trust to have (daughter) a little bit more, overnight or whatever. (Husband) has expressed that he wants to work a bit more on a work night so it would give him a relief, that I could have (daughter) and he could go to work. And I could have her a bit the next day and he could have a sleep in…and it would be great. That is what we are going to try to work towards.

So do you think that felt guilt while you were away in [omit], or in hospital or (rehabilitation unit), and you weren't there to provide and do all the washing, and that was connected in some way to the way your mother raised you…that that was what the mother was there to do. There might have been the anger there that you weren't going to be there to be the mother to your daughter?

Yeah, like I can see that…no actually it is different because I always say to (daughter), you know, I love you and I mean it with all my heart, I give her butterfly kisses and we hug and cuddle and that sort of thing…I call her darling…never had that with mum. So I can see a lot of differences with what I have done with (daughter) even though I am not there all the time…but when I am there is that difference there.

Do you see the self-harming more related to what happened with your dad?

With dad, and with I think, a lot of build up of stress over the years. Because I felt I wasn't being treated fairly by mum. I would ask dad at one stage 'why does mum hate me?'…that is how I felt; that mum hated me.

Did he console you?

He just tried to explain that she is just under a lot of stress…

Did he say 'no she doesn't hate you?'?

No, no. He knew she treated me differently as well. And that is why I felt that what mum couldn't provide, he provided. That is why I felt the sexual behaviour with him was a natural thing…I thought that was a learning about sex and a natural affection and that sort of thing. Like I had no idea. I was so naïve. I am still naïve a lot till this day…even though I have had a child. Before I teach (daughter) about things, I am going to have to read up and get books and things; and go through it with her. She will probably know more than I do! I would like to get her books and go through that together with her and that sort of thing.

Almost correcting what should have been done?

Mmmm. I still remember with mum. One day we were doing the dishes and I was drying, and she was washing I think. And she told me about bleeding, and I would have to get padding, and don't have a bath, have a shower. You know, that was about it. Mmmm.

What was your family's response to your self-harm when they found out?

I mean they were good with me at first. I think that everything has happened…like they didn't understand it but they were there for me, sort of thing.

At that time they were giving you support?

Mmmm. But as time went on and it kept happening, it sort of…the love wore off.

They became frustrated by it?

Yeah. They weren't accepting of it. Like now, mum gets very angry…she lets you know.

Is it openly discussed with your mum?

No.

With husband?

Well we haven't really had the chance to talk about it because (daughter) has been around. We don't talk about that sort of thing in front of (daughter). And I certainly haven't let them know about this last instance. They seem to think that I have had the skin graft done…mum was in hospital every day, like I was in there for 5 days, and mum was in there every day visiting. It was a different thing…I hadn't done it myself. It was a positive move that I had made. But she could accept that you know.

So perhaps the way she responded in the past was the way she was trying to stop you from keeping on doing it? She would get anger and tell you off…

And thinking that that was going to pull me into line. It doesn't. When the time comes, you have this tunnel vision and you just don't see outside of it. You just have…this is just what is going to happen, there is no way out of it.

Do you think that if your family had an understanding of that tunnel vision that that would be helpful for them?

I don't know, I don't know if…I don't discuss that.

Do you think it would be helpful?

Yeah, yeah, like I have spoken to someone else who cuts up a bit and she said the same thing; it just happened to her in the past couple of days…she cut up a little bit; it is only superficial but she gets the tunnel vision and can't see outside of that. It is something that happens…that is a really major thing that I wish people could understand. Like, as much as you have a daughter, or a husband, you are trying to get back to or whatever, your family, your life, your job and everything; but you can't see outside that tunnel vision and it just hits like a…this thing that you just…the end result is that you are going to cut and that is where it is; there is nothing outside of it.

What do you think reduced the tunnel vision then? As you said, the last incident a few weeks ago was the first in a number of months, what has reduced that?

Just um, I have just had to pull it together. Knowing that I was going to be moving out and living on my own. Which is scary.

Do you think the understanding of it you have developed has helped?

Yeah, also like when we spoke of control. That cutting is not control; it is a loss of control. I have learnt that that is a really important part. I have had to consider that and in a way…to bring something positive out…it is not about what happened a few weeks ago, as it made me realise that I am still vulnerable to cutting and that sort of thing, if things get to me too much it can still happen…just like that…and my life is in danger or whatever. It is a reality check I suppose. Overall, I am doing ok. I keep getting positive feedback from (case worker) and I am seeing (clinician) this afternoon about the alcohol, which will be really good. I am trying to put in a few plans myself as well. I am looking forward to that. Trying to get my life back on track.

Interview 2

Any thoughts from last week?

I didn't pull up too well...I ended up ringing [case worker] at 4.30pm. We spoke and...just I drank and...a lot of things coming back to me...and I have had strange dreams...

Do you think that is why you went home and drank? To stop the thoughts?

Yeah...yeah...you know, I have had really strange dreams...a lot of things to do with family and that sort of thing...but I didn't cut or anything like that though.

Do you think it is from talking about family or self-harm that has raised these issues?

Look it is probably to do with both...the self-harm definitely comes into family, that I'm cut off from them and that sort of thing...so when I have self-harmed, I don't see my family. It interrupts that sort of thing...I would say it was a bit of both but also wanting to be part of family again...that is really important to me.

So you don't feel the same sense of family than perhaps you were used to years ago?

No ,.. like family has always been important...they're a stable part of your life. I feel like I need that now...living out in the community again in a flat. Trying to make a go of it...I feel like the family are a really important part of my life, you know. I've got friends but a couple of my friends have been through the system and that, and they have their ups and downs and that sort of thing...I've got to try to be strong for them but I need my family for that stability for that everyday thing...a normal day. Normality. To me, it is important...I want to get back to normality.

A lot of people, family, clinicians, don't like to talk about self-harm to the patient because they feel that it can cause it. What do you think of that idea?

We have spoken about different things last week and I didn't self-harm. I think that I am really getting over that now. Probably the odd occasion it will happen a bit...like two or three weeks ago. But to me, it is one of those things that I have overcome. I see it as more as a problem now...it causes grief. You get cut from your family, you end up in the acute unit, I don't want to end up there...to me it is not viable. You just don't want to do it because of all these things. There are consequences of cutting now.

By talking about the self-harm you have come to that realisation? You have had therapy and case management where the self-harming was a focus and openly discussed. If you had not have had that, do you think...

Oh, I would still be doing it. If no one...if I hadn't have had the treatment that I have had, I don't know where I would be at this stage. All the help and everything I have had.

There is always that concern with people that if we talk about it, it is going to happen.

No, no, I am at that stage now...before it might have but I am at that stage where I am better to talk about it and have that control. That has been happening for a few months now. It has gradually come together. It was only in the last couple of sessions that we had that it sort of came together.

That idea that instead of using cutting to regain control, which is what you always thought that it was, it was actually the opposite?

Yeah, yeah…when I cut those three weeks ago or whatever it was, I realised that I lost control and that sort of thing. I am concentrated very much on having that control back…it is control and relearning coping skills I suppose.

Do you think that there has been an increase in your drinking to cope?

Look I have certainly been drinking heavily and that. And I am getting some help with that at the moment…that is the next step. Learnt not to cut now…control and that sort of thing…the next step is the drinking. To cut that down and certainly have control over that. That is my next step.

So you can see some parallels between that idea of cutting to control, although it was a loss of control, and the drinking...at the moment you are using it to control feelings?

Yeah, like I want to shut up a lot of my life…I don't want to think about it. Even now, with my daughter, I miss her a lot. I have a full day on Sunday with her but it's now Monday…and I have a week without seeing her and be able to get back to that normality. It all comes back to that normality…that family life. I spoke before with my family and that…getting back to everyday living and normality. I feel like I have been out of that for so long.

If I said to you the word 'family', what sort of things come to mind?

Love, normality, everyday people…my family are normal people. My brother is doing well. They're just hard working…and that love.

It sounds like a connectedness idea…you need them to feel connected?

Yeah, which you know they haven't come around to see me at the flat yet though. But I know they are busy and work and have families and have their lives. I have to make the effort to ring them and just catch up with them, and it makes me feel really good when I actually do. It is like…I just want to get back out there and be an everyday person. I don't feel like that at the moment. I just want to feel like a normal everyday person. I know that I can function like that but then I have my downfalls where I can be up one day, I'll be really positive and I'll do all this, and then the next day I can be really down. And everything goes wrong and I fall in a heap…and I drink too much. Why I don't know. I am still sort of fighting that instability…there is instability, something not quite right still. I am still fighting the ups and downs.

If I gave you another word...what about 'support'?

Yeah, I get that from [case workers]…but sometimes I think that because all my life I have relied on someone, who was going to get me through…like parents, and then [husband] took over the role, and I still find it hard to come to terms with being independent. And rely on myself. And I am battling with that…it is hard. And I think the support…yeah, like if I had support I would rely on that support and I would become independent. So, at this stage, it is a good thing that I am trying to work through this. I'll get there. I will get there.

What about 'guilt'?

I have a lot of guilt over a lot of things. Guilt now is if I missed access on Sunday or something like that…the guilt is overwhelming. I get palpitations, can't sleep properly…that sort of thing. It's a really big thing. I get guilt over something, I suffer for it. No matter how small it is or how big it is, it doesn't matter. I get really stressed over it.

Is it a common experience for you?

No, I don't have a lot of guilt these days. Things have been going really well. Access has been going really well. Because I have tried to turn my life around and put a plan into place. And prepare myself for Sunday. I still…to think that I have to do that, to even plan and put a plan into place for Sunday you know, to see my daughter and that. I have to do that. It is something that I have to do. A bit weird when you think about it. Should just happen naturally but I have to prepare myself for it.

It would take a lot of energy from you to have access with your daughter? It is not just showing up, there is a lot of planning to do?

Yeah, like Saturday I prefer not to do anything, unless I catch up with a girlfriend for coffee. That sort of thing but basically go to bed early, get up early and get going, and walk up there…it is a fair way, and just sort of prepare myself mentally for it, you know. Because I want to be at my best for her. I can do at least that…yeah it is hard.

What is I said 'punishment'?

I don't punish myself now, as in self-harm and that sort of thing, but I think that in certain ways it still happens. Like Tuesday was a really bad day, everything happened on Tuesday…and I think that I got punished enough…I don't know what for but it was just a bad day and everything went wrong and I feel that I am getting punished in other ways. That might be a bit strange, sound a bit strange, but I think that I get punished in lots of other ways. Punishment is in a lot of ways, being in my flat, not being with my family and that, being a wife and a mother. I think that is punishment enough.

So you are no longer punishing yourself with the self-harming but do you feel that in your life there is enough instances of punishment around you?

I feel like I sit there of a night and think 'why am I here', 'what is going on', 'why is this happening', 'what is going to happen in the future', that sort of thing. I think that that is punishment in itself. When you just want to be there, you just want to have a clean house, and cook tea, [daughter] comes home from school and be there for her, or go and pick her up from school. Be there for her…I am not going to experience that and I think that that is punishment enough in itself. Because it is something that I always wanted to do. It has all gone wrong. When I think about it now, and have to make a new life myself now, trying to have that confidence…I find it hard to have that confidence to get back out there again.

Do you see that you are rebuilding your life or that you are modifying your life?

No I have to rebuild my life. I have to rebuild it and get on with it. Try and find work. Try to find somewhere better to live, and have some money. Money has been tight, under state trustees, it has been tight. It is really hard. And I sort of think that I have worked for many years, and I have nothing for it. Nothing to show for it. I have to rebuild my life and to, I think with me, and [husband] show that I am trustworthy. I can achieve and I am not just a hopeless case…it is all very well to just go around there on Sunday and play with [daughter] all day; I try and do dishes, and do this and do that, sort of help out where I can. I just need a job to prove that I am able to do something and that I am not just on a pension and that is it. To prove to [daughter] that mummy can work, and that daddy works, mum can work as well.

What about if I said the word 'therapy'?

Been there. Done that. I think that I have had that much therapy over the years, I probably have got to the stage where there is nothing more that can help me, I have to help myself.

Is it a positive thing or has it been a negative?

Yeah, certainly when we worked with each other, that was a big change in my life. It changed my cutting. Working though family situations and that sort of thing. It helped a lot, as I said, I have been there and done that…now it is time to help myself. I just know in myself that I need to help myself.

What if I said 'trauma' then?

My trauma now is trying to get through day to day. It is not about what happened with dad, or anything like that. It is getting through day by day. Sometimes I wake up in the morning and I think that 'please god, help me get through the day', just get me through. I have days like that. Trauma to me now is actually getting through day by day, trying to achieve something. As I said, I don't think it is what happened with dad, it is just getting through day by day and if I can achieve something positive, that is really good. I feel good at the end of the day. Sometimes I don't. To me that is trauma.

What about 'self-harm'?

Knife, yeah I can picture a serrated knife. Cutting something; bleeding; cut in deeply. But again that is something that I am trying to control, and that is just not happening anymore…I just can't allow it to happen anymore.

It is there but you try to control it?

Yeah, like it is there. I have thoughts like just then when you said it…I can just picture a knife and a serrated edge and really cutting deep with it but I can't allow that to happen anymore. Look I am going to probably still have like three weeks ago with my leg…mishaps…definitely going to have them once in a while but its dulling on me. It is a dying thing…I don't want it to happen anymore.

So the drive to do it is not as strong as it used to be?

No. no, only once in a blue moon it happens still but no, no, no I don't want that anymore. It is not part of my life.

What about if I said 'coping'?

I am coping. Yeah, got back out there in the community and living in a flat…trying to be independent. Coping…I have troubles with that like I don't cope as well as I could. But I am getting there…I keep the place clean, do my washing, shopping and all that sort of thing but I do have problems there…drinking, I fall in a heap sometimes with it and I don't cope as well.

I just want to finish up talking about how different people over the time have responded to your self-harm. What you think different people might need to know about self-harm, to provide you with the sort of support that you said you need. If we start with your case manager, therapist, counsellor, and clinician – what is their usual response to your self-harming?

I end up in the acute unit. My family don't have anything to do with me – she might ring but she is angry with me.

We will come back to family in a moment. In terms of mental health workers, what is their response when you self-harm? Things that they might say to you, how they behave?

I have had experiences where I have had to go into emergency and that. I have had different doctors or nurse give me the short shift.

What do you mean by short shift?

Rude, and 'oh, she's done it again'

Have you heard them say that?

No, but they sort of just wipe me. "oh yeah, we'll just suture it' or 'not suture it', or whatever and then send me over to the acute unit. But very arrogant and rude in their response to me. And I can understand that because they have more important people there, more urgent clients there, but I mean overall I have had good response…when I was at [rehabilitation unit] they were great, good response from them. Got me to emergency if I needed to go and that sort of thing.

Do you think that as far as mental health clinicians go, they have understood you?

Not really, I think that they are a bit scared by it.

So you sense some anxiety in them?

Like I know that at [rehabilitation unit] when I cut seriously a couple of times, it took sort of all four of them to work on me, or treat, or work on me. I felt they were anxious and really didn't know what was happening. And even when I cut superficially, just they would come in and find me cutting, there was anxiety there.

What do you think that anxiety is about?

I think that seeing blood and how far I have gone…not really knowing me, how far have I gone? It does cause concern for people who do not understand self-harm. You know yourself how far you have gone, although a couple of times this year I had gone a bit far. But you can't blame them for not understanding just how far you have gone or why it is happening; they don't understand why you are doing it. For me it was probably guilt, concerns and loss things building up and I would just go and do it?

Did any of them ask you why to try to understand?

No. No I have never had that.

Do you think that would have been useful? Would you have been able to explain that to them?

I don't know if I might have been able to explain that to them but it may have been useful instead of 'what have you done?' you have to explain that you have cut yourself and that sort of thing and blah blah blah.

So you have never had something say 'oh my god you have cut, what is wrong?'

Yeah, no they don't. No you never get 'why?' or 'what's happened?' or anything like that.

Is that with emergency as well?

Yeah, yeah.

I know with emergency there have been different techniques in trying to stop you from self-harming. Plaster…leave the wound open. What do you think about those sort of strategies?

It doesn't work because like I know when I would just get out of plaster, I would go and cut again. It was just that relief…I couldn't get the plaster off, and I tried. No that sort of thing doesn't work…it has got to come from within yourself. You have to accept what is happening and stop yourself; which is what is happening with me at the moment, trying to really stop myself, and I am trying. You just can't keep living the life of cutting up like that. And with living independently, out on your own…if I cut to the bone, like I did at [rehabilitation unit], it just bled and bled and bled. I went through towel after towel after towel. I don't know where I would have ended up.

If you think of any positive experiences that you have got from mental health workers, what sort of thing has been useful or positive for you with regard to the self-harm?

Just I think having the workers there was the main thing. I know at [rehabilitation unit] when I self-harmed, they rang the police and ambulance…rather than going up on my own, there was someone with me. They would hold me back. I think that getting some sort of positive feedback from them is an important thing.

Like, 'look, you have been doing really well'?

Yeah, yeah. Just something, a positive bit of feedback from them.

You didn't mind that they had to restrain you?

No, no. because I could have ended up anywhere and usually I had been drinking and didn't have all my thoughts with me. I could have ended up in a serious situation. I could have crossed the road and got run over you know.

At the time though, did it make you angry?

Oh yeah, yeah. Because I wanted to go and do my own thing. I had only one thing in mind and that was cutting...and being on my own and wanting to just so that...expressed myself in that way. I didn't want workers around, I didn't want to be held back. I just wanted to do my own thing.

What about being shackled in E.D?

Sometimes I think that is unnecessary but I leave that up to them, they know what they are doing but I think there was times that I had calmed down and accepted the situation that I was in and, which I had cut and in E.D., that they could have taken them off. And they wouldn't.

Did you feel punished by them during those sort of episodes?

I felt 'this is not right' and I couldn't expressed myself enough to say 'look take them off because I am alright, I have settled down'. It was a different scenario with them. They wouldn't do that, and I couldn't express myself enough to say that I was ok.

What do you think that created that inability to express yourself? Because you were highly emotional at the time?

Oh look it was dreadful...emotion...the whole lot. There was always something behind why I cut and why I do what I do. And it is a matter of knowing what or why I have done it, and I have to know myself now why I do what I do.

Did you ever get the comments that you were just doing it for attention?

No, no. it wasn't anything like that. No I can't remember if I had ever heard that.

Was there any strategies or techniques used by E.D. that you found particularly useful?

I think that just getting that service that you need, like sutures, instead of getting 'oh no I am not going to suture that'. Like I have had different doctors say 'no we are not suturing' and then you get other doctors say 'yeah, I will fix this'.

Why do you think they would not suture then?

Because I think that I was coming in so often and I was coming in so many times that they couldn't understand why.

Do you see that as a punishment then... 'well we will leave your arm open then'?

Yeah, yeah. And I also probably expected it from them. I thought that they are going to be sort of...can't be bothered with me, like 'she's self-harmed and we have another person out there that has had a car accident' you know, so you are not worthy.

That must be really hard though, to go into a service that is to treat everybody and to be made that you are not worthy?

Oh yeah, and it happened numerous times. And I have had the nursing staff in there from [rehabilitation unit] and they have sat there with me and thought that the doctor and nurse were really rude to me. And they said afterwards, you know 'they were really rude'. They felt awful sitting there like that. It was just like, never mind how I felt.

So you see a lack of understanding in both mental health workers and E.D. staff but with E.D., they would react differently to you?

Yeah, I think that they would really benefit from having somewhere over there, I heard this yesterday about [city], they have got a special section for mental health patients and they have a worker on board and nurse, and they specifically work with people that have done what I have done in the past. I think that that would really benefit here.

So if you had some specially trained in mental health, like [rehabilitation unit] staff that was working out of E.D. you would find that quite useful?

Yeah, yeah. Just someone that would understand mental health and why someone has self-harmed. Because they don't understand that over there, they don't. They get quite annoyed by us, 'you are a nuisance'.

Do you think that anytime it might have been useful to sit down with staff there and say 'look, I am going to be doing this, but I am working on this. If I come in, this is perhaps how to work with me'?

There was a registrar that kept coming, he was very arrogant and I explained to him that I am trying not to do this. I am trying not to, but he was very rude and arrogant and didn't have any understand of it. I don't ever want to see him again. There needs to be a special section cordoned off for mental health.

In particular, as you know I am putting together this education package together for emergency staff and mental health clinicians, what do you think they need to know about why people self-harm?

They will never understand because being a patient yourself, you do not understand yourself why you do it. You get this tunnel vision; you cut yourself off, because of stressors in life bring it on. That is the only way that I can explain it is that you get so many things in your life and stressors that you cannot deal with, and no matter how small or big they are, you get a tunnel vision…I have spoken to someone else, a friend of mine who does the same thing and she also said she gets this tunnel thing. You just can't see outside. You are just going to do it and that is it. It is the only relief. And whether it is a build up of guilt from over the past, or of things you have done recently, or whatever, you just cannot help it. The thing is you not only physically hurt yourself, but mentally you are hurting. There is a lot of hurt there.

I always conceptualise self-harming, as a lot of people call it attention seeking, and I say well of course it is attention seeking because the behaviour or the act of the self-harm indicates that there is distress there. It is an indication of distress; you need to find out what the cause of distress is rather than judge, not work on the behavioural level, you need to understand what has caused it.

There is distress, there is something that causes…like I said there is guilt or distress in your life that has happened that you go into this sort of almost like a zombie state. You know you can't see outside, you don't think of consequences, you don't think of anything else you just go ahead and do what you have to do. And for some reason, it is self-harm because you feel like you have done something wrong, or even though you haven't…you feel like you have done something wrong and you have to punish. It's like the punishment, you punish yourself. But it is an awful stage to be at because as I said you can't usually seek help or anything because you cannot see outside of this tunnel. You don't see outside and someone that might be able to come around and help you and get you through it, you can't see consequences of not seeing your family, or ending up in the acute unit or whatever. Or hospital…you can't see that. The only thing you can see is usually the knife…for me it is the knife…and that is it.

You have only had one instance of self-harming over the past few months, how did you get to that point? To the point where it is only once in that amount of time?

Control...yeah, and as I said, the last couple of weeks we had before we finished up, a lot of things came home with me. Yeah it clicked...I thought 'I have to have this control'.

So it is something that prevents you from tunnelling?

Yeah, although obviously it can still come back if I get too stressed over different things that have built up and I don't talk about them. They just build up and I go into a tunnel.

So talking about what creates the stress can help reduce the stress?

Yeah, yeah. Like it really helps...I had the problem for years that I could not really express what was going wrong or what was happening. I probably know myself...I had to learn what was happening and what had happened.

You had to learn to create a dialogue with someone else?

Yeah. I had never been taught how to talk...that sounds silly but you have to be taught to be able to talk about things you know?

Is that where childhood development is so important?

Yeah, I was never able to. I know with [daughter]...what she gets away with! If I had done that when I was young! Belted, and sent to bed. It is good to see her expressing herself, and when she is angry she expresses that, then gets over it in ten minutes and she is fine. Send her to her room and she is over it. That's it. I never had the chance to do that. So I guess that is where the cutting came in and that sort of thing.

Interview 3

I'm struggling a little bit.

What is happening?

Just...different things but [case worker] and I have caught up this morning. I didn't see her last week. It was good to catch up with her...struggling a little bit. At the moment I have early warning signs of having a bit of a setback. So I am aware of what is happening.

In terms of the self-harming do you mean?

No, no, just not coping. I have really gone past that self-harming stage so, which has been wonderful, but just not coping in other ways.

You did have the cutting a couple of months ago, and before that it was February.

Yeah, and I have certainly got no...even when I am down like at this stage...I certainly don't want to cut. It just is feeling down on myself.

Is the drive there to still self-harm?

No it is not so much there. Which is really interesting. It's become another stage...it is really interesting to know that I don't want to cut. But I am taking it out on myself in lots of ways...like drinking. I have tried to reduce the drinking in lots of ways. Because of access on Sundays I am sort of cutting down, but I might have three days of heavy drinking and its taking its toll on me. It is not working.

Can you see any parallels between the drinking and your self-harming?

Well I am starting to I think. That is what is starting to happen...is that I am starting to see that physically and mentally I cannot handle the drinking.

Do you think that the drinking is another instance where you think you are gaining control? Try to control how you feel?

I only drink to forget what is happening in my life.

Current? Past?

Like my family and [daughter] and [husband] and that, you know. Yeah I am starting to realise that it is not doing me any good. Things are starting to come to a head again, different things, this is another new one coming out.

Like another symptom to deal with?

Yeah. But I have gone to [employment agency] and looking at work. So I will get a case manager in the next week or so.

Is that is because you want to do that, or to prove yourself to the family?

No, I want to. I know in myself I need to get back out there and do something…I have to do something. To get out there and do something again…find something appropriate. Yeah I just feel lost at the moment…a bit lost. Best way I can explain it…I just feel a bit lost. I am trying to get through to Sunday and have a good day with [daughter] and everything feels natural and normal. As the week goes on I go down. Then I have to bring myself back up again. It is a struggle.

Have you noticed any changes in your family relationships at all?

Yeah, like mum called around Monday morning. Had a coffee with me which was good. We usually catch up once a week. Things are pretty good but I just feel like that at the moment I am not looking physically right and things have come to a head a bit and I have sort of realised what is going on. It is a matter of getting on top of that…it is another struggle I have to get through…but I have to get through that.

Has been there been any specific feedback from your family on how you are going?

No, no.

Do you think you need that?

Yeah well [husband] was a bit quiet on Sunday. And I sort of sensed that but he had also worked Saturday night so he was tired and that, so I thought that he was just tired and that. I have to realise that. [daughter] was great. Mum called in Monday and had a cuppa…that was good. I think that [case worker], talking with her this morning, I have been spending a lot of time with other people with mental problems and that, and they are sort of dragging me down a little bit…well, probably a lot. I have to sort of try to restrain a little bit from them. Yeah, like I know one of them I can have three calls in a day from her. She gets down and that sort of thing and that drags me down. I have to look at that.

There is no specific feedback from your mum like 'gee, you have been going really well lately'?

No she…I was talking about [employment agency] and she said 'only you can do it'…it is up to me. It is more a thing that I need to do myself.

Does it make you feel alone?

Yes but then I sort of think, come on get yourself together and do it. Yeah, and that is what I did earlier in the week but now I have come down a bit of a cropper during the week. But I can do it. I know I can. And talking with [case worker] this morning was good, made me feel a little bit more positive in what I need to do. I still need that…I need [case worker] working with me. I have realised…we didn't catch up last week and I think that is where I have really come down.

That regular contact is really important. Even if you are feeling good.

Mmm. But I just feel a bit of a mess at the moment…got to get myself back together.

You mentioned that idea of feeling lost. Do you find [case worker] like a guide that helps steer?

Yeah, yeah she does. And we talk about what needs to happen and I think I really got lost last week and early this week. It has been good to catch up with her again.

That idea of lost, is that 'you feel lost in this world', 'don't know who you are'?

No I get lost as to myself…like [case worker] keeps saying that I am literate, I am capable, you know. But in myself, because I am associating myself with certain people that are through this system as well, I get a bit lost.

Do you start to wonder who you are?

Yeah, this friend of mine is in the system and she is going to marry someone who is in the system as well. But like they don't do any housework and all I see is mess, and I get back to my flat…having stayed there for the night…and then I can think 'oh, I have to clean'…it is a funny thing but I think that I am lost between the two. I get involved in their world but I have my world to…I get lost between the two…if that makes sense. I get to the stage where I have to move on with things. I want to get back out into the workforce. I just feel the need to be…like when I am around home, or with mum, or talking to my sisters on the phone, I just feel normal with them and I have to keep that up…but I haven't had enough stimulation from them you know. Like, I need that. Just not being with people in the system and their problems…being back out there again.

Do you think then that your family still aren't providing you enough?

It doesn't happen. They are busy with their lives. I rang my sisters the other night…they don't ring. Hopefully they will. They both sort of said that they would like to catch up with me and have a coffee and that sort of thing.

Why do you think they don't ring?

They are busy with their own life. I know one of my sisters works full days and then she still has family to go home to, to cook and clean, and do all that. And then the other one…she's also the same.

Do you think that on their side there is an anxiety about ringing you?

No, because when I ring them we talk and talk for half an hour…have a great conversation and catch up on all the news, nieces and nephews. Yeah, there could be a little bit of apprehensiveness as to how I am…I don't know. I am not sure.

Because you are ringing them, you are in the right frame of mind to be ringing and want to talk when you are feeling good about that. But if they ring you, they might be unsure of how you are feeling at that particular time.

Yeah I think that they have just got caught up with their lives, and that is how it is these days. They're busy. You don't feel like talking to your sister…I think they appreciate it when I ring and it's good to catch up with them. I think it is just the way life is now these days…you just don't catch up a lot.

Do you still see your friends you had before you 'entered this other world'?

Yeah, we caught up on Saturday…she called around and had coffee. That is what [case worker] and I were talking about his morning. Keeping in contact with these friends I have got…and there is another in [city] who is a [occupation] and I rang her the other night and we talked for an hour. And we just talked and talked and talked. And with this other girlfriend we talked on Saturday. We will catch up again this weekend. She seems like she wants to keep contact with me and make sure that I am ok. They are really good friends. We are always going to be friends.

So you have been open about what you have been through?

Yeah, and she…this one from [city]…lent me this book 'The DaVinci Code' and I have been actually reading that which has been good because it is getting my concentration going again and reading and that. So every day I sort of pick it up and read. It's really a good book. That is one thing I have had going for me this week…I have been able to keep reading but as I said I feel like I have gone down a bit.

But these two friends, have they ever said harsh words about what you might have been doing or have they always been the more positive?

Yeah, very positive. Always positive. Well one of them as I said is a [omit] and she is very positive in herself. We talked for an hour the other night. And the other one, we talk about both putting weight on and that sort of thing. We might go down the street and look at a couple of shops and that, coffee. We just sort of…we are pretty open about things.

Did you ever speak to them about the self-harming?

I know this girlfriend from [city] knew about my self-harming and I showed her my arm. Sunday was the first time I didn't have to wear anything on it. I went and saw [plastic surgeon] this week, and he reckons in six months time he will see me again and do more with it again. It's going to get better as time goes on.

Did you ever feel judged by your friends?

No, no. she doesn't…she is very down to earth and has never judged me.

Has she ever offered advice?

Yeah, like she has said about [husband]…with him, perhaps wanting more than what I …with him, he is sort of getting what he can out of the place. He sold the two cars and bought himself a good car…and I haven't got a car and all that. But you know, I take that in hand but I also have to weigh up as to how I feel with [husband] and that too. What he is doing for [daughter] and that. It's a bit of a tough one. It has been a year of a lot of tough things happening. It has been hard. I think that is what is playing on me at the moment…where I am headed with a few different things. I am sort of facing things a bit more…like work, and myself, being in the flat on my own, and what has happened here, there is the reality.

Does it create the need for adjustment to the world as it has changed so much?

Yeah, I suppose I have been in my own little world and reality is coming out and it is really hitting hard. It is hitting hard. And like I was tears with [case worker] this morning which I haven't had tears for ages you know? Today for some reason I am breaking down with them a bit. It is silly. But I wondered why I did not cry with everything I kept thinking about, like [daughter], [husband] and that. I still hadn't broken down. I think things are starting to…

You need to give yourself permission to do that though. If you look at your self-harming, there was that build up. You would store all this emotion and frustration and you would be like a volcano. I think we all have bad days and end up in tears, but you need that I think. Let yourself feel.

Yeah I can't…I can switch them off. I know there is going to come a day where I am really going to have a really bad day probably, or not so good day.

Do you get scared by your feelings?

Yes.

What sort of feelings?

Vulnerable. Just being on my own. Pretty scared by that. And as to whether I can manage. I do get scared. That is probably what is happening with me a bit too…getting back to normality. I am finding it a bit scary and a bit strange.

Since your childhood, you have never been allowed to feel your emotions. So that now you are older, they can be quite intense because of the significant changes, they scare you. You haven't been able to learn how to cope with your feelings. Perhaps that is related to the alcohol…you control the feelings because you are scared and you are feeling vulnerable. You try to control that by drinking and forgetting it.

Yeah. You just feel vulnerable and you think 'what if someone tried to break in' or what if something happened and you are on your own? I keep thinking, I am safe where I am. And I need [case worker]…I do need her. I probably, apart from my husband, [case worker] has probably been the most inspiring person. I missed her last week, and fell in a heap. She is great.

Did you have any other thoughts or queries that have come up from the earlier discussions?

No, I have dreamed a bit. I have been dreaming a lot about family. And it has been like family back in the family home. That has been happening a fair bit. But not bad ones, just unusual. Family, conversations and different things happening but not sort of going back to dad. But more sort of family. And that is playing a bit on my mind…I just want my family. It has been good to catch up and talk about all this…put everything into perspective. The only thing is I am not having a good day today.

Perhaps even from our discussion today there might be something you might want to take up with [case worker].

Yeah, like crying, and the drinking. I haven't cried for so long. I feel like I have kept putting it off and today I have had my tears. Perhaps I do need to have a good cry, you know. But I have been holding it off for so long.

You will feel some emotional relief from crying.

Yeah, yeah, and I think in some ways I need to do that. Because every time I go up home, [husband] and I are sorting things out, and I find that hard. The separation and what belongs to him, and what is mine. Just sorting things out.

But you need to grieve that. It is healthy to grieve over losses and changes like that.

Yeah. But I haven't allowed myself I suppose. I get back home on a Sunday night and I just put the television on and just switch myself off. I can switch myself off. That is what I feel I need to do, and yet I know that I have to let it out sometime.

Appendix C: Interview Transcripts for Patient 2, Helen

Interview 1

[She handed across a personal writings book before the interview started, and said "If you want to photocopy it…it goes backward; I did this last year and I ended up in the unit, because I've had about 13 or 14 suicides in my life so you're welcome to read this later"]

If you think of when you first self-harmed, what age do you think you were?

13.

What was happening at that time?

My grandmother died and I'd broken my leg, but my grandmother wasn't close to me, she did a lot of physical things for me but wasn't a close person. A boy down the road died. But I remember writing notes to my mum and dad as soon as I could write you don't love me. We had a very strict but loving family.

What type of self-harm did you .... On an arm or a leg?

Cutting. On my leg.

What did you use?

A knife.

Were your parents aware of that when it happened, when you were 13?

Yeah but I told them I cut it on a barbed wire fence. Like I always made excuses.

So what age do you think you were when people initially realised you were self-harming?

In my late 30's. There were periods I'd go through and I was fine and then something would happen. I remember I overdosed in [hospital] because I was involuntary...everything was out of my control and when we went to the pictures I said I can't cope so they let me walk home, except I went to the supermarket and I overdosed and I didn't tell them...I told my friend.

So you used panadol to do that?

Yes...that is a pretty classic with me. Because I knew my liver was stuffed.

Can you remember the first instance that people realised that it was an active self-harm?

Yeah, that was it, in [hospital]. But I think that was because I was really sick when I first had [omit] disease. All the help, I looked after myself, I didn't drink, didn't smoke...Like I would wake up one morning and would be failing my grades in high school, like chemistry in form 5, E minuses in form 6. But I didn't know what was going on, the teachers knew that something wasn't right. I just knew something wasn't right and burst into tears and, but that was due to [physical illness]. Like I got flown down to [city], I got photographed in front of a total stranger in my knickers because I was so jaundiced, I basically wasn't supposed to survive. And lost my dignity. They did a load of invasive things and then I got told you have [physical illness], to go home and take these tablets for the rest of your life. The foods you were actually eating were killing you. It was a slap in the face...

As you said there were already changes before that.

Yeah,

And then you were told you can go home and...

I wasn't told about the psych side of it, like this was 25 years ago. I had no counselling, nothing. All the research I did was off my own back, and off my parents' own back.

Do you think that in the past, when people first realised, was that a suicide attempt, or was it more that there was no intent there to die?

I can't remember, that was 20 odd years ago.

Because often when people overdose on medication, some people don't have that intent to die, it's a different form of trying to punish themselves or hurt themselves, or relate to others "Hey I'm distressed here".

Yeah, I think it was like that, and I found that continuously, like "hey I need help" but no one hears me. And I've been before heaps of med students and I have always said "listen to your patients" because they know what it's all about.

What forms of self-harm have you engaged in?

I've tried to hang myself, strangle, cut, stabbing, overdosing...

Was the hanging and strangulation a suicide attempt?

I didn't want to die but I didn't want to live. I just wanted to hop off. But the last episode, 3 weeks ago, was a definite suicide attempt.

And I think that there is that myth amongst health workers that if someone engages in self-harm that there not likely to commit suicide, but some attempts of self-harm are actually suicide attempts and aren't taken seriously enough, which is unfortunate. What circumstances do you think are you more likely to use self-harm?

When I'm tired, when I've been used and abused, when I'm not listened to, because like my IQ is in the top 10%, and I don't know anything. Like I was six weeks off sitting my finals for nursing…and that was another big let down. I had to go to equal opportunity to finish my child care even though I'd been credited. I got through the intellectual disability services training…like I had been in a wheelchair, I know how I had been treated, and I thought 'no' I don't want anyone else treated…I believe everybody has a heart and has feelings.

I get the sense then that you feel you haven't been looked after, so you therefore want to look after others to make sure they don't experience what you have.

Yeah, like I have survived but people say "she complains", but I would need a tree and a half to put all my complaints to. I am a caring person and I give and give and give but at my own health's expense.

Can you give an example of when someone hasn't listened to you and you self-harming?

Oh yeah, I was really down and friends came around, we rang up psych services and said that I was very close to self-harming. "Oh, she'll be right". They were so worried that they bought me up here and the workers sent me home, and I thought I was scared…they were intending to stay the night and when I thought they were asleep, I started stabbing myself.

So what do you think drove you to do that?

I was asking for help and no one was listening to me. I know that [case worker] knows me very well…he has known me for eight and a half years…and he can pick when I'm going downhill and I just clam up, I don't talk to anyone, I block out my friends, I block out my social life.

And you'll often find that with self-harming that you can't express it outward so you turn it inward, so that all the thoughts and concerns and stresses that you have, you can't talk to someone and feel better, so it comes inward.

I don't like talking to my friends about it because they get scared, which is quite natural. I tend to listen to people and sometimes I take on their problems. I don't mean to, but it's my nature. And then I turn it into my problem.

Why do you think you actually use self-harming behaviours? What do they actually do for you?

Because I need punishment. To remove the pain. Guilt.

The sense of guilt and needing to be punished is a common theme. What sorts of things do you think causes you to feel guilty?

Like I've been accused of doing things I haven't done, when I should have stood up for myself…and I used to be very assertive, be school captain, I won three citizenship awards, so I was very outgoing until I got the [physical illness].

There would have been a lot of loss associated with that. Do you think that part of this need to be punished, that you've done something bad…

I feel guilty that I haven't got kids, like grand kids for my parents, I haven't got a stable job. I'm in the age group…the old ones get looked after and the young ones get looked after…and I should be working and the government doesn't provide for 42 year olds. When I first went on to disability pension, I thought no, because I felt guilty about it.

Did you ever have any counselling at the time you were diagnosed with [physical illness]?

No…none whatsoever.

Do you think that would have been really useful for you, because it is like a grief reaction, you have these goals and dreams that disappeared with this diagnosis and the loss associated with that?

Yeah, in that I couldn't have kids and I couldn't finish my nursing. My nursing sister dragged me off the ward because she told me that I was sicker than the patients I was nursing. I've got to learn to say no and not feel guilty about it. And that's what [case worker] and I have been working on.

I think that working with [case worker] on that concept would be very useful for you.

Yeah, because I'm a giver…

You said before that you used self-harm as a punishment. Is it day to day things that you're punishing yourself for, or is it more long term?

Both, like sometimes it's a build up of things, sometimes it's something like… I'm very sensitive too and before I got [physical illness], it would just go over my head and I would think 'hey that's fine' but I find when people can't accept, I can understand them not understanding my psych side of it, but I do have a genetic disorder and it's not my fault. I like to treat people gently. Like my brother, I haven't seen him for three years. I've asked him to my place when they come home…"oh it's out of our way". People like that that put people down. It makes me feel [err]…I try to make everyone feel even.

At the age of 13, when you first cut your let, do you think that was a punishing act?

I can't remember. I remember a boy died of a brain tumour, my grandmother died and I had broken my leg and it wasn't diagnosed as broken for ten days. I had 16 weeks of plaster and no physio. Like this was 30 years ago..

But do you think anyone was listening to the stress you were in at that age?

No.

So with no one to talk to about how upset you were and how much pain…

We lived out in the middle of the country and miles from anywhere and my dad, I love him to death, he's a very closed person, he's not a hugging person and doesn't express emotions, but I put that down to his parents and I don't blame him. He'll do physical things for me and you know, when I'm home I like to kiss my parents goodnight and he'll just go [turn head to side and present cheek], like that. But when I was nursing I was like that too when I look back. I didn't have a very large personal space until I sort of palled up with a friend who had a real big family and she'd come and give me a really big cuddle, sort of like this, and then I got used to it and thought through the experiences I'd had…they weren't nice.

So how did you parents respond to you after you'd broken you leg and you were upset about your grandmother and you know, the boy that died?

They were very supportive. My mum is my best friend. She's really deteriorated and I am finding that hard at the moment. She's fine but overall she's deteriorated. She's got auto immune and also she had two strokes, her mother died of a stroke and a cousin had a stroke.

So that'll be a big concern.

Yeah, I know that I am going to lose her and that will be hard. When I was living in [town], I didn't have my own identity. In [that town] was when I started self-harming. I used to sit on the road and hope someone would run over me. I had a neighbour who knew, she understood what I was going through. She was great.

What do you mean you didn't have your own identity?

I was [father's name]'s daughter or "that sick girl". Because I was living at mum and dad's, and because I became sick the day after finishing HSC...[town hospital] had me diagnosed with hepatitis, the whole works, before anyone did and that was very hard on my parents and I was a lot younger then. Mum spent the whole 6 weeks down with me and dad was going between [capital city] and, he hadn't driven in the city and he wasn't that confident. The second time, he wasn't that confident, and he was in a car smash, but it wasn't his fault.

That changed things?

Yeah, my ambition when I left school was air hostess, join the army, and see Australia. I've seen Australia now.

It's very hard?

Yeah, I'm still going through the grieving. People are saying get over it. I've had a lot of experience with death with personal friends and relatives and that girl that went over the edge of the [hotel], I know her mum, and two days before her, another friend dropped dead at home.

You don't experience a sense of guilt about these deaths, do you?

One that you'll read about [in the personal writings book], I did. I was the last one to see him alive.

You mentioned before that you feel guilty before you self-harm, do you feel guilty after you self-harm?

I feel really relieved.

Just like a discharge of that guilt.

Yeah, I've punished myself. Like my parents were very strict and at the age of 4 we were smoking behind the hay stack, it went up and the haystack burnt down, and we were black and blue from dad's belt. But he never hit us for any reason but for punishment.

But there is that strong sense from your childhood that it you did something wrong, you deserved to be punished.

Yeah, I'm not blaming dad, but it's just the way I am.

In your family then, was it very common for that era to be disciplined, you'd be smacked?

It was the formal turn of events.

They use a lot of time out strategies now, so there was not a lot of talking about what you did wrong?

No. And we were not locked in but we had to stay in our rooms for a week and were only allowed out for meals, toilet and that.

What did you do in the room for a week?

Play with my dolls.

But that would have been really distressing?

I knew it was punishment because we'd done wrong. But indirectly, it wasn't our fault because it was our neighbours and he got off scot free.

Do you think that looking back now, that the punishment you received for that was justifiable or do you think it was too extreme for what had happened?

I'm not a person for hitting, I see mums and dads in the supermarkets hopping into their kids. If they get carried away, I report it but I walk away because I'm not a mum, and a lot of it is their mum's frustration…the kid doesn't understand. They don't say "put that back" or "I haven't paid for it" or "we don't need it". You don't talk don'ts, you talk dos, because when a kid's doing something wrong, "don't do that",…well they don't know what to do, they don't have a paper with directions.

So do you think that you deserve to have punished yourself most of the time?

I wish I knew.

Is there any times where you've looked back and thought that thinking it over now, I didn't deserve to put myself through that, but at the time you just driven to do that.

Yeah,

But afterwards, you might think I think I was too hard on myself there?

Yeah.

So that's a common experience. Is there any other ways you would punish yourself, like depriving yourself of anything?

Well, I have suffered anorexia, but that was anorexia. I still fight with it. I don't starve myself, but when I get stressed, I just don't eat. You get to a stage where you can't. I used to fall into two forms of depression. I would eat and eat and eat, or I didn't eat, or I just couldn't be bothered. I've spoken to the dietician about eating and she said it sounds like anorexia. Like I fight it daily. I've lost 4 kilos in three weeks and that wasn't through starving myself, that was through the operation and not being able to eat and I said my main goal at the moment was to maintain. I don't want to get any thinner or let my weight to go down.

There nothing else that you do like buy yourself some clothes and think no I don't deserve to treat myself to that…is there ever those sorts of ideas? Your self-harming is more like you said, you feel guilty, you punish yourself, or if you feel guilty you try to talk to someone and they won't listen, so you have no other choice but to relieve yourself that way.

Yeah, or I clam up. I do deprive myself of my social outlets.

In your lifetime, has anyone seriously harmed you?

I have been, not sexually abused. But like [older person] trying to touch me. I don't tell my father…he was a local [identity], he would make excuses to come back to the house. He found out where I lived in [town] and I wouldn't answer the door. I had a silent number here because he'd look in the phone book…dad wouldn't understand but mum knows.

What age were you when that started happening?

Late 20's.

And did you tell your mum what was happening?

Yeah.

How did she respond to you?

She was very protective but because he was a local identity, and it was a very close community and he was so respected, I felt trapped. Then when I moved to [another town] and a 75 year old kept coming around. He thought I owed him something. Because he gave me a job. I ended up going to the police and he never sexually abused me but he invaded my personal space which is nearly the equivalent…and his wife was so lovely and so I just quietly said to him…I just said if you don't mind not coming to my place and that was the last I saw of him.

There hadn't been any earlier forms of sexual abuse or...

When I was very young, mum and dad had boys from boys' homes or orphanages here and I don't know how old I was, but one exposed himself to me and that freaked me out because I was a very closed person.

Do you think that was the beginning of the personal space that you needed?

Yeah.

You are not used to your mum and dad encroaching on your personal space?

Mum would, she's a very kind person.

But having a man do that?

When I was born, dad had a broken leg, and mum had me and my brother all under 15 months. And mum had to milk the cows, run the farm and I'd get put onto dad to feed me. Dad would not wake up to [brother] crying but he could not tolerate me crying, we had a special bond but it is a very unusual bond. I have been told that he still has a lot of guilt about my disease. And that is probably why we have...it's a very unusual relationship.

You mentioned before about when you were younger, you'd write letters to them, asking them why they didn't love you.

Yeah...'You don't love me, I am leaving'.

Why did you think they didn't love you?

I think at the time my sister was born...it's typical. My older brother, I can't remember much of him. I just think it was, as much as I love my sister, it was a typical childhood thing.

You grew up in a farming family. Did you get any idea that the son was very important to the family to take over the farm, did you ever pick up any of that?

No.

There wasn't that drive from your family?

[Brother] always wanted to be in the army. He came home 5 or 6 years ago during shearing; like he was always lined up for the farm and he said no and left for [city]. Dad's still on the farm. Mum isn't well enough to be so far from the nearest hospital. Particularly when dad whinges about petrol prices and mum tells me how she wants to be in town and I tell her "you've got to talk to dad" because us three kids have said our piece.

If you could describe overall how your childhood was, what would you say?

Overall very happy, secure but very strict. While I lived under mum and dad's roof, I did what they said and that was how we were brought up. But dad does tend to still treat me like a two year old. Like he just bought a new car, he would get [brother] to drive, get [sister] to drive. I went to move it 3 metres the other day, I started it and he said "no I'll move it", I said 'no I'm in it, I've got a licence". And like I don't like dad driving around town...particularly in [town]. He doesn't see things on the road. I say "dad look out for that". But I don't know, I'm dumb.

You mentioned that your dad was someone who would use the belt if you were naughty, would your mum also punish you, or was that just dad's job as he was the authoritarian so to speak?

No. I was a little devil, I was defiant, she could be say we needed to be disciplined but dad had to deal with it.

So that would be "wait until your father gets home"?

Umm, I can't remember.

You mentioned that you'd had a broken leg that wasn't picked up for 10 days.

It was x-rayed and nothing. 10 days later it was…like we need to have another look at it. I was actually opening up the crack further and further.

So that was a misdiagnosis?

Yeah. At a country hospital

That would have been very traumatic.

Yeah, it was. Now I've had a total knee replacement.

Was there any neglect do you think, in your life, like were you provided?

My parents couldn't afford to send us away on school trips, we were allowed one trip a year, which was fair enough…Another thing that happened when I was 13, my cousin suicided…But we went to [town] twice a year, my mum would pick out my clothes. As far as neglect, we were provided for. Dad was still paying off the farm.

Things are certainly different with farm life, aren't they? Just going out and earning a wage and bringing it home, where anything you benefit from the farm needs to go back into the farm to keep it going. It does make that free financial money, it's just not there, it's invested in the farm.

Yeah, our house was comfortable but it wasn't flash because dad's priority was the farm. You don't make money from the house. But now, because mum isn't so well, they have put in a split system air conditioner. I said "well enjoy the comforts, you've earned it".

What your family's response before even now to your self-harming?

Dad does not want to know about it. He's attitude is that if it's not rosy, he blocks it out. That is his way of dealing with it. I don't tell them everything or each time I self-harm. I had a case manager that rang up mum and dad every time I walked into A&E. That was why I ended up stabbing myself because I thought I didn't have any rights, or control. That is why [rehab team] took me on. And [case worker] and I have discussed the life threatening situations that he would ring up my parents but he always says to me "I'm going to ring them up" or "who do you want me to ring?".

How does your mum respond to you?

She worries, but she's got to because she's an ex nurse as well. But now she tries hard. Like this last week when I went home there wasn't any extra travelling, I didn't demand any change from the routine in the house, I slept when mum slept.

Do you think they understand when you self-harm?

Dad doesn't. Mum I think does. We haven't really talked about it.

It's not something that's openly discussed?

No. I asked [case worker] to tell them this time that I had [physical problem] which was not a lie. But they didn't know why. Because I don't want to be the cause of mum having another stroke.

So there is a very protective thing on your behalf that you don't want to distress them with this?

Yeah.

Do you think that 20 years ago it would have been useful to openly discuss it with the family?

With mum yes, with dad no.

So your mum would try that 20 years ago?

Yeah, they kept me at home. And they went through guilt that they couldn't handle me at home. I ended up in [hospital].

But you would actually sit down with your mum and discuss why you were cutting?

No.

There was no dialogue about your self-harm? It was more…

She asked to care…"Are you comfortable?"…but I am fiercely independent. And I just take after my mum. I have a mixed gene that I close off like dad, but fiercely independent like mum.

Interview 2

Last week we were talking about how you like to care for people, but sometimes I think we do that and we don't look after ourselves first.

Yeah.

And then we get so run down.

Yeah, I just give and give and give.

So you're able to notice early signs that you need that time out

Yeah. But it is not always possible.

Do you think then that you're more likely to go through the cycle of self-harm if..

When I'm tired, that when I'm most sensitive and most vulnerable.

I've had a look at the interview from last week, and you mention that when things are out of your control you, for instance, you took the overdose when you felt that everything was spinning out of control.

Well I was going through a phase then, I had to take this medication, I had to have ECT.

Is that a common thing that when you don't feel in control and you feel low, you're more likely to hurt yourself ?

Yeah.

You mention that with the eating disorder…in those low times you won't eat either…

That's not deprivation, that's stressed out.

You lose your appetite

Yeah.

Does it affect your sleep?

When I'm at a low weight, yeah, when I was anorexic I was sleeping two hours sleep a night.

I had a look at the pages that I photocopied and certainly there has been a lot of misfortune and a lot of trauma that you've been exposed to. Are there any of those in particular that you think stays with you more than the others do?

The one that committed suicide and I was the last one to see him alive. Looking back there were signs there, that at the time he was happy go lucky.

Do you think you carry guilt that you hadn't noticed it, or that you haven't been able to help him?

More helplessness. Not so much guilt. He had made up his mind.

Do you think that when he said he'd made up his mind that he understood that the feeling is that you do want to suicide?

Yes. Hop off the world.

Yeah, to hop off the world, so you can see where he might have been at that stage?

Yeah, and I pride myself and my friends because like number 1, I don't want them to see me like I am, and number 2, I don't deserve good friends.

Why don't you think that you deserve them?

Because it's just me.

But often we think that we don't deserve something, we have this idea that we've done something bad or something wrong, so we don't deserve that. What do you think did wrong?

Let them down. I could have done more for them.

Does it come back to that idea of caring? You perhaps haven't cared for them as you should have?

Yeah, and I'm very sensitive to people about the way they look or the way they feel or what they're saying and in a way I expect people to pick that on me and I get disappointed...like I've had a lot of obvious physical disabilities and I hate asking for help, and like one girl, I went over there and did her dishes and helped out, and then I though I'm not really helping her because she is just sitting there. I had my arm in plaster and I said "would you mind helping me do the dishes? I suppose you'd do that for me".

Where do you think you might have learnt that ability to read people, the body language, what they say? You're obviously very good at picking up on things. It's almost like a sensitivity thing. Where to you think you might have learnt that?

I thinks it's a trait from nursing, my child care, the way I was treated.

In your childhood, do you remember watching your parents closely to figure out what sort of mood or how to approach things or how they were responding to you early on?

Not that I remember, but dad always had a large personal space. Mum was the loving one and she was the one that always told, and she continues to tell me, that she loves me and dad loves me, although dad hasn't actually said that to me.

I just wondered that if your dad had this large personal space, if you have to watch his response because you couldn't just walk up to him and cuddle him because you wouldn't know what his response was. You'd have to say something and watch him. And often these traits as you prefer to call it, do develop as kids through our childhood and you probably needed that to be able to think "how's dad doing to respond if I say this" anyway, you do become very aware of other people and you learn to read them.

Yeah, like I have a girlfriend who owns a shop and I just dropped in to drop off a birthday present and I said "look you get some sleep".

What I want to speak about today in particular is how professionals have related to you or not related to you. If we just for the moment talk about counsellors or other professionals who obviously have different training than the emergency department. If we just concentrate on a counsellor, what sort of experiences have you had with those sorts of professionals?

When I was in [town], they queried schizophrenia and I was self-harming and I remember one of the psych nurses, he was my case manager, he was really arrogant and seemed out of touch. I didn't accept that I had borderline personality disorder, until about three years ago, I was in denial because I really had something else.

That would have been really hard.

Yeah.

What do you think it might have been that meant he was arrogant to you? Not being able to help you? Not being able to stop you self-harming?

Frustration. Yeah.

Do you remember any specific things he might have said to you? Can you think of anything if particular that he might have said that you felt that arrogance in him, or that frustration?

I was in A&E in [town] and he said he is just sick of me.

Straight out like that?

Yeah.

How did you respond to that statement?

I fought, kicked and bucked because they were holding me down.

Something like that increased your anger?

Yeah. Well I didn't know what he was doing. Before it was diagnosed, it was attention seeking and all this sort of thing…and that was the last thing I wanted because I don't like being the centre of attention, I don't like people feeling sorry for me because people feeling sorry for me doesn't get me anywhere, empathy and understanding does.

What do you think the understanding does?

It probably relieves the helplessness, like one of my friends, when I stabbed myself, after I had been up here and got turned away. He said "I don't know why you do it" and I said "because I had done all the right things and I just got shit in my face", I thought that no one cares.

Do you understand why you might have? What did that do to you at that time? What is the level of understanding of why you stabbed yourself that night?

I was frustrated, rejected, angry, alone, because I couldn't explain to my friends how I was feeling. They knew that I was very suicidal, and they did their best, I needed help.

Have you ever really been able to talk freely about your distress?

Not to them. It scared some of them.

Did it scare you?

It did in the beginning. Now I see [Priv Psych], I talk quite openly to him, but the last time I hurt myself, I actually wrote a suicide letter and I gave that to him and he said "Do you want it back?" and I said "No".

Can I ask where you stabbed yourself?

There and there and there [stomach/bowel].

Do you know why you chose to do that rather than overdose or cut your arm?

Because I knew that I could kill myself…I did hit an artery and my intestine.

Do you think others saw it as a self-harm attempt or a suicide attempt?

No. The only people that knew were the police, the ambos and you guys here.

Did they think you were attention seeking and self-harming or do you think they honestly thought "[name] has tried to kill herself"?

No, I think they thought it was attention seeking…especially the second time the ambos came up.

Because that's a quite severe injury and a quite severe episode of self-harm and I certainly do believe that it is attention seeking in terms of a communication of distress.

Yeah, yeah

For someone that distressed to do that, you need to pay attention to them.

Yeah, yeah.

I certainly think the borderline diagnosis or the disorder, that people with that disorder, find it very difficult talking to people. To talk, you continually have the door shut each way, and we all have problems and fight with someone, and we talk about it. But if you've got no one to talk about it with, it builds up and the distress just becomes higher and higher.

Yeah, one night I rang up triage, and yeah, it was hopeless and I gave up. I felt rejected because I was being passed from pillar to post. I was in the too hard basket, which I have said to some people I may as well be dead. I said I've got [physical illness].

Did that make you feel more alone? That you were put in the too hard basket or that no one put in the time to know or to learn what is going on?

Yeah, to know what's going on.

In general, from mental health staff, what responses from them, after your self-harm, were helpful?

That time I was in the unit, I'd rang the week before, and I wasn't going to ask for help. I just wanted to talk to someone who knew, or I knew that cared and I kept saying "you don't want to listen to this garbage" and she said "Yes I do, you need help". I spoke for ¾ of an hour. The police came around and they put the knife in the sink for me and they talked me through a little while and then said "we've got to call an ambo" and I said to them if they make any snide comments, I am gone, and so they went out and talked to the ambos and they were as good as gold.

So that's, as you said, is showing some form of caring or empathy is really important in getting you to open up and accept help.

I was talking to one of the cops and he said you're having trouble finding the kind of help, because of the shortage, and I said yes.

For him to say that, he's obviously thought of how difficult it is for you and the idea that someone's thought about it will obviously have an effect for you, a positive effect.

Yeah, and that's my first step of hopping off the merry go round.

Are there some things that we've touched on there that's upset you?

It's that someone actually genuinely cared.

I think that just my spending time today with you, that it's probably something worth talking to [Priv psych] about, the drive in you to want to care for people, but also that you get cared for and I think there something very eminent in that for you.

Like I have never fallen in love.

Is that because you've always felt very separate from everybody else?

I don't know. I love my parents, I love my brother and sister. I love my nieces and nephews but I've never actually fallen in love and I've broken off the relationship because I feel that I am wasting their time. I want someone to love me for me.

And perhaps that idea of being cared for is something you might benefit from speaking at length with [Priv psych].

Not physically cared for, but…

Being cared for, someone cares.

Yeah.

Someone has thought about me or done something for me?

Yeah.

And that's how we build our self esteem because we know that people care, so I think that interview aside; I encourage you to explore this with [Priv psych]. I think you'd benefit a lot from looking at that and resolving a lot of the issues you have with him. You know, that wanting to be a nurse and care for people and with the [physical illness], and then you became the patient and not the nurse, and it all comes down to that idea of caring. When you become the one caring for others and then become the patient that needs to be cared for. And it's been very difficult for you because you felt good about caring for people but because of your illness, you are the one being cared for.

Yeah, because I'm fiercely independent, I always have been since I was this high. I'm very much a mixture of my parents.

I know that with a lot of treatment plans or crisis plans or management plans, that there often devised so there is a consistent level of care, that everyone treats you in the same manner.

It has never worked for me.

Have you ever felt any of them to be punishing?

Yes.

What sort of things have made you feel that?

When I was first with MST, they had a contract that I went into the unit, I wasn't allowed to go away over night. I wasn't allowed to see family, I wasn't allowed to go home overnight, in a month's time or if I'd been going OK, I'd be allowed to go home for a weekend. I could have just screwed that piece of paper up.

But you felt that in some way that was a punishment because you were in the unit you were unable to see family, and working off management plans, with a lot of people with the diagnosis, I would see that that was a protection thing, to make sure you were OK and caring for you basically, making sure you were in a secure environment. Was the rationale behind that decision explained in those terms?

Yes. But like when I came into the unit, if I self-harmed in the Unit, I would be locked in seclusion for x amount of time…then brought out into HD for a couple of days. I was locked in seclusion for 56 hours once and [psychiatrist] was looking after me then and he maintains that that was sheer hell for me and him.

Was that adequately explained, why they were doing that?

No, they'd come in and walk out, I'd ask them a question, they didn't even talk to me.

So, I think that at times, where I've agreed to the use of HD and I've agreed to the use of emergency use of seclusion, particularly because people at certain times are acting in a way that normally they wouldn't, and so to protect them, that needs to be done. But I think that if there is any sort of restriction at all, it needs to be explained that it's the need to look after you.

But they weren't listening to me, I'd get claustrophobic, out of control because I can't get out of that room. Even with my last admission, they didn't listen. It wasn't pleasant to stay with them. I had two med students and the last thing I said to them was listen to your patient.

So, at times, if people had taken the time to listen, do you think that that would have reduced the stress, so that you don't get to the self-harming stage?

Yeah, and there was one in particular who would sit and listen and not say "I know how you feel" or anything, just say "it must be hard for you".

So those statements though, you value and hold dear to you because they are indications that someone is listening. Would that be right?

Yeah.

I think that, the project that I'm looking at, there are a lot of negative attitudes towards patients that self-harm, and as you said, it brings up ideas that I'm hopeless because I can't stop you from doing that.

Yeah, frustration.

Yes, this develops into frustration and I think that if we have a framework to understand any illness around, it can reduce that frustration or what I call anxiety. Often people get anxious if they can't help someone else and they get frustrated.

And that just worsens the problem.

Yes, and you have had difficulty with mental health staff, as far as case managers go, have you always found it easy to discuss the drive to self-harm?

No, last year I was in continuing care and she would just tell me what she would do and she would just walk into my house without knocking; woke me up. "This is what we're going to do". I think I mentioned to you that when mum had a stroke she wanted to talk to her about it. And I wanted to change case managers, there was a lot of red tape and I just felt that no one was listening, no one cared and that was my first instance of stabbing myself.

So at that time I know there were periods where you have felt so alone that that sounds like a very significant incident where you've got someone who's there to care for you but is not listening.

No respect for my parents or me.

What do you think she may have done that would have changed that? If you had the magic wand, and you could hit her on the head, what do you think you'd want from her that would have made…

Asking me what I thought. I should write out an ISP because I wasn't involved in it and she'd written it. She said my doctor being involved, [support agency] had been involved, and none of them had, because I asked them and I didn't agree with the plan.

So you've obviously had some good experiences with mental health professionals, although some very difficult ones.

One, it was my last case manager, we just couldn't communicate, like she was very professional and everything, and she respected my rights, but I just didn't feel comfortable with her.

Was that, as you said, she may have been professional and everything, but do you think she understood, or had some empathy for what you were going through, do you think that was what was missing?

No, a personality clash, which happens in life.

Yeah, I think it comes down to finding someone you're comfortable with, you'd certainly progress further and quicker than if you are having that struggle.

In three weeks I had three case managers, three different psychiatrists and two support workers. That's when there was the change over to MST from continuing care. Like I know all the political stuff that goes on here, I am not silly but I don't say anything to anyone except when I get really cheesed off because I know our case managers are stuck and they can't do this and that because of the political stuff.

In terms of general hospital staff, how in general have you found their response to your self-harming behaviour?

"Why don't you finish it?" "Do we care if [patient] goes out for a smoke and doesn't come back?" I had a total stranger, and I hadn't self-harmed but it was a result of self-harming, this was last year, I was throwing up and everything and she made a comment, about me deserving that.

What do you think drives someone to respond like that?

Not understanding, because I had two very complex conditions, and instead of saying look I don't know how to help you they cover up. I stabbed myself, like I wanted to go home and the doctor said ring if I need to. I rang the hospital, and I could take two Panadeine Forte. I had to call an ambulance and they said "oh hurry up it can't be all that bad", and I knew I was sick, very sick, and normally I would have told them to shove it then, but I didn't have the strength, I could only walk out to the ambo, they were going to make me sit in a seat, I said I need to lie down. They took me up to the hospital and one of the first comments was that I looked very pale. They didn't do any obs, put any blankets on me or anything and I have put in a formal complaint about it.

Why do you think they've done that?

Because most of them know me and most of them know I self-harm.

So it becomes "then it can't be that bad, we've seen it before"

Yeah. But I knew.

I think that there a real danger then thinking that way over time, particularly when it comes to physical health, that there's a focus of care. Have you found any responses from the hospital to be helpful?

Not really. I just hate hospital because I should be a nurse.

Can you understand, with your training in health care, their responses to you?

No because I, although it was 25 years ago, I would treat each patient with respect and empathy. Now, that's not taught. It's all out of a book. You can't get out of a book how to treat or how to sit with patients. I sat with a patient who was dying of cancer for hours on end because she didn't want to die alone. And you can't get that out of a book.

Working with the students that come through here, they've never experienced Psych, and some of them just love it and some can't deal with it.

When I was doing nursing, I couldn't deal with [nursing home], which was for the intellectually disabled, you know, the kids that weren't meant to survive. Everyone's got feelings, they could be quite severely disabled but still loved a cuddle.

You mention that, in particular [Priv psych] is fantastic; he will listen. what happens if things aren't going well, with your appointment next week, how do you contain your distress until you see [doctor], what other things do you use to work that through?

I try and learn natural…burning lavender oil. I hate ringing triage, there is two on triage in the day and one at night that I can talk to.

What makes them different?

They listen. Instead of "just keep doing what you're doing".

What sort of responses do they give you at [support agency]?

Same as [priv psych] basically. Like I don't go on. Like when my friend got killed and another friend died, I just got to a point I needed to talk to someone and you can't talk to your friends at 1 o'clock in the morning, so I rang triage and let go.

There is a difference between somebody feeding back, that must be really hard, there's a different between that and someone saying "You just go and to this." How do you respond to that more sort of solution focused technique that you're stressed when they suggest different things for you to do?

Because I'm usually frustrated and I have tried them all.

Does it become frustrating then for you?

Yes.

You ring and they just tell you to go and try all this stuff?

Yeah, that was one of the things I had with case manager in continuing care. She had ten things for me to do when I get stressed out; when I get to the bottom and I am still stressed out, I was to start again.

So at times, it's very common in the literature, that need for relief, you are so pent up emotionally and stressed that there is a need for relief.

Yeah, but I'll won't do it to my friends because they've got enough problems or different problems.

What sort of things can help you then release?

Relaxation.

But is that something you've learnt to do over time?

Yeah.

Self-harming, is that release?

Yes.

Initially, or is there long term release with that?

Both.

In terms of natural therapies, lavender and things, do you find them more of a distraction or a release?

A distraction.

They don't do anything to reduce the stress or try to take your mind off things?

Yeah, I like the smell in the house.

Like watching a TV program, or?

No. When I get [case worker] she takes me through relaxation, because I don't have anyone unless I'm absolutely desperate…and when I say to MST I'm meant to be on CATT alert, I'm stressed out trying to deal with it. And I don't abuse it.

Do they respond to your request for CATT alert?

A couple of times, because I just started asking for it or before this last episode, because I know they are busy.

Is it almost like permission that you can ring them then if there alerted to what's happening?

Yeah. I don't what to go through it with triage because it is too easy to just hang up, which I had in the past.

So if you're on CATT alert the response is quicker?

They don't tend to say they're too busy, like they might only spend ten minutes with me but it's enough to relieve that pressure.

But sometimes it is as little as ten minutes that you need?

Yeah, because I know they're good people and I don't like taking up their time.

What do you notice in yourself that you think you need to let [case workers] know that you need to be put on alert?

Just stresses. If I'm not dealing with things.

So you can sense a change in your mood, you become more anxious and stressed, and you become aware of that and become very aware of people's body language and small changes.

Yeah and ignore the signs of my own body. [case workers] encourage me to listen to my own body instead of everyone else's and I feel very selfish but….

I think though, at the end of the day, it's like a ripple effect, if you look after yourself, then you can be a good friend and you can be a good daughter, but if you're not doing well, you find it difficult to be good to your friends.

Yeah, that's why I lock them out.

So if we do want to care for others, we need to care for ourselves. I think that's something that in my work as being a psychologist, I'm always aware to look after myself because I can't help anyone if I'm not feeling well, I'm useless to anyone else. So I don't feel selfish for needing time off, but it can be very hard if you're not used to that...

I remember my nursing sister dragging me off the ward saying you are sicker than the patients.

And if you need time out, you allow yourself to have time out.

Yeah, I'm so tired, I'm so looking forward to it.

INTERVIEW 3

How have things been since I saw you last?

A bit rocky.

What does that mean?

I went down to [city] on Tuesday to my specialist. Someone had upset me on Friday, and I sat back and thought no that wasn't me, so I went and talked to her the next morning and she apologised. Then [city], just going down there just freaked me out, with all the changes, they tried to show me how to catch a train...

Yeah, it's very busy there.

And it's changing, and it just freaked me out. I don't think he caught on that I really was. I have lost my confidence, I saw [specialist]. And this kid started, not abusing me but making comments that hurt and she's got problems herself and I had to bite my tongue. One day I was with her and it's not my place, she's not my child. How about if I said those comments to you, how would you feel? And on Wednesday I had my new protective mechanism by taking the phone off the hook. I called psych services three times and from ¼ past 4, I asked [omit] at the front desk I need to speak to [case worker], ASAP. That was ¼ past 4. I rang [case worker], I don't know where she was. 5.20 I rang triage, they were busy, they got back to me at 7.15 and by that time I thought well no one...they are busy. I put myself at the end of the line.

Did you feel bad with triage because you knew they were busy but when they rang you back at 7.15 you still had that guilt that you were taking up their time?

Yeah, because I didn't answer the phone but the comments were "I've been flat chat, I've still got a lot to do" and it made me feel like...

Yeah, certainly I've heard that before from people that even in an emergency, they feel as though they're not worthy to be in there receiving treatment, they're talked down to, or "oh you're back again"

Yeah, I have a classic on that one! Anyway Wednesday, I took the phone off the hook, which I found worked, I rang up [case worker] and said "don't worry about coming around", and that was when I cancelled out on you, I cancelled out on another appointment too. I took the phone off the hook, drew the curtains and just did my own thing. The way I figured it, I can't hurt anyone else and no one can hurt me because I only needed that last little push.

Do you think perhaps the ability to recognize you're breaking point is a lot better now than it might have been?

It varies. Thursday I saw my own GP, And I said to [doctor] "I'm losing my independence" and he said "yes". My disability…and that was the icing on the cake and I couldn't talk to anyone about it, like a friend of mine works with people with disabilities and she said "oh you knew that all along" and I said actually someone telling me, like professionals, and friends, like everything goes over their heads.

And I'd imagine you'd spend a lot of your time just pushing that to the back of your mind and want to know about it now, today.

Yeah. And then Thursday night I got out in the garden and a friend came over and it was dark and my routine at night I light candles and just relaxed and I put a skewer, because I was trying to put a hole in the end of a candle, that's the second time it's happened. I went to hospital, I went to triage. They said "what did you do that for". I said "I didn't do it, it was an accident" and they took me straight in and got security, the whole drama and one of the doctors that knows me, he's helped me a lot, he provided me with info, I took this friend with me to back me that it was an accident when she was there and anyway…

So you felt you needed someone to back up your story?

Yeah, I shouldn't but…and I said about the reception I got and he said the questions shouldn't have been "what did you do that for", it should have been "what happened" or "how did it happen". Then another nurse comes in "what did you do that for" and started, I said that my coordination is going and I was getting ready for a party blah blah. He is one of two doctors I've had in the last eight years that has stood up for me.

What is it in particular that you find really helpful, that that non-judgemental attitude?

Understanding. And I bit my tongue, but know I feel I should have said to the nurse that mental illnesses are allowed to have physical illnesses, they are allowed to have accidents. I could write a book on the receptions I got in A&E.

There is a lot of journal articles and things like that where people with borderline personality disorder have written down their experiences to help educate people. This is something people do do.

Yeah, and I told you about the incident with the ambos. My friend followed it up because I hadn't heard anything. It's being investigated because it was totally uncalled for. I mean potentially I could have died.

Do you feel better in yourself putting in the formal complaint?

Yes, in that I hope they don't treat other people the same way.

Do you think many years ago you would have had it in you to complain or speak up about things you were unhappy with about your treatment?

I don't know because my life has been that jumpy and last Tuesday night I got about three hours sleep, and Wednesday night I got zilch. When I saw [priv psych], I went in there about ½ an hour earlier and there was a bombing in Bagdad or somewhere I saw on the news, and they repeated it every five minutes and give the nitty gritty gory details and I just burst into tears and went and had a smoke and composed myself…in the end I asked if she could turn it over and she said there's only cartoons on.

Do you find that a lot, in the past, or that it's not just the stress that you're dealing with today, there's a lot of things from the past that come up all the time that complicate things like things could be going well with friends and family and the house is all neat and tidy, and you're feeling good, and then these thoughts of the past sort of intrude, so it's not stress from now you're dealing with, it's almost like you've got stress from the past you're still dealing with.

Yeah. Like I said to [case worker], I said to [priv psych], I need to deal with [friend's] death because I feel I (crying) carry it. And that was nearly 12 months ago.

But I suppose that's the thing, where it wouldn't matter if it was 15 or 20 years ago, if you don't resolve things, they do come back?

Yeah, like the guy I was the last one to see alive. I still haven't. It's still inside.

As far as past things coming back, does it ever stem back as far as your childhood, when your leg was broken, when you first cut, the punishment you received from the haystack?

Yeah, from feeling unloved.

As far as the family goes, I know you've told me that your dad isn't someone who shows physical love, your mum would, but were your parents people you could talk to if you were worried about school, or...?

No, if things were rosy, if it wasn't they didn't want to know about it. Like my mental illness.

That been consistent throughout?

Yeah. When mum was sick, I didn't know what to do. I said to dad "you're not coping are you", "yeah yeah", that's typical of him.

Yeah, that's how he coped?

And I can't change him.

Would your mum spend time when you were little talking about anything that worried you or you sort of kept that to yourself, or best not to say anything?

Yeah, I spoke to mum about the man harassing me, I felt she was the only one, I couldn't talk to dad. I knew I couldn't. And mum sort of protected me, when he come in she would warn me.

But she didn't make it clear that he wasn't allowed?

No.

Not in the house or anything, to put you in a safe place, she'd just tell you when to come in?

Yeah.

Would you have liked her to have done more than just tell you he was coming?

I don't know because he was a so called respected person and it's very difficult in a small town.

How old were you when that happened?

That would have been ten years ago, 15 years ago, with a 30 year old guy, 20 year ago with a 75 year old guy. But there is a line and when people cross it, I feel bad.

What I wanted to do today was to give you some words, and just get from you what comes to mind when I say these particular words, so if I started with self-harm, what do you think of when I say self-harm?

Punishment.

For what sort of things?

Things I've said, things I've done, me, being me, things I deserve.

Why do you deserve?

I don't know, that just how I feel.

Have you always felt like that?

Yeah, like when I treat myself and feel guilty about it I turn about and punish myself.

What about guilt?

Guilty. I have a lot of that. When I think logically about it, a lot of it is unnecessary, like the Friday incident when my girlfriend rang up and said "I know you're there" and hung up. I feel guilty because I should have been there. Then I think no, I'll improve my life, I shouldn't have to answer to anyone. Like I was in control and I've sat back and I've thought "no I'm not guilty of anything".

Are there times where you're unable to challenge that though?

Yeah, when I'm very tired.

And you don't have that mental energy to run through scenarios and look at the other side?

Yeah.

Punishment?

With me, unlike someone said last year, I usually, for me, I don't like giving it to anyone else, I just cringe. But for some reason it's OK for me....because [priv psych] has asked me about it too.

Trauma?

Death. Suicide. Sickness. Accidents. Unhappy. It can be physical, emotional...

So you see yourself as a victim of trauma?

No.

You don't see that you've been through any sort of trauma?

I've been through trauma with other people.

What about family?

I don't really know what the word family means. I had a family but to me a family is love, caring, brothers and sisters to love as well, and they couldn't give a shit because I have a mental illness.

So there's no nurturing from your family, no caring, as you've said there's people there that you're related to?

My mum is family, my dad as I said, he's shows his caring and nurturing in a different way. I just feel like dirt when I go and see both of them.

So how do you feel when you do go home to your parents now?

It depends on how well mum is and what dad's....I'm very much like dad, I'll give and give and give. But I give at my health's expense and he gives at his family's expense. There's a difference.

Has there been times where your dad has, as you said, cared for people outside the family and not shown so much care for his own family?

Yeah, it doesn't mean I love him any less.

I know, I'm not saying that. What about therapy?

I don't know because I've never really had any.

Do you see what you're doing with [priv psych] as some form of therapy or what you might have had with Psych Services as some sort of therapy?

I don't know, not at the moment, not really, because every time I'd start something there was a disruption where there was change of case managers.

So there must be that idea that with therapy comes some sort of stability?

More strategies. Yeah.

What do you see therapy as?

I don't know. Releasing in a controlled way.

Support?

Inconsistent.

Sometimes it's there, sometimes it's not?

Yeah.

It's been fairly variable?

Yeah.

What sort of support do you think you need?

Support through my degeneration, my physical condition, be able to talk…

I'm someone that always believes that you work within your patient's reality, so if it's overwhelming for them, it's overwhelming for them. It doesn't matter if I'd respond differently in that situation, at the end of the day, it's how the patient's responding to the situation, you deal with that.

Yeah. Like [priv psych] is working with me, it's been 12 or 13 years. I had him here when I was in the unit here and I was locked up in seclusion for 56 hours, and he said it was sheer hell for him as well as me and he showed me his notes that he wrote on me and he acknowledged how terrible it was for me.

What about if I said coping?

Variable.

Sometimes you can, sometimes you can't?

Yeah.

In terms of the when the self-harming started, you said it was when you were 13 and you had the broken leg and you cut yourself.

Yeah, and my grandmother had died, a neighbour my age had died, a cousin committed suicide, it was all in that era.

At that time, was there anyone there to talk to you or listen to you about how you were feeling at that time, coz that a lot of loss for a 13 year old?

No, we went to school, spend hours on the bus, did our homework, had tea and went to bed. We were 17 miles from school or anyone. When dad won't talk, and mum was very busy, who do you talk to?

How did you break your leg?

Playing netball. I'd broken it playing netball, playing squash, when I was on tablets I can't remember when I smashed my car up and broke both legs. It just seems to have got worse, my self destruction. Even though I hit rock bottom, the self-harming is getting worse.

My opinion is that there was the emergence of the borderline symptoms before the [physical illness]. That inability to talk and open up, keeping everything to yourself, your mood would have been quite variable before that…

……….and my personality,

Yeah, and then I think the [physical illness] has certainly complicated things dramatically like it's difficult for anyone to work through with a personality disorder itself without the complication of having a physical health issue as well.

Yeah.

And you have come a long way, as you have only just met me three hours ago really but your ability to now open up and talk, providing people listen, I think that is really going to be beneficial for you.

Because it can send you in the other direction so at the moment I talk to professionals like [priv psych], yourself, and [case workers]. Before I hurt myself the last time, I knew that something was about to erupt and I wanted to talk to someone and [case worker] just happened to turn up and he was really interested in hearing about my holiday. I said I needed to talk instead.

But often I think that people become a little bit anxious, clinicians become a little bit anxious, and try and distract people into talking about what they think are the good things in their lives and the good times, and not actually address the bad time. So at that time you probably needed to talk through something whereas [case worker] probably felt that let's talk about your holiday and that'll cheer you up.

Yeah, it didn't.

No.

I basically needed debriefing. From holidays. It was stressful, although I never let on to anyone. And things just piled up even before I went away.

Are you going to have concerns then with your new case manager then?

I expressed this to [team] about it. I highlighted some things and said we need to talk about them. Don't distract. I need support with this deteriorating physical condition as in 12 years – talking that through. Just acknowledging that when I was younger I was the healthiest, happiest kid and I had a career ahead of me…goal setting and they set goals and I say why because I set myself up to fail!

And really, if you're looking at building your confidence, you set small goals and it might be that you just clean out your refrigerator for example; if you achieve these small goals you do feel good in yourself, so it helps your confidence. But if you set goals that are unrealistic for you, you just feel shattered every time because you can't reach them. Do a lot of people know that you've been through all that?

No, because I think they would be scared…………..(crying)……………

Because I'm aware of that, I'm able to piece it all together, why you feel so traumatised all the time. It's not just now, its ten years ago, six years ago, even 12 months ago that you are trying to deal with and I think it's fantastic this ability of you to try and open up. But what your treatment plan here needs to do is encourage if that, it shouldn't make you stop doing that. It should make you feel like you can't do that and keep it to yourself.

Yeah, and that's why I did what I did on Tuesday night.

But I think that sometimes, I think I said to you on the last appointment that we had, that taking time out and looking after yourself can be really helpful and is really healthy to do. You don't have to feel bad that they "I don't want to see anyone today", I just want a me day, leave me be to chill out, and as you said, you do that before you get to your breaking point when it's just one more thing and you're exploding.

Yeah.

If you can do that it will reduce.

Well that's the first time I have done it, like because I don't like taking the phone off the hook with my parents, but I thought well even then, it was a protective shield, no one knew I was home.

I did mention to you that common theme, needing to care for others, needing to be cared for and looked after yourself and I think this ties in quite nicely with that because at that time it would have been hard for you to take the phone off the hook because "what if someone needs me to care for them" but to take it off the hook was a "well I need to care for myself at the moment"

Yeah, I felt very selfish about it.

But at the end of the day, you know from your nurse training, and I know from my work, if you don't look after yourself, you can't look after and care for anyone else. So you do need to give yourself permission to do that, to say "now hang on, I care for me".

Yeah, I find that very hard though.

And you will, but what I'm saying is its OK, you can give yourself permission because I think it would be a good choice, in my professional opinion, it would be a good choice for you.

Yeah, like tomorrow my parents are coming up to do a few odd jobs and help my neighbours shift. But Friday and Saturday is just for me. I did that last weekend, last Sunday, because it was a nice day and I thought I'll do my own garden, and I did a bit and thought now I need to keep going. I hate doing it but I need time out. I just wasn't physically or mentally up to seeing anyone. I don't like people to see me being down.

But you need to, with retreating, it needs to be picked up...it's OK to do it for you. And there is that secondary gain that people won't see you when you're like that but the core reason should be that you're looking after yourself, and you do come from a background where you had a broken leg, there was all these stresses going on and no one actually took the time to care for you, so you get to this position where you think you don't deserve it, you haven't had it before, why should you, but what has happened is earlier on you weren't cared for and that was the wrong. The wrong was the childhood, the wrong was that you weren't cared for the way you needed to be.

Everyone is different and I know my parents love me, though dad was walking around in circles when I passed out. He thought I'd died and he was in tears. Mum was the cuddly one, that is the difference............

But everybody's different, just because you've got five people in a room with borderline personality disorders, doesn't mean that they are the same, and your treatment or your therapy is always based on [you], I'm not treating borderline personality, I'm treating [patient].

It's to me the old way of nursing. Everyone's got their problems and are different, I know that, I cope with it in the wrong way but I'm learning, its trial and error, and when I can cope, I'm coping more.

Appendix D: Interview Transcripts for Patient 3, Eve

Interview 1

What age were you when you first used self-harm?

It was eight years ago. So I would have been thirty-two.

What was happening around that time?

I lost a baby. Through an ectopic pregnancy...aborted at about two months. And I was severely depressed after that.

Do you understand why the self-harming might have occurred at that time?

I am presuming that it is just the stress of the situation that triggered it. And it was a way to relieve some of the pressure of the moment. To self-harm and relieve some of the stress.

There were no previous episodes of self-harm?

No.

Even denying yourself certain things or...?

I had anorexia when I was a teenager so I guess that is the ultimate denial. That was when I was fifteen/sixteen but after that, no.

At 32, did other people notice that you were self-harming at that stage, or was it sometime after?

No, it was some time after. People always thought that it was a suicide attempt. I mean in a way it was but it wasn't a serious suicide attempt. It was more a case of 'I can't take this anymore'. I cut myself, and if I end up dying, I end up dying but that is not my motivation behind it – it is just that I can't cope with this anymore.

So, what sort of people were involved at that time?

My husband and my immediate family.

Was there any contact with the emergency department?

I was with a private psychiatrist in [city], so I was at the [omit] clinic, rather than in the public health system.

So there were periods of cutting for a while before people realised that it was more self-harm than suicide attempts?

Yeah, a reasonable period I think. Perhaps six-eight months.

Whereabouts were you cutting?

My elbow, cubical fossa, and my wrist.

With?

Razor blades usually.

Were they something that you would store, or have with you?

Generally, yeah. So I would sort of pre plan for it, yeah.

What other forms of self-harm have you used?

Just cutting.

Just only the two sites then?

Yes. Oh, I have done it once on the vein on my leg but that was desperation because there was nowhere else to cut. Both my arms were in plaster cast so I couldn't do anything.

What had happened at that time?

That was the treatment they did at the time in the psych unit. For people who wouldn't leave the stitches alone. They would put you in plaster cast.

Both arms?

Yeah.

Was that to protect the injury but to also stop you from using the other arm to cut?

No, you could still reach the area but you could not get to it. It would stop you self-harming in that area. Protect the stitches.

How did you feel when they did that?

Incredible frustration but there was some sense of relief in that I couldn't do it anymore. There was no possible way that I could get to them. But it was frustrating because you couldn't feed yourself. You had to bath in a bath with plastic bags over your arms.

So it was just the one occasion on the leg?

Yeah.

And that required suturing?

No it didn't. Just strapping on it.

What sort of circumstances do you use self-harm in?

When the frustration level comes to the point that I cannot stand it anymore. Where I don't want to live anymore…I just can't stand the tension and pressure inside. I feel like I am going to burst if I don't do something. Generally it is also attached to the feeling that I do not want to live anymore. And if I do happen to kill myself, so be it. But it is not usually the primary motivation.

Can you think of the last time you used it as a coping strategy, what was happening in your life to create that high level of stress?

It was about ten weeks ago, I had a job. I hadn't been working for a long time. I had a fulltime job, and I was trying to cope with that and my husband and my children. Looking after the house and all that…it was too much.

Is that a common thing, the daily responsibilities just overload you?

Yeah.

That is when you go into that crisis point?

Yeah.

So it doesn't necessarily have to be tied to some sort of trauma or anniversary date?

Not so much things in the past coming back to me, more current day stressors are just too much.

So, in summary, why do you think that you use self-harm?

To relieve the pressure…just to relieve the pressure. And secondary as a suicide tool.

How does it actually relieve pressure do you think?

Just the act of cutting and the pain that is associated with cutting. Just releases…lets go of some of the pressure. I can't explain it any other way than that.

What sort of feelings do you have before you self-harm? Is there any guilt or just sadness and frustration?

It's unbelievable depression. Just the feeling of futility.

How long do those periods of depression last?

Usually ongoing for a little while…for a couple of weeks beforehand. And they will continue until I get over the episode. That can be eight weeks or whatever.

So these depressive phases where you are more likely to go into shutdown and self-harm, they are around a couple of months long?

Yeah.

How much time in between do you get when your mood is ok and you seem to be on top of things?

I had two years in between last episode and the time before. That was the longest break I have had. That is why I got a job because I thought that I could handle it. Before that, it would have been about every four to five months.

Do you use it as a form of punishment?

No.

So there is no thoughts of 'oh, I shouldn't have done this' or…?

I guess that combines with that feeling of futility. What's the point of going on when it is not going to work but it is not out and out guilt.

So there is no sense of guilt prior to cutting, do you have it after?

Maybe slightly but not overwhelmingly. I generally feel more embarrassed than anything else because you have to go to the emergency department and then you get all the condemnation from the people in the emergency department.

Is there any feelings of regret? Do you wish after that you could have handled it a different way?

No, the relief is generally there that overrides that.

Do you think that you deserve to harm yourself?

Yeah, I think that I am a pretty useless person. I don't deserve to be on this planet at all. So I deserve what I get.

Is it something you always have felt?

Yeah probably.

Where do you think that idea might have come from?

I suppose it stems from my father whom I was always trying to please and never seemed to achieve that. Always had no worth to anyone. Yeah.

What was your childhood like then?

Well, dad molested me…and I was always seeking approval for what I did. Thinking that if perhaps I could do something right, it would stop. But it was all my fault anyway.

Did you have any brothers or sisters?

Just a brother. He is older…two years older. So yeah, it wasn't a very happy one.

Your mother was around at that stage? How was that relationship?

Mum and I are close, really close but she doesn't know anything about what happened.

She still doesn't know?

No, and I don't want to see her destroyed by her knowing it. Because I know she would be.

Was your brother aware?

No.

There was not touching of him or…?

I don't know, I haven't talked to him about it. It has only been a very recent thing that I have realised happened.

So growing up, what was your understanding of what was happening then?

I have very little memory of growing up, I have only flashes. I just know that I was not happy…I can remember a few instances with dad. That distressed me greatly.

What ages was that happening?

When I was pretty young. Starting at about three and a half, four and I am not sure how far it goes. I don't have any memory for anything up until about the ages of ten or eleven. It is all just blank except for the few instances that I remember.

Do you suspect that it was something that was quite regular that was happening?

I don't think that it could have been because dad was a [occupation]. What I gather from mum is that he was away a lot. I just don't know why my memory is just so constantly blank. But I don't know.

The instances that you do remember, was it just fondling and touching, or did it progress further than that?

No, it was just fondling and touching.

But it was something that you felt at that time was wrong, and obviously felt uncomfortable with him doing that?

Yeah, very upset. I don't know how mum could not have noticed. But um, I don't know. Whether she chose not to…block it out I guess.

How does that make you feel towards your mum?

Oh, mum has always been totally dominated by dad and I guess this is another case of mum being completely dominated by dad. It is just a case of mum not being able to say anything…even if it was the welfare of her child, she would not have been able to say anything.

Does it make you feel angry towards your mum?

No, I pity her more.

You do recall things from the ages of ten and eleven though, is there just that seven year period that is missing?

Yeah.

How were things later on when you started to grow up into a teenager?

Well I had anorexia and that was the biggest trauma of all and I missed a year off school. I was in hospital for three months and crap like that. They didn't really know how to treat anorexia in those days so they sort of fiddled around and did what they thought they could do…it didn't help in the slightest. And I just stopped going to the shrink after a while. I would just go and sit there and not say a word…and he would let me just sit there session after session and not say a word. And I said to mum, this is pointless going so I stopped going.

What there any discussion in that treatment about the earlier abuse?

No, the only thing that was discussed was that they assumed that I was trying to get my father's love. And that he wasn't noticing me. And as hard as I tried that I did not want dad to notice me, that is all that they assumed it was…I was a child crying out for their father's love. To me, it was more a case of starving yourself so he won't notice you, rather than a case of starving yourself so that he will notice you.

So to starve yourself, you will just diminish and disappear?

Mmmm.

Where you close with your brother during that stage?

Not really…it has only really been since we have grown into adults that we have become close at all. Yeah, we are fairly close now.

But around that age, your mum was a fairly good support, although she might not have understood what was happening?

Yeah.

You suspect that she might have had some idea but she chose I suppose not to open that can of worms?

Yeah.

What about grandparents or…?

No they were all over in [another capital city]. We lived in [omit] so we didn't have anyone close to us.

What about friends?

Yeah I had some friends when I started at primary school, but they dropped off when I got anorexia.

Is that from you shutting down and moving away from them, or they didn't understand?

Probably both. The lines of communication were totally cut off when I was in hospital for three months. And then because I left school at that point because I couldn't keep going, I took a year off. I went back the next year but all my friends were in the year above me. So I didn't really have any contact with them.

How was school for you?

It was really hard when I went back because I didn't have any friends and I was really skinny. Shy and reserved, lacking in confidence and all that stuff.

Was there ever any sort of bullying at school?

No.

You felt left alone by that?

Yeah. I went to [omit] college and there wasn't any bullying at that stage then. There just wasn't…not that I was aware of.

Was there corporal punishment there?

No.

How did you go with school work?

I had this desire to do well, I always have had, so I studied my guts out. And I did pretty well.

And you went on to do college/uni?

Yeah, I am a [omit] and I am doing my Masters at the moment.

How do you cope with that?

I had to defer this semester as I was in hospital for eight weeks. But I will start it again next semester. It is not that hard.

You seem to get a sense of comfort from your studying?

Yeah, I like it I really do. I always have. I get a sense of achievement out of it. Because I know I can do it, and I can do it well…it is the only thing I can do well. I usually get pretty good marks because I study really hard and pay a lot of attention.

Has anyone beside your dad seriously harmed you?

No.

And you are married?

Yes.

Is that like your first boyfriend?

Yeah. It is a first boyfriend thing.

Where did you meet?

We met at uni so we met when I was eighteen. We got married when I was 22…been married 18 years.

How is that relationship?

Mmm good, except for the sexual side of it which I still struggle with. But my husband is very supportive and he is a very intelligent person. He can work out my moods and he knows when problems are happening. So he is very supportive. Can read me pretty well.

And that is obviously very reassuring for you?

Yeah it is.

Does he give you feedback when he notices that things aren't going well?

Yeah. We work on it together rather than him telling me what to do. He will make suggestions. And he is very good in the recuperation phase…trying to get me motivated and getting me up to do stuff. He is very good at taking time off to look after the kids if I simply cannot do it.

Does he understand why you self-harm?

No I don't think so. He has never asked me about it…I think he just assumed that they are suicide attempts. But I have never tried to enlighten him and he has never wanted to know. Whether he is…not that he is not interested…he probably just sees it as not his business.

Do you think it makes him anxious?

I don't think anything makes [him] anxious. No I don't think he does. He just accepts it as part of life…

So you have just the two kids?

Yes.

How old are they?

Seven and three.

And how was it during your pregnancy?

I had a really bad pregnancy with my son. I had contractions from five months and I was in hospital. When he was born he was really sick. But when [daughter] was born, it was a dream pregnancy. It was a total accident…pleasant surprise.

Was there any periods of self-harm during pregnancy?

No, they are too precious to me to ever want to hurt them. That is why I personally do not believe in abortion. I don't believe in forcing my opinion on other people but I could never abort, even if [daughter] was down syndrome or anything like that.

Was you mood different during pregnancy?

It was pretty elevated. I was pretty happy most of the time…delighted to be pregnant. Delighted to be having another child.

So there were no two month phases of depression during the pregnancy?

No.

Has there been any form of neglect in your life?

No not really.

So you have always been provided for? financially? Emotionally?

Emotionally by my mum. Not by my dad…just my mum.

Your mum was an affectionate person towards you?

Yes, very.

How does she go understanding the self-harm phases and the depression?

Umm, the only thing that she would think about the self-harm is that it is a suicide attempts and nothing more. She is pretty accepting of most things and I think she just accepts the fact that it is a suicide attempt and that is it…nothing more, nothing less. I don't think I would like to explain it to her…what it actually is because I don't think she would understand. She would try her best but I don't think she would understand.

So, you are quite at ease with letting those around you think that it is a suicide attempt rather than a release of frustration? Like a coping strategy?

I think the general population find it easier to see it as suicide attempt rather than a coping strategy. Cause I think that if they saw it as different from a suicide attempt they would call it attention seeking.

Have you ever had people give you that impression that they think that you are attention seeking?

Yeah like my in laws.

How is the relationship with the in-laws in general?

Not the greatest. It is more of a case of keep each other at arm's length and we are happy. I feel she is very condemning of me, thinks that I am not good enough for her son because of what I do. Not looking after her son properly and stuff.

Does that feed those ideas of the worthlessness you described earlier?

Yeah, yeah.

Do you think that it would be useful for them to have some sort of understanding like your mum and husband do? Would that help reduce some of that frustration?

Umm, yes I guess it would help. Whether they could be bothered making the effort is another matter. I imagine any information…they are pretty intelligent people…would be of some benefit.

The self-harming started when you lost your first baby. Can you see any connection between the use of self-harm and that particular loss?

Oh the fact that I wanted to punish myself for the loss of the baby, I think that it was my fault even though it was ectopic. I felt that I should have died with the baby; rather than aborting the baby…even though the baby would not have survived anyway. I feel that if I was a proper mother I should have died with the baby and been there for the baby in heaven…rather than leaving her alone, I pretend it is a girl even though I don't know, I pretend it is a girl.

So you were forced to make a decision at that stage to terminate the pregnancy?

I really didn't have any choice in the matter, it was just purely accepted. I would die if I didn't, so it was just done. I didn't have a choice.

Where do you think that idea that you had done something wrong comes from?

I don't believe I caused the ectopic pregnancy but I believe that I should have died with the baby and gone to heaven to look after the baby. Rather than aborting it…which I feel is inherently wrong…all life is precious. But I had no right to abort the baby.

You mention that all life is precious, does that apply to your own?

No it doesn't apply to me.

Why do you think that is?

Because if I die, I am in heaven looking after the child that I lost. And I will eventually see the rest of my family anyway. I know I am some worth to my children, but that feel is often overweighed by the other feeling of worthlessness.

But that is an ingrained notion, that worthlessness?

Yeah.

Was there any periods in your childhood that you wished you could run away, or that you were dead, or that you didn't exist?

Yeah, I was pretty suicidal when I was anorexia, which is probably why I was in hospital too.

There were no attempts on your life at that stage?

No.

What about when you were going through the abuse, can you think of any times that you wanted to leave the family or not be there?

Umm, I didn't want to run away, I just wanted it to stop. No.

What do you think about that idea that you just wanted to please your father? You mentioned that idea before that 'if I do things well, he might leave me alone and notice me for the right reasons'?

Yeah. I can understand why I felt that way…if I could possibly get him to notice the worth that I am…he acknowledged my brother and my brother's intelligence…my brother won a full scholarship to [college] and I just didn't seem to be in the same league as my brother in my parents, no my father's, eyes. I just didn't seem to be worth what my brother was worth.

Do you think that was related to being a brother?

Yeah. Looking at it.

So the male child was considered the more superior child from your dad's perspective?

Yeah.

What about your mum? Did she show any favouritism towards your brother or do you feel she tried to compensate for your dad?

No, she didn't show any favouritism…she if anything gave me more confidence in myself as a person. Because I could play music and my brother couldn't, and mum had a great love for music, so she made me feel worthwhile because I could play music and neither my brother or father could. My father appreciated music too so that was something I could do that could prove my worth.

Did he recognise that talent?

No.

Is your dad still alive?

Yeah.

With your mum still?

Yeah.

How is the relationship now?

I don't speak to him unless I have to. He picks up the phone and says 'hi [omit], here is mum'. No 'hi how are you going?', 'nice to talk to you' or anything. I don't like going near him at all, or hugging him at all, or any physical contact with him whatsoever. I feel uncomfortable in his presence. I feel uncomfortable if he does anything towards me – be it physical, emotional, or verbal…I don't want to speak to him, or to touch him…anything.

What do you think that it was that got you through that time, because that was obviously very stressful. You have obviously blocked most of it out, although you have had pieces come back to you. What do you think it was that got you through that time to now?

To now it has been my husband's support. He has been unbelievable my entire life, just in his ability to support me. So I came from anorexia at eighteen, to my husband who got me out of anorexia just by his support. I know that he loves me for the way I was, not by what my shape was. Didn't require anything of me, just loved me for who I was.

So he gave you a sense of worth?

Mmmm.

Do you think that [husband] gives you what your father should have?

Yeah. Unfortunately he is in some ways quite like dad, in that he is very capable and very intelligent. He is very matter of fact. I don't know if that any of my current sexual problems with him have to do with the fact that I picture him somewhat like dad. Yeah, I don't know.

Do you recall any times when he has wanted to become intimate that thought of 'no, you are reminding me of dad' or?

Yeah, I do. Yeah, particularly at the moment. When all this stuff is coming up, yeah. I just can't bear the thought of [husband] touching me. It is not revulsion on the part of [husband], it is revulsion on my part that I let it happen.

So it is almost that replay of what happened years ago?

Mmmm.

Have you spoken to [husband] about it?

No. Well, not in that sense…he does not realise that I have any issues with regards to sex.

So you just allow him to touch you and just try and tolerate that feeling that would go through you at that time?

Mmmm…and fake the rest.

So not try and push him away and raise it as an issue?

That is right yeah.

Did you have any things to add to what we have talked about this afternoon?

No.

Interview 2

What I didn't ask you about last time was, you met [husband] at 18, and you were struggling with the anorexia at that stage, how did things progress from there until 32?

Really well…I didn't have any problems at all. My anorexia improved and pretty well I had finished with it.

Was that within a couple of years of meeting [husband]? So about 20?

Yeah, around that. I was studying part time and that was what occupied most of my time.

Were you working as well?

Yes.

What sort of work?

I worked in a [omit] because I am a [field of science].

How was the work environment?

It was ok.

So the work was not stressful and time consuming?

No, no. it was good. I had quite a few jobs because I kept finding a better job to move onto.

Did that result in you moving a lot?

Yeah we had about three houses before we lived in [present town].

They were all in [city]?

Yep.

How was the relationship with your parents when you moved out and you were living with [husband]?

The same as they always are. They haven't changed…I still get on really well with mum, and nonexistent with dad. It has always been like that.

So the relationship then, with your dad, is like it is just someone that lives with your mum?

Yeah.

Face to face contact…how does that go?

Neither of us know what to say to each other. Neither of us, well at least I don't want any physical contact with him, I don't want a hug or a cuddle. It is just very awkward.

Does your dad relate to [husband]?

No [husband] can't stand him.

Is that because of the abuse or more than that?

[husband] doesn't…isn't sure if I have been abused or not. And he has just formed his own opinion of dad…and that is that he hates him. Because of the way he treats mum, and women in general, and his opinion on things and all that sort of thing.

How does that make you feel that [husband] is not sure if you have been molested or not?

Pretty disappointed in him, yeah.

Why do you think that he questions that? Is it because the memory around that time is also hazy?

Yeah…and that why he says he questions it. He doesn't say that he doesn't believe me…he just says that he is not sure. He doesn't say 'no I don't' believe you' or 'Yes I believe you', he says he is not sure.

I know of family members who say 'if you can't really remember, how can you be sure…if something like that happened to me, I would remember it?' Looking back at the last interview, you were saying that it is a recent thing that you have worked out. How ago was that?

Oh, that was only my last hospitalisation…so the last three months. And I think that is why [husband] is questioning if it really happened because how could something that dramatic happen and I not remember it? But it is so distressing and clear the memory that I had that is not just a dream…it wasn't just a dream. What I felt. The reactions that I had to the feelings and the thoughts that I had, was so strong. It wasn't like just a dream…it was way more than that.

Almost like a reliving?

Yeah.

The relationship with your dad, that "I don't want him near me or to touch me", was before the last three months, what do you think was behind that? The way he treated you?

I always felt sexually uncomfortable around dad…I always felt there was…I always felt so uncomfortable in the house with him growing up. I never felt safe with him. Um, I felt safe as a human being but not as a female around him. There was always that feeling that it just wasn't right. And I just very uncomfortable with him as a male being near me or anywhere in the house with me. And I dread the time that he would come home at five o'clock every day. As soon as I heard his car in the driveway I would go straight to my room and shut the door. Just to get away from him…so I didn't have to see him. Then the only time I would see him would be at dinner. And then I would go back into my bedroom.

Is that at the time when you threw yourself into your reading and your studies? Because it was to occupy yourself in your room?

Yeah.

Have you been discussing these memories with anyone?

No I haven't because I am debating whether to or not. Because I am concerned that sitting down and discussing all this will end up with me back in hospital again. And my conflict at the moment is that if I don't do anything about this, will it be a never ending cycle? With me ending back in hospital every six months…twelve months? Or if I don't do anything about it, will it just fade away? Or if I do do something about it, will I end up in hospital again? At the moment, I am opting not to do anything about it and just see how it goes.

So did you disclose it though to the staff on the ward?

Yeah.

Particularly with some of the work that I do with people, it's "well I am going ok...there is a recurring issue for me, but I know if I start to open the wounds so to speak, I am going to feel worse before I can feel better".

That is exactly it.

Which can be pretty scary if you already feel like you are quite cyclic, and one minute you are like this and the next not...why make it worse?

Yeah.

It can be really difficult. The memory gap you call it, the haziness, has there been periods of the images that are getting bigger or is the haze lifting on it as time goes by?

I get some more flashes of memory but they are still hazy and not clear. But I have had more flashes of memory than just the one.

Would it be daily it comes to you?

No, no. Probably once a week or something like that.

And how do you deal with that?

Usually I am really distressed. Yeah, I don't really know how to deal with it. It just really distresses me...I feel dirty, feel like it was my fault...feel like I must have done something to earn it.

Listening to your comments there, that you feel like you deserved it, how you feel now, do you agree with those thoughts? That you must have earned it or encouraged it somehow?

Yeah when I hear it when I am not, absurd basically...in the moment it feels like it.

And it is often to harder to challenge your thoughts if your mood is low or you are distressed, you can see the illogical pattern in it, but at the time it is hard to work through. Do you think of self-harming when you become distressed from the images?

Usually yeah. I just sort of think...what am I going to do? Why is this all happening? I can't take anymore. I want some way to relieve the pain of how I am feeling.

So replace the emotional pain with physical pain?

Yeah.

If self-harming occurred in that situation, would you see it as a punishment sort of thing? Particularly if your thoughts are "I deserved it"?

No it is more a just a desire to remove the stress of the moment...I can't deal with it. Just life isn't fair...I can't take anymore.

When you were in the unit just recently then and you disclosed these flashes that you were having, how did the staff respond to you?

They were really good...really good. I was really distressed. They gave me medication and that to calm me down, they were really good. I thought that if I told anyone, they would not believe me. That was my biggest fear but I had to tell someone because I could not cope with the memory on my own. So I told one of the nurses that I trusted and she believed me. Everyone I talked to believed me. Which was my greatest fear that no one would believe me.

But now I suppose you are going home to, not that [husband] is saying that he doesn't believe you, but he is just a little unsure about what this is about.

But he still supports me…he is just unclear about what actually happened, or the extent of what actually happened. How much of it was actual event and how much was associated with the trauma with it. Not being clear about what actually happened.

But there was that general uncomfortable feeling around your dad before these memories that just came to you; was that based on as you said the treatment of women by your father?

It is a 'oh I believe that women should be doing all the work and the men should sit back and put their feet up'. Mum will get dinner, put it in front of him, get up and do the dishes, all that…do anything for him. [Husband] hates the way that dad expects mum to do everything for him.

A woman's worth is based on her domestic capacity?

Yeah. And there of no use for anything else…oh except for the sex.

Do you know much about the relationship between your mum and dad?

Mum treated me more like a friend than a daughter…when I was older and she would tell me in graphic detail, often well too much…she always told me that she and dad had a very active sex life.

Why do you think that she would tell you that though?

I don't know….

What ages did that befriending between you and your mum occur?

About 20.

So it was more that you had moved on with [husband] and were out of the home. The relationship changed and she saw you more as a confidant?

Well I had a sex life with [husband] then and I guess that she figured I now knew what was happening, that I could therefore relate to her.

Your mum didn't have any other close friends?

No not really.

We had a brief talk last time about your family's response to your self-harm, and how they probably don't understand it, that it is like a suicide attempt not like a coping strategy, have you got anymore thoughts in general about what might be useful for families to know about self-harm?

Just that it is more than a suicide attempt…it is so much more than that. It is not through any want of attention…it is just a need to release the pressure…coupled with suicide desires. But not suicide on its own.

I think you mentioned last time that there is not that desire to kill yourself with the cutting but there is that apathy that "hey if it happens, it happens; I really don't care".

Yeah.

It might not be the purpose but if it is the outcome I really don't care?

Yeah. Yeah.

It is almost like a passive suicidality that is there?

Yeah.

Although you are actively self-harming, the suicidal behaviours are passive, they are not the driving motivation there.

Yeah.

[Husband] is talking with you and working with you, you find that very helpful. Open communication, feedback if you notice you are sliding…that working partnership. Do you think [husband] is enough or would it be useful if more of the family had his sort of approach or his level of understanding?

Oh it would be fabulous if the rest of his family had that sort of understanding. I feel like that think that I am just an attention seeker. I hate the opinion his mother has of me…I am disrupting her son's life and just being an attention seeker. And I know that my mum doesn't understand. [husband] does not really understand either…he thinks that they are suicide attempts. I haven't really tried to set him straight.

Are you concerned that he will see you as an attention seeker?

No not if I explained it to him…I guess it is hard for a lay person to understand the desire to just get all the tension and stress out of your body. Just not being able to cope with the pressure anymore and that is just a way of relieving pressure. Like kicking the cat…but it is a different way of doing it.

What particular responses from your family tend to exacerbate the problem, or increase your frustration? Is there any particular comments that they make or actions that they do?

It is mostly [husband's] mother. Oh she just makes comments that I am not looking after him properly and I am not good enough because I am not looking after him properly. Obviously, my role is to look after her son and not do anything else in the relationship. She does not think that I am a good influence on the children and that.

And she says this directly to you or through [husband]?

Through [husband]. But she said to my face that I am not looking after [husband] properly.

There is a lot of similarities between her line of thinking and your dad's thinking about the role of the wife.

Yeah...

As you said, you are not looking after him; you are there to look after her boy. Whether that is a generational thing?

I think that it is probably a generational thing…that is the way it was in the seventies.

What particularly would be helpful as far as your family goes?

Well the early response is just ringing up mum and having a chat to her. Saying that I am having a crap day and just having a chat. I talk to her everyday or every other day anyway. Just [husband's] support when I say hey I am feeling really down and I just can't cope today, he will say "what do you need from me…do you need me to come home right now? I will come home now if you need me? Do you want me to grab some tea on the way home? Do you need me to pick the kids up? What do you need from me?" and that is really good because he just knows the right questions to say. I guess he has been there long enough.

So your mum will provide time for you to ventilate and talk through what is distressing you?

Yeah.

Whereas [husband's] approach will be a little bit different...he has been there so long that he has gotten to the point where he does not need to give you the time, he just gives the possible solutions to help? So instead of talking to you on the phone for half an hour about what is wrong, he jumps to the 'do you need this, this or this?'

Yeah he is more practical on the what can I do for you side than sitting down or talking to me emotionally. I don't think he fully understands…I go up and down like a yo-yo even across a day but he is on an even keel. I don't think he understands the highs and lows, even what it feels like to even have a high or a low.

Which is more useful or they are both useful in different ways?

They are both useful in different ways. I don't think I could cope without either of them.

So your mum's response is more a validating response?

It is more a reassuring response. You know, 'you will be right', we will talk about it. Try to just chat about her day and get my mind off things and try to cheer me up in general.

So she doesn't problem solve like [husband] does?

No, no problem solving.

In general, as far as professional help goes, how have you found the response to you?

Really positive…the only people I have had any negative ones from are the doctors in emergency. Who do not understand why I have done it and who chastise me for doing it. Maybe they are just frustrated. I don't know but I have had that a fair few times.

So with emergency, when you say that they will chastise you because they don't understand, what sort of comments do they actually offer when you have attended there?

Comments like 'what did you need to do that for' or 'why did you do this' or 'whatever possessed you to do this' or 'what are we going to do so you do not do this again?'

The tone of voice you use then is quite interesting because my reasoning would be that if you had come in and that you have self-harmed and I asked 'what has happened' or 'why have you done that', that would be different. Often it can be as simple as watching your tone of voice that can make all the difference. No one is going to open up to someone that they feel is judging them. And obviously, as far as your family's responses and the nurses in psych unit, talking about it can help.

Yeah.

But basically if the question is loaded with that sort of tone it is more difficult. Does it generally make you more anxious and distressed to have that response?

Oh yeah, yeah. I feel like I am wasting their time and that I am just a nuisance.

When you have self-harmed, is there that anxiety about 'oh no now I am going to have to go there?'

Oh yeah.

So by the time that you get there, are you fairly settled in yourself?

Generally because the ambulance drivers are pretty good and calm me down a bit…because they are talking to you all the way asking you questions and that, you don't have to focus on what is happening and that you are going to hospital. Once you get into casualty and you know the type of response you are going to get, and thinking that all they are thinking is that you are attention seeking, yeah.

What sort of waiting times have you had in emergency?

Usually about an hour to get sewn up and anywhere up to three hours to see the CATT team.

How do you find the CATT when they respond to a referral?

They are usually pretty good.

So, you are put into the ambulance, and that is pretty good?

Yeah.

You come into emergency and you have the silly questions…

Which distress me.

Is that from a wish that they would understand or?

Yeah I wish they would understand.

Up to three hours later, you have the CATT come in that you feel reassured by?

Yeah.

Is there any sort of periods where what emergency have done has been useful?

No. Other than sewing me up. No.

So that is doctors or nurses?

Both.

You wouldn't see any understanding from them at all?

No.

So if I said to you what do you think that ED need to know about self-harm, what do you think?

Nothing…they just see it as attention seeking and a waste of their time.

What do you think they need to know about why self-harm occurs?

They need to understand that it is not attention seeking, the person is in real trouble, and needs their help…not their chastisement. Need understanding …not to be told off.

Do you think psych services in general need to know more about self-harm, or you think that their understanding is pretty good?

I don't think a lot of the people in the unit understand it because I have been told off…I have been told to behave myself like a grown woman, I have been told to grow up, act my age…things like that.

There tends to be a tone of judgement in those comments. Can you see an anxiety in the workers when faced with self-harm?

More of a frustration that they are having to special me or sit in the room with me or expend all this energy on me…stuff like that. If I behaved myself, I would save them a lot of trouble.

Interview 3

You mentioned that certainly there was this gap in your memory, are you finding that more and more pieces are coming through?

Yeah.

How vivid are they?

Some of them are really vivid. Last week was really vivid and really distressed me. I came very close to killing myself last week. Some are very vivid.

What made you think of killing yourself?

I felt so dirty…I just didn't think I could handle living the way that I felt.

The return of the memories, is that during the day or at night, or asleep? Or nightmares?

Usually nightmares. This one I was just sitting down and having a cuppa and thinking about christmas and about dad and the family and that.

And Christmas is a hard time of year, being a family holiday, it does raise some issues for many people. Is it just instances of the molestation coming back or is there other things?

Just the molestation.

Are you getting support from [husband] with that?

Yeah I am.

You mentioned last time that he was up in the air about whether or not the abuse occurred, is he starting to move with you as things keep coming back?

I don't know where he is at. I haven't put it to him again because I don't know if a really want the answer.

So you feel dirty?

Yeah.

Like, parts of guilt, that you had attracted it, or done something to deserve it, are they strong themes?

No, they are only really strong when it happens. Realistically I know that a little girl cannot do much to attract a male.

What sort of emotions does it cause?

Just absolute revulsion…trying to block it out of my mind but not being able to. Overwhelming revulsion and just feeling so dirty.

Is that causing you to act in certain ways? Showering? Trying to do things to distract yourself?

I try to do things to distract myself. Listen to music, get out of the house and go for a walk. In ended up being able to get out of the house with [daughter] and went to the shops for a while because I thought that if I stayed at home I would end up cutting myself.

I know the query was do I dig around and resolve it, or do I leave it, where are you sitting with that?

I am still sitting with leaving it, because of the emotions that it stirs up. That I don't think I could cope with that…I would end up back in hospital. Just I don't think that the timing is right yet. Particularly with needing to go up to mum's just after Christmas. And I will have to see my dad and stuff like that…so I don't want to be anymore stirred up than I already am.

There needs to be a planning around that – to make sure you have the supports in place. And if you look at things like your self-harming, you use that to deal with distress or when you get overloaded. Strengthen your ability to cope before you open up wounds.

Yeah.

Today I just had some words to give you and for you to just talk about what comes to mind when I say these words. Given the week you have had, some might be more difficult than others. I might just start with the word self-harm?

Oh that just brings back all the memories of cutting myself. Yeah the lack of understanding…you feel like you are all alone because no one understands. They think you are just doing it for attention and that is it.

And that has been more a theme with the family, as in extended family, and emergency?

Yeah.

Family.

That brings more distress with it than anything. Because I have got dad in the family. Our family was never really close anyway. My family does not bring thoughts of reassurance or warmth to me.

What do you see I, in the ideal world, what is family supposed to be?

Supportive. Loving. There in times of crisis.

So is there people that you would term as family that you are not necessarily related to, or family is just an idea of people that are related?

Just people that are related. It is what I would like my family to end up being.

So there are some ideas there of how your family was and how your family is, but particularly with the new generation, how you would like that to be.

Yeah.

Is that something you are working a lot with raising your kids, is it a conscious thing that you are aware of?

Consciously aware of always telling them that I love them. Reassuring them that I am there. My son gets very distressed if I have to go away and go into hospital and stuff like that. I want him to see that the family can still support him if I am not there. Dad is still there and [sister] is still there. He hasn't worked that out yet.

So to him, the family should be more than just you?

Yeah.

Can you see some parallels between that and your childhood where you just had your mum?

Yeah.

So you would like to correct that pattern?

Yeah. I mean [son] is very attached to his dad, it is not that he isn't, but I just sort of have the nurturing role where he draws reassurance from me but he draws fun from his dad.

Do you wish it was the other way around at times?

I wish there was more of a balance. Because it worries me that [son] can't cope when I am not there. He can cope alright when [husband] is not there but he can't cope when I am not there. If he had more of a nurturing relationship with his dad, then that wouldn't be quite the same.

How do you think that you can achieve that?

It is just trying to get [husband] to soften his stance a bit. Not be so down the line with so many things.

So [husband] is very black and white in his parenting?

Mmmm.

Guilt?

I guess that is more associated with dad. I don't feel guilty for cutting myself. Or for even trying to have killed myself in the past. I don't want to feel guilty for any of my actions that I have done. I feel guilty that I…that still I must have done something as a little girl.

I have found that a lot with the work that I have been doing that there is that guilt there but it does not make sense, you do not really understand what it is about but you can identify it as guilt?

Yeah.

And perhaps I have done something wrong or encouraged something but it is not fully understood. It is something that drives to act in certain ways such as self-harming and there is a lot in the literature about unconscious guilt…that it is there but it is not reachable to you at the moment, but it is something that with therapy later on, would be worth exploring. Speaking of which…therapy.

I have had lots of therapy over the years! I see the benefit of talking to someone. But it is a case of finding the right person…I used to see [psychologist] and I just found that it didn't help…I didn't get anywhere, it didn't resolve any issues. For me there is an advantage in therapy but I get so distressed initially that I have to watch out for the ramifications of the therapy.

What is it about talking that helps? You have obviously put talking and therapy there on a parallel. What do you think about talking to a professional?

You can sort out the issues in your mind so that they are less jumbled. Get them out in the open. Just the fact that I said to someone that dad molested me, the fact that I said it to someone made all the difference. Up until that point I had not said anything and it was really distressing me. When I said something I felt so much better.

What sort of things would you expect from your therapist in relation to that talking?

I suppose guiding me through it…trying to make sure that I don't reach the point where I get too distressed. Trying to stop me from getting to that point. Trying to help me to see the reasoning…not dad's reasoning…the fact that as a little girl it would have been impossible for me to have encouraged my father. To have that pointed out to me…the illogical nature of some of the reasoning that I have.

Punishment?

I am a great one for punishment…I always seem to be punishing myself for something. I am not big on punishing the kids…I am not very good at that. I am big on punishing myself. I guess that partially that is what the cutting is about too. That I do not deserve to be a mother and I don't deserve to have children. Don't deserve to be living…that sort of thing.

I have noticed some sort of a change in that idea about punishment from the first interview we did. So whether the return of the memories is sort of helping with things fit together? It is like a jigsaw; you don't want to see the end picture but it is starting to piece itself together?

Yeah.

The self-harm was described initially as a way to cope, a way to survive. Now because of these feelings of guilt, are you starting to see some connection between it all?

It is my stress coping mechanism…most definitely…but I also feel like I don't deserve what I have got. I don't deserve to have a husband who is as good as the one I have got, I don't deserve to have such great kids. And if a cut myself and I die, then so be it. Yeah. I don't suppose it is really a punishment…if it happens it happens. I just can't deal with life anymore… the stress is too much. If I die, I die…I probably deserve it anyway.

Support.

I don't know what I would have done without the support of some of the people I have had. [husband] has been the best supporter of all. And my mother. It is so important that it goes without saying…if you don't have support then you are not going to cope out there. You can cope well enough in hospital but if you don't have the support out there then you will never get there.

So there is something protective in the support?

Yeah.

Trauma.

I don't really know what to say about that one. I don't really consider it trauma what I am remembering but I guess it is. If you rate trauma as great distress? I guess I have created a lot of trauma amongst my family from the actions that I took and ending up in hospital and that.

Coping.

I guess that it is just a matter of coping with everyday life…the stress which is pretty hefty for me sometimes. I take most stuff to heart and [case worker] is getting me to learn coping strategies, working on a plan of things that I must do if I start to get traumatised, distressed, stuff like that…

working on an action plan.

So there is something of a necessity in having something to help you cope?

Yeah.

It is like support and coping mechanisms need to be there, at all times…not just in hospital but when you are home in everyday life…?

Yeah that's right.

At the moment perhaps the self-harming seems to be tied to the coping issue, but I suspect that it is also tied to the guilt and the trauma…it is all intertwined in there somehow.

Yeah.

Therapy should be about untangling that. When you are thinking about everything in your head, there is no-one there to say "hey hang on, let's have a look at that". We are not very good at controlling our thoughts that way…Why don't you think that you deserve the husband and children that you have got?

Well I just don't think I am a good enough person, good enough for them.

Why?

I don't think that I am a good enough mother. I have ended up in hospital. I have put my kids in jeopardy by cutting myself while they were around. Not having support for them. I have been in hospital and I haven't been there for them. So I try to compensate by giving in to them too much…which I think makes me a bad mother too so I can't win. I don't think I deserve [husband] who has stuck by me, and all the crap that he has had to stick by me through.

What you are essentially saying is that you are a bad person?

Yeah.

Where do you think that comes from?

I don't know really. Don't know.

And I think we get our sense of confident from our idea of self worth and if you feel you are a bad person, you do not have a good sense of self worth. I do suspect with your upbringing, there were themes of that in our earlier interviews: that 'I tried to please', 'no-one noticed me for the right reasons', if that is what you have known since young, that is all you have known. We tend to accept that idea of being bad and that "I don't deserve this", instead of looking at where it comes from, you just accept it. You must deserve a good husband because he is still there.

Oh I think he is just stubborn!

INDEX

A

B

C

D

E

F

G

H

I

Q

R

S

T

U

V

W

Y